ILLUSION
The true story of a dog who did it her way

Brenda Tilsley Gibson

*This story is dedicated to two very different,
but equally remarkable vets;*
Nigel Williams of Lincoln
and
Christopher Day of Oxford,
both of whom have raised their Science into Art.

Text © Brenda Gibson
Photographs edited by David Lingard
Published in Great Britain in 2005
by TUCANN*books*
All rights reserved
Design ©TUCANNdesign&print

ISBN 1 873257 61 9

Published by TUCANN*books*,
19 High Street, Heighington, Lincoln LN4 1RG
Tel & Fax: 01522 790009 • www.tucann.co.uk

For their help and encouragement in producing this book, my grateful thanks go to:
Jemima Harrison,
Jenny Bird, Peggy Grayson, Janet Harding, Mary Haines, Malcolm and Ann Kilminster, Karen Maitland, Joan Mason and Shirley Payne.

During my years with Fern, I met many wonderful people. A few appear in this book. To those who do not, I offer my apologies and sincerest thanks for their kindness and friendship, especially Jo Chambers, Liz and Jim Colley, Stephen Elwood, Renée Harcourt, Rhona Harris, Tony and Christ Higgingbottom, David Hopper, Sarah Jackson, Joy O'Flanagan, Clare Porter, Fiona Redworth, Betty Turner, Keith Whitelam and Chaz Worrall

Illusion

"A real fun dog" SJS

CHAPTER ONE

"She's putting two fingers up at you, Brenda!"

I risked a quick glance across the hillside to see if anyone was close enough to witness my embarrassment: a jogger skirting the pond, two golfers searching for a ball. Only the horses were near enough.

"Keep calling her."

"Come!"

No reaction.

"Come! Come!"

She raised her head. At last!

"Ferny, come!"

"Her name's Fern."

George used his exasperated trainer's voice.

"Fern, come! Come!"

She lowered her head to resume minute inspection of all things grassy.

Surely now, there was someone laughing at my futile efforts? Everything was going wrong. The sun was too hot, the grass too thick. Even the distant traffic was too noisy. In growing desperation, I waved my arms above my head.

"Fern, come!"

She turned to watch with some interest. Encouraged, I waved frantically and began trotting backwards, lurching clumsily over ankle-wrenching tussocks of grass. Puppies were supposed to race after owners who looked like disappearing, weren't they?

"Come!"

Not this one! Having satisfied her curiosity, she resumed her grassy inspection. George stepped in

"Fern, come!"

Fern came; immediately, joyfully. Sitting at his feet, she gazed upwards, happy and confident. He bent down, scooped up the eleven-week old bundle of shining black mischief, and began making the wonderful, cooing, laughing sounds she so loved.

I watched in silence.

It had been a long and unhappy road to that Tuesday morning in the summer of ninety-one. The decision to have a dog, which many people take so lightly, had not been easy. Even as a child, I had never lived with a dog, but now, as I kept telling myself, there was no one else to please. I could do exactly as I wanted.

The only child of older parents, the family died as I grew up. Last of all had been Mum, almost ninety and far out-living everyone else. I was entirely alone.

The year following her death had been utterly desolate and became ever more so. Having given up full-time employment to care for her, I taught at the local college part-time and it was time, which once I craved, that now weighed so heavily on my shoulders. Neighbours were most supportive, but as Time diminished their concerns, so my feelings of isolation grew.

Mornings were the very worst. Who cared when I got up to start a new day? Or even if I got up at all? Only Monday and Wednesday afternoons and on Friday mornings would anyone care and the students could soon get a new teacher. No one actually depended on me. No one needed me. Evening brought the comforting shroud of closed curtains, and night the brief suspension of painful reality.

"You've coped so well."

"You've kept going."

"You're so sensible."

Sensible? Even a simple thing like shopping had become an ordeal. I imagined other shoppers were analysing the contents of my supermarket trolley, deducing I was alone and staring at me in their efforts to work out why.

Perhaps if I did something for others, I reasoned, then I might feel valued again. So I threw myself into voluntary work, but everyone, even the saddest hospital patient, seemed to have someone to call their own. After a while, not even that sopped my despair.

Loneliness had me imprisoned behind its glass wall. There was a whole, wonderful world out there, but I did not feel part of it. I could see, I could hear, but I could not join in. If only I had someone: someone to talk to, someone close, to go places with, then I could break out of the glass prison.

When I stood at the top of my garden, I could just see through the trees into the garden of the house beyond. Sometimes, I caught glimpses of the Border Collies living there. I thought there were three. Neighbour-speak told me they belonged to George Clapperton, a retired R.A.F. dog handler, who now trained dogs privately and an idea began to take shape. One day, I plucked up courage to call through the trees.

"Mr. Clapperton! I wonder if you could help me? I'm thinking of getting a dog."

He turned to face me at once, an enormous smile spreading across his weather-beaten face. Arms akimbo, legs spread, he listened carefully, as I recounted plans for a Rescue dog. We who had no one, would have each other.

"Ye might like to look at the breeds though, Pet."

Forty years in England had done little to soften his Scots accent, and the look in his fiercely blue eyes suggested I had no choice!

Books of all sizes began to flood through the trees and across the fence; books on breeds, books on physiology, books on psychology, books on working dogs, gun dogs, problem dogs. I ploughed through them all.

"Do you think this is wise?"

Mary frowned when I told her. I had kept in touch with a retired colleague and had to tell someone my exciting plans!

"They're very tying. You'll never be able to go anywhere."

It had not occurred to Mary that I not only wanted, but needed "ties", or that "going anywhere" was no fun at all by oneself, but she wouldn't even listen to my reasons, let alone try to understand.

"So you're going to hide away and give all your love to a dog?"

No, no! I was going to get a big, friendly, extrovert dog and we were going to do all manner of things together!

But her opposition grew. In the end, it became totally implacable and I was faced with the unexpected and unwanted choice of losing a friend, however distant, or losing my dog-to-be. I made the choice.

The last of George's books was returned over the fence.

"Now ye can make a list of the breeds that tak' your fancy."

What had happened to my rescue dog? My alter-ego? I didn't want a pooch born with a silver bone between its teeth! I wanted a dog who, like me, needed loving and together we could face the world! But in gratitude for George's time and interest, I would make such a list. Actually, it was easy; Golden Retriever, Labrador Retriever, Rough Collie, English Setter and Airedale Terrier.

"My grandfather used to have an Airedale," I offered by way of explaining the odd one out, "and my father used to tell me wonderful stories about Rex."

Coincidentally, George happened to be working with an Airedale who had a behaviour problem; he tried to make mad, passionate love to anything on legs!

"I'll tak' y'out wi' me if the owner agrees, then ye can get a taste of what they're like. I'm about done and the lad's goin' to be fine."

So for the first time, George's cream Mercedes estate drew up outside my home and I slipped into the passenger seat. The car reeked: a scent unknown to me. It was the warm scent of dog. In the back, sat the three Border Collies, an Airedale and a ten-year old boy with an ear-to-ear grin. It had long been Tom's dream to ride in the back with Wisp, Gus and So, and my appearance had given him the opportunity!

We spent the next hour on Lincoln's South Common, weaving across the hillside between joggers, golfers, and what seemed to me, an enormous number of horses. How George's young pupil loved to show off his newly acquired skills! If a child could do so much, then how much more could I do? Suddenly, I felt elated, confident, feelings that had long been absent. There was even a tinge of happiness as we dropped the Airedale and his child-handler at their home.

As we drove, I pondered the things I had seen. The future no longer yawned bleakly ahead. There was a shaft of light piercing the gloom and that light was in the shape of a dog.

But which dog? I realised George had been talking.

"….So I know just the breed for ye, Pet. The list's fine. They're all good, they'd all be fine for ye, but ye've no got the best."

He turned those piercing blue eyes on me.

"What'd suit ye best is the Flatcoated Retriever."

I had vague recollection of a large, all-black dog. Perhaps it hadn't made the list because it was all black.

"Why?"

"Because they're more fun, Brenda!"

But that night, I rapidly forgot George's surprise recommendation, as my mind filled with thoughts of that huge teddy bear of a dog, an Airedale. George's reasons for a breed did make sense. Within certain parameters, I would know what I was getting. There would be no nasty surprises of temperament, health or size for a first time owner. I could have my rescue dog next.

Only two days later, I was overjoyed to discover there was an Airedale breeder just down the A46, towards Newark! Surely this was meant to be, I thought happily as I drove to the boarding kennels which was also the home of Sujoncla Airedales. And there were puppies ready and waiting for new homes! I could not believe my luck!

I warmed immediately to Susan, an attractive young lady, very proud of her dogs.

It was in the kitchen, and not in any of the kennels, that I met mum Amy with her two pups which had been delivered by Caesarean section. I knelt down to see them better. Rejoicing in the (albeit temporary) names of Gertrude and Gladys, they squirmed, wriggled, took a few tottering steps, fell over, staggered up, then set off again in a different direction.

Suddenly, unbelievably, the tip of my right ear felt incredibly warm, rather as if a hair-dryer had been switched on! Puzzled, I turned my head to be confronted by two unblinking brown eyes. Amy!

"She's a very good mother," said Susan, wide and knowing smile spreading across her face.

Amy remained right next to me as I surveyed her pups from a respectful distance. But my delight vanished when I learned they would be ready in four weeks and it would be eight weeks before I broke up for the long summer holidays! George had emphasised the supreme importance of the formative eight to twelve weeks in a puppy's life and the tiny Airedale would be fourteen before I could be at home all day. Could I possibly leave a tiny pup alone for up to four hours at a time?

I returned home, short-lived elation replaced by familiar despondency.

Conflicting thoughts raged in my mind. Gertrude and Gladys grew. Now they looked like Yorkshire Terriers, which is I suppose, what they were. Finally, I decided.

On a lovely, sunny morning, I went to the kennels to tell Susan, and to see those beautiful pups for the final time. I left, choking back tears. So very easily, I could have had the dog of my dreams, the dog I most wanted, yet I had rejected that opportunity! How I wanted to turn around and tell her I had changed my mind, but it was as if my legs belonged to someone else. I cried that night, trapped once more inside the glass prison, but I stuck to my decision.

Exams were coming round at college. I was so busy marking course work, filling in endless forms, devising what I hoped were interesting revision exercises, and coping with students in varying degrees of panic, that I had little time to pursue my search for a companion, but a few weeks later, an advert in the freebie newspaper caught my eye.

"Cocker Spaniel puppies. Blue roan. Ready in four weeks."

Perfect timing!

The address was near Grantham, and even though Cockers hadn't made my list, and weren't very big, I'd always liked them.

A gentle breeze sighed in the tall trees that shrouded the house at Cherry Tree Kennels. The entire place looked unloved and untidy, but what struck me most, as I picked my way to the front door, was the smell; a smell of staleness, of dampness and of dogs. The pups I was told, by the rather forceful, middle-aged lady who appeared from around the back of the house, were outside. As we made our way to a long, low, brick and stone outbuilding, I could hear several dogs barking. The sounds came from the other side of the house and somewhere beyond the trees. The barking suddenly ceased as abruptly as it had begun. Perhaps they were a neighbour's dogs.

Floor to ceiling bars along one side of the whitewashed outhouse, gave it the air of a small gaol. Imprisoned in its far corner, was a large, plastic dog bed. It was the only thing there. In the bed, lay Mum with her babies. And that was where they remained. I felt uneasy.

"Aren't they quiet?"

"All my dogs are quiet," she replied with pride.

I thought her pride misplaced. There was something wrong: the smell, the untidiness, the quietness. This owner had no joy in her dogs, and they had no joy in her, or in being dogs.

She strained down to the bed and unceremoniously selected three pups, setting them on the bare floor. Mum merely watched, resignation dulling her sweet, brown eyes.

"There's only these three left; all dogs."

Two pups plucked up the courage to approach, but I was taken by the third. He stayed back, watching from a distance. Gently, I picked him up. He sat in my arms without demure. I could make you happy, I thought, gazing down at the little black and white pup. I could make you run and jump for joy. Yet I knew this was wrong. This was not how a novice should choose a dog, out of pity. I looked at Mum. She didn't seem to care that a stranger was holding one of her babies. How very different this was to Amy, secure in her warm kitchen. I needed time to think.

"If I have one, it'll be this one."

"You'll have to leave a deposit, otherwise I'd have to let it go. I don't have any trouble selling my pups."

"I'll let you know."

I was glad to escape: glad and yet so very sorry.

As I put my car away, I heard George in his garden. Perhaps he'd have a look at the little Spaniel! He'd be able to tell me if it was all right.

"I've seen an advert in the paper, George; Cherry Tree Kennels."

He was instantly alert.

"Grantham?"

He dropped his spade and faced me through the trees. His expression was grim.

"Ye don't want to go there, Pet. It's a puppy farm. Don't go there." He leaned forward.

"Ye see, that's another reason I want ye to go for a breed. Ye go to a reputable breeder, and get a good type o' dog. One breeder wi' one type o' dog. You tell me who you've found. I'll find out if they're worth seeing."

I never did tell George I'd already been.

That evening, I thought a lot about "my" black and white puppy. I wished with all my heart that he and his brothers would find good, loving homes. I tried not to think about Mum.

Two more weeks passed. The students took their exams.

"In June. Have you any puppies ready in June?"

Thoughts of the phone bill filled me with dread, as I scoured the country for George's recommendation. Yet every listed breeder of Flatcoated Retrievers seemed to be either taking time off, or their pups were already spoken for.

"Have you any puppies ready in June, or July perhaps?"

I was stretching those formative boundaries. I was also getting desperate.

"Then, maybe August? Early August?"

Now I was really pushing it, but I could see my hope of a family and a new life slipping away. I worked through to the mighty Shargleam kennels: same response, but this time, with a glimmer of hope.

"I could give you a few numbers of good breeders who are known to us. One of them might have something."

Heaven knows which part of the British Isles these codes were for! Then I recognised the final one! It was here, in Lincolnshire!

Forgetting I had promised to tell George first, my fingers actually shook as I dialled the number.

The female voice was precise, almost curt.

"I've a litter due the end of April. They'd be ready in June. You've had a Flatcoat before?"

I wasn't about to make much impression.

"What have you had?"

My hopes vanished.

Yet the formidable voice continued. It was made clear that I would have to be interviewed before I could even be considered for her list of potential buyers. Would ten-thirty on Thursday be convenient? The middle of the night would have been convenient! To my utter amazement, the address she gave was almost local. My dog could be but twenty minutes way!

I told George I had learned of a Flatcoat breeder in Lincoln, but not that I had already made contact. I needn't have worried. Back came the recommendation;

"She's fine, Brenda; excellent reputation. Only the very best quality dogs."

He beamed and his blue eyes sparkled. He seemed genuinely delighted. But what had happened to my Rescue of unknown parentage? Not only had I settled for a pedigree, I now seemed to be heading for the top end of that market! I felt as if I was being driven along a particular pathway, yet I didn't want to resist. There was a strange feeling of inevitability about it all. Somehow, it felt right.

Thursday crawled into reality. I prepared very carefully. Smart, so that she might know I would care for my dog, but not so smart that she could think I might not be able to tolerate the inevitable grime and grit that come with four paws.

The address took me to a long row of large terraced houses in the west end of the city.

My first reaction was one of disappointment. How could anyone breed big, active dogs in a terraced house? But it was merely a matter of yards from the West Common, a huge area of grass, trees and ponds that led to the now disused Carholme Racecourse.

A cacophony of deep barks greeted the doorbell. Through the green Victorian glass, I could make out several heads which appeared to be bouncing in all directions. Footsteps sounded in the hall and the voice from the phone spoke sharply.

The barking ceased. The bouncing heads disappeared. A door slammed, then the footsteps returned.

Jill Saville was quite tall and bonny, with dark hair and an incongruously tiny nose. She wore a long denim skirt with a plain green sweatshirt embroidered on the left breast with a small gold logo: Fossdyke Gundogs.

"Hello. You're on time."

Relieved the first hurdle was over, I followed her into the lounge, disappointingly, a dog-free zone. She invited me to be seated, then took her place with her back to the big bay window.

"You've not had a dog before. Why do you want one now?"

My feelings of relief began to evaporate as I tried to think of reasons she might find acceptable.

"Why a Flatcoat?"

This wasn't so much an interview, more the third degree!

I told of my large garden, the ample space within the bungalow, the time and energy I had for long walks, and that I already had an excellent trainer, willing to take us on. Mrs. Saville's expression was invisible against the light and I could tell nothing from her detached tones.

"Dog or bitch?"

"Oh, bitch. My trainer says they're easier for a first timer and they're more affectionate."

"I've always found my dogs more affectionate."

With that, any feelings of ease I had left, vanished completely. But the interview was not over.

"You'd better meet my dogs."

She took me down the hall, opened the door to the breakfast room and stood back.

Those bouncing heads I had seen through the green glass held laughing brown eyes and were attached to gleaming black bodies, quivering with excitement. Four luxuriant tails wagged furiously. Four great tongues and eight huge paws made a full frontal assault and I disappeared beneath a warm onslaught of sheer happiness. So this was the Flatcoated Retriever! Wow! Mrs. Saville watched silently as her dogs sniffed me, washed me, pawed me and seemed to find me to their liking. The only way I could survive was to get down on my knees and use my arms as they used their paws! And I hugged my first Flatcoat! They were big. They were strong. They radiated pure joy. They were simply wonderful!

"Think you could cope then?"

I struggled to my feet, pulling my coat straight. If memory serves me right, the only answer I could manage was a strangled gasp, through an ear-to-ear grin!

Mrs. Saville nodded.

"I'm not saying you'll get one. Depends how many she has, but I'll put you on my list. Come and meet Mum."

Back home, I sat in a trance! Not the miserable limbo I had known for so long, but an excited, near-disbelief that one of those gorgeous, boisterous, loving beings might one day be here with me. Above all, I thought of mum-to-be Fossdyke Finale, Magic.

She, too, had greeted me with boundless enthusiasm. She had pushed her fine head into my hand, and licked with long and slow sweeps of her warm tongue. I imagined she was approving that I might have one of her babies; a daughter of Magic!

I tried to concentrate on jobs in hand, but with little success. A quotation I must once have read appeared from nowhere to go round and round in my head.

"When man is lonely, God sends him a dog."

I was lonely. I pondered on the tortuous route I had taken to find this, the ideal dog, on my very doorstep. Surely this really was the one that was meant to be?

Time passed, oh, so slowly. I imagined the sleek black form of a Flatcoat beside me as I walked to the supermarket, as I did the gardening, as I moved about the house. I imagined saying goodnight to my new family, and waking up to find someone waiting for me and wanting to be with me.

When April arrived, I allowed myself to start turning the dream into reality.

First, there was the bed; Mrs. Saville had told me the correct size. Then bedding; I already had old blankets and sheets. Then there had to be a brush for that shining coat, and a comb; two combs, one with wider teeth so as not to pull fine baby hair. And toys! Toys for exercise, toys to stimulate a developing mind, toys for a teething puppy to chew.

And a name! I needed a name. George had said short, single syllable names were best. Names that could be called, easily distinguishable, an out of the ordinary name, yet all I could think of were boys' names; Sam, Moss, Ben and I wanted a pretty, feminine name.

Then it came as a bolt from the blue! There was no doubt! My daughter of Magic would be Fern! A Flatcoat named Fern.

I punctuated those final weeks with calls to Mrs. Saville. Was Magic well? Was the pregnancy going to plan?

Finally, the response I longed for! April 29th and the puppies were here! There were twelve of them. There were enough! Fern was here. She would soon be at home with me. My loneliness would be over, and a new life would begin.

I first saw the pups at four weeks, when I could resist the temptation no longer and turned up, unannounced, at the green glass door. Although not allowed inside the breakfast room, I was able to peep from the hall, through the briefly opened door. I had no clear idea of what to expect. An infrared lamp shone from above the whelping box onto what appeared to be umpteen tiny black commas, each twitching in its own space, endlessly wriggling, going nowhere, but forever trying, each stretching into the unknown. How could any of these black grubs possess the beauty of Magic?

Three more long weeks struggled by and during that time, I visited the pups twice more. The first time, I was allowed right in and to stroke the babies. Now they looked like dogs, with roly-poly bodies, thin waving tails and needle-sharp teeth!

I wondered which would be mine. Had I touched her yet? Had I stroked her?

On my second visit, Mrs. Saville decided to demonstrate the finer points of the Flatcoated Retriever, and lifted several puppies, in turn, onto the top of an adjacent cupboard, so that I might appreciate their profiles. Each stood to attention, like a small, black soldier, apprehensive of their new and elevated station. To me, they all looked perfect, but Mrs. Saville never seemed fully satisfied.

"See the top line? Could be a bit straighter, perhaps."

"His brisket isn't as deep as it might have been."

"This bitch's tail's set a bit high for me. Could grow into it, though."

She searched the pen for one pup in particular. He, too, stood to attention, but did not receive any criticism. I was led to appreciate the straight top line, the deep brisket, the shoulders, the neck, the set of his tail and so many technical details that were completely lost on me! This pup was perfection. She returned him to the pen.

"There's a bitch in here, too. Like that, but even better. It's her feet. She has marvellous feet."

The target was found, but this pup made it crystal clear that she resented her sudden elevation to the cupboard top.

"Look at that head--"

Marvellous Feet shot backwards. Mrs. Saville tried again.

"Look -"

Marvellous Feet twisted sideways and skidded to the edge of the cupboard. Mrs. Saville grabbed her and again replaced her in the middle. Marvellous Feet promptly belly flopped and slid forwards, eyeing the drop back towards her siblings.

"Oh, no, you don't!"

The small Houdini was swiftly scooped up. Mrs. Saville laughed. Was it my imagination, or was there just a hint of the very slightest embarrassment?

"You'll soon have her now. Only one week to go."

The determined pup was returned to the pen. Mrs. Saville turned and looked straight at me.

"Until you have Fern."

Silence. She continued to look at me. Then a smile warmed into life, grew, and I knew I was missing something.

"Her," she nodded towards the pen, "that was her, Fern. You just met Fern."

CHAPTER TWO

One week had never been made of so many days! A countdown at N.A.S.A. had never been watched more closely! It didn't occur to me to question the choice of Fern. All the books I'd read had gone into great detail about how owners-to-be must select the right pup for themselves, yet I had been told which was mine! But all Magic's babies were black and wonderful. Only one had stood out and that was simply because he was smaller than any of the others, and he was already spoken for anyway. With hindsight I believe I would most likely have chosen the pup who didn't want to stand on the cupboard top: I liked her style!

The week passed. It was time.

Yet I was in turmoil. Was I trying to buy Love? What would Mum have said? Would she approve? I'd always wanted a dog. Would she be happy that my solitude was ending? Of course she would! But did I really want this? Wouldn't it be easier and safer for me to stay as I was, bound to no one and no one bound to me? Sealed against the pain of any worry, or illness and the agony of inevitable bereavement. But did I want such safety? Hadn't I come this far because I did want to care? Because I did want all the risks which caring brings?

I needed desperately to talk to someone. Margaret and I had become friendly only a few months ago, meeting after Mum's death when I entered hospital for surgery. There, an entire group of middle-aged women together faced the indignities of bedpans, throwing up, surgical stockings and the race to fill a catheter bag, because that meant one's waterworks had survived the rigours of hysterectomy, had pledged unending friendship. Only Margaret and myself had remained in contact. She worked as a volunteer at the local hospice. Anyone who could do that I reasoned, would understand.

Her unqualified joy when I had phoned to tell of my plan to have a dog suddenly flooded over me as I drew up in front of the green glass door. Still time to change my mind? No! Never!

The door opened. Mrs. Saville must have been waiting.

"Hello. You're on time."

Another interview, not too unlike the one of a few weeks ago, made certain that I had everything in place. She gave me a diet sheet, and explained that Fern was already fully insured for six weeks. More importantly, should it all go wrong, I was to return Fern to her. I must not, under any circumstance, sell her on.

When the finances were complete, we went together into the breakfast room and I was invited to pick out my puppy from the tumbling mass of excited bodies that greeted us. For no good reason at all, I focused on the two largest, who were wrestling each other with great vigour. Finally, I pointed to one of them, but he turned out to be Perfection from the cupboard top. Mrs. Saville had already decided to keep him and had given him the pet name, Skipper, in honour of a famous role played by favourite actor, John Thaw, in the T.V. series, "The Sweeney." Skipper was destined to become her favourite dog of all time, and would live up to his registered name of Illustrious. The destiny awaiting his wrestling partner and sister was to be very different, for this was Illusion, my own Fern.

She sat happily in my arms as we headed for the door. The cage, loaned by Mrs. Saville, was already in the car and its new occupant swiftly installed.

"What's that?"

Mrs. Saville peered at an object in the corner of the boot.

"Fern's brush."

I had brought it along just to make certain it was suitable. Mrs. Saville's expression of surprise turned to amusement, then erupted into laughter.

"That'll do for a week or two! Hang on a minute. I've got a real one you can have."

Still chuckling, she returned through the green glass door. Feeling such an idiot, I picked up the brush. It fitted in my palm and had a strap to go over the back of my hand. I suppose it was a bit small. Mrs. Saville returned.

"Here you are. You can keep it."

"It" was about ten inches long. It had a thick, wooden back. Some of the varnish had worn off from where it had been held. The bristles were bright red, very long and very, very stiff. She read my thoughts.

"Oh, you'll use it alright. You'll use it and you'll lay on with it, believe me."

I dropped it in the boot. It was a horse brush!

But nothing could dent my happiness! All doubt had vanished! I felt excited, confident! I turned to say goodbye.

"Let me know if there's any problem. I like to keep in touch with my owners. It's Jill, by the way."

And so we set off for home; our home.

We had travelled barely fifty yards before Fern voiced her opposition. She began to howl, loudly. Whenever we were forced to stop, so did the howling. Perhaps she thought she had won and I would stop taking her away from her mother and siblings. But that howling was as nothing compared to the din which erupted when we hit roadworks and she had an audience! People began to look round. What on earth was this woman doing to such a. little puppy? By the time we'd negotiated the go-stop-go, my face was as red as the car! Yet I couldn't help but admire Marvellous Feet's determination. She hadn't wanted to stand on the cupboard top either!

At last we reached home. Closing the gate behind us, I lifted her out (from a dry car!) onto the drive. She was so tiny! She looked around without any sign of fear, and saw; grass! The first she had ever seen, she scampered to its edge, then stopped dead. Nose twitching, she tentatively extended one marvellous foot onto its surface. How different it must have seemed from the concrete she was used to! A second paw followed, a pause, then she was off, racing back and forth, fast as her little legs could carry her! This certainly met with approval!

The surrounding plants next took her eye. Again, this was something totally new. Green plastic fencing had temporarily protected most, but one large heather was accessible. After eyeing it with curiosity, Fern sniffed it with care, judged it to be suitable, then rolled onto it with great glee!

By now, it was time for my first efforts to feed her. What on earth would I do if she refused to eat? Or to drink? As I prepared her food, she became almost demented with excitement, and tried to clamber up to the worktop, towering above her! But she did eat in a most ladylike manner and cleared her bowl. Throughout her life, I remember Fern failing to clear her bowl only once! Then, we went outside immediately, up the drive and back onto the lawn.

"Fern, go wee."

I was following George's instructions to the letter. As yet, Fern had no idea of the command, or of her name, but the sooner I started the routine, the sooner would she understand, and know what was expected of her. Eventually, the action coincided with the phrase. Lots of praise and a short play followed, then back indoors, for I thought it high time my pup had a nap. Or was it me who needed one?

I lifted a cardboard box bed down to the floor. The adult bed could wait and hopefully miss the attacks of puppy teeth. Fern seemed to know what it was for at once and inspected it carefully, but found it fell short of her expectations. She raked out all the bedding. Still it did not meet with her approval, so she decided to ignore the box and bedding altogether, and lay on the bare floor tiles. And she laid on her back! Slowly, her head tilted to the floor, and she fell asleep, but without closing her eyes. They simply rolled up into her head! She looked terrible! Flat on her back, legs splayed outwards, and showing the whites of her eyes!

I sat on the kitchen stool and sorted through the paperwork Mrs. Saville had given me. I read and re-read Fern's pedigree with growing awe. Far from my intended Rescue of unknown parentage, Fern was born of many champions; father, all four grandparents, and liberally gracing the past five generations. Great grandfather on both sides, was none other than the legendary Shargleam Blackcap, top Flatcoat of all time, and Best in Show at Cruft's! I gazed at the little sleeping pup, innocent of the world and of her immaculate parentage. Remembering what Mrs. Saville, or Jill, had said when she explained the finer points of the Flatcoat, then surely Fern must be what was known as, "Pick of the litter." Why on earth had she chosen this pup for me, a complete novice? Maybe I should show Fern? There must be somewhere to learn how. Perhaps she might become famous in the new world I had just entered! Perhaps there was something else we could do together?

Together! What a wonderful word! I broke the silence by speaking it out loud, savouring each syllable, tasting the love and joy that the word held. Together. Together. Who says you can't buy love?

The rest of Day One was spent in a similar, delicious fashion: watching Fern sleeping, playing, exploring, rolling on the ever flattening heather, feeding, and "go wee-ing". As darkness fell, she took herself to the cardboard-box bed and curled up in the replaced bedding. I spread newspapers on the floor and headed for bed myself, thoroughly worn out!

Lying there, I mused over the day's events. The realisation that the comfortable, yet excited feeling, wrapping me in its warmth, was happiness, came almost as a shock. I realised I was smiling as I lay there in the darkness. The future glowed. What did it hold for us? I was delighted Fern seemed to have such a strong and individual personality: just what I needed! Yes, George must be right: Flatcoats are more fun! And you can buy love!

I don't know how long I slept, but I was jolted into awareness by a sound, the like of which I had heard only in a B-rated horror movie. A full, yet piercing sound which started high, and soared even higher! So this was what a first night puppy sounded like! Poor, little lost Fern, crying for the warmth of her mother, brothers and sisters. She howled in loneliness for hours on end. I wanted so much to go and cuddle her, to tell her that all was well and that now I loved her and would always care for her, but both George and Mrs. Saville had warned me against such action, explaining that it would merely prolong the puppy's distress and make for future problems. So I pulled the duvet around my ears and pretended I couldn't hear a thing.

Necessary sleep eventually claimed us both before another bout of howling broke the silence. This time, I stayed awake. Four o'clock. Five o'clock Five-thirty. The new neighbour from across the road left for work in his noisy diesel. The howling finally subsided, but I couldn't sleep again, and eventually headed for the kitchen. As I approached, I heard a strange grating noise. Quietly, I opened the door and peered around it towards Fern's bed. With her back to me, she was engrossed in chewing the cardboard box, and judging by its battered edges, must have been hard at work ever since she stopped howling!

"Fern."

She looked over her shoulder, realised I was there and ran towards me, stringy tail waving with delight. Opening the back door, we both rushed out into the sunny morning and the "go-wee" ritual began our second day together.

Day two also saw the beginning of another ritual, thankfully a temporary one; that of scraping tiny bits of dried Weetabix off the kitchen floor! Perhaps it was the puppy milk that changed this cereal into vegetarian cement!

The postman brought some unexpected mail: a card with bluebirds and a bottle of champagne on the front. Inside it read; "Congratulations on your new arrival." Underneath was written; "May you have many hours of fun and laughter together. Margaret."

Dear Margaret! She always seemed to know the right thing to do.

On the third day, George came to see us. The moment he entered the kitchen, Fern stopped in her tracks, took one look, then promptly keeled over onto her back and began to urinate. In a flash, George had picked her up, and deposited her outside for her to finish.

Down on his knees, he cooed soft sounds and spoke gently to her.

"Good girl, Fern. Good girl."

She looked directly at him.

"Oho! That's ma girl! Good girl, Fern."

Perhaps he wasn't quite the terrifying, Super, Mega, Alpha pack leader she had at first thought. Her tail slowly began to wag.

"Fern, there's clever. Good girl, Fern. Fern…"

George stood, trotted past, turned to face her, and backed towards the garden, arms spread as at the start of a hug, laughing and repeating her name.

She watched for a moment, then threw caution to the wind, scampering after him with glee. A new relationship had been born. It was a relationship which would have a profound effect on our lives together.

George was keen to start work with Fern. He had never trained a Flatcoat before, and I think he was itching to find out about the breed which is at once known as the "Clown Prince" of dogs, yet also the finest hunting retriever of all! I, on the other hand, wanted to wait until Fern had been vaccinated, and those vaccinations had "taken". But the important formative weeks in a puppy's life were already here, and passing, so we compromised. I wanted a healthy dog, but I also wanted a " bomb-proof" dog, one who remained totally unfazed by life's surprises, however sudden or noisy. I knew that intelligence depended on the physical number of connections between neurones in the brain, and that stimulation, through many and varied experiences, developed these connections, so we really needed to go out. And we did. I carried her everywhere!

"Come on, kid. Let's go connect some neurones!"

Not the most common thing to say to a pup, but that is what I did say to Fern at the start of each foray!

First, we made friends with the bin-men, who were quite happy, though somewhat bemused, to allow this small, black puppy to peer intently into the awesome jaws of their crusher and to watch and listen as the wheelie bins crashed up and down.

We sat on the wall beside the local primary school playground at lunchtimes, and I held Fern on my knee so that she might see, as well as hear, young humans tearing around, yelling and shrieking.

We even braved the School Run with its depressed clutches, depressed Mums and revving engines. She found that fascinating!

Then two strokes of educational good luck came our way. The first was a really good thunderstorm which growled its way in towards the end of an afternoon's gardening. Fern was apprehensive of the distant rumbling and when the first crash reverberated between the houses, she was ready to panic. I carried on weeding, without a word, and Fern took her cue from that. She returned to dismembering her "dolly", the knotted inner tube of a bicycle tyre thrown over the fence for her by George. Large raindrops began to fall as the thunder muttered into silence. Much as I wanted, I couldn't dash for shelter. How would Fern know that my human frailty was driving me out of the rain and that I was not fleeing from That Noise? So I stayed, going from damp to wet to soaked and praying for just one more crash.

It came with such an explosive and vicious crack, that I feared a nearby house or tree had been struck. From the corner of my eye, I saw Fern whip round to look at me. I didn't react, so she resumed chewing the large strip of inner tube, formerly known as her dolly. I was watching Fern, wondering why she was so determined to chew all her toys to pieces, when the thunder came again, and this time, I saw her reaction clearly. Or rather I didn't, for there wasn't one. Zilch. Nothing. I gathered my tools, called to her, and together, we walked unhurriedly, to the back door. I was wet, she was wet, but a "bombproof" dog was surely well on the way!

The second piece of good luck was that the council decided to dig up our road. Although never staying long, for fear of damaging tiny ears, Fern found the digging, drilling, shouting and traffic noise much to her liking. I thought the hammer used to flatten things was her favourite, for she not only heard, saw and smelled it, but felt its vibrations, too. Exciting stuff!

It was around this time that Fern met Fred, another ex-colleague of mine, and he pointed out what he thought to be a totally ridiculous anomaly: her name!

"Illusion?" he had gasped after their meeting, specs skewed on his nose, "Illusion? Some b*** illusion!"

Ever after, Fred would always refer to Fern as S.B.I.!

My outings with Fern met with George's full approval, but I needed his direct guidance to get her to accept the car. Our first excursions were just round the block; all of eight hundred yards and she howled the entire way! But I had to keep repeating this, ignoring the howls and remaining totally silent myself, until we were back home, when I would open the rear door to praise the now silent pup. The next stage was to drive a little further, still ignoring the protests, still remaining totally silent, but stop halfway, get out, go round to the back and praise the quiet pup. I endured this for almost three weeks, twice each day, before we reached our goal; an entirely silent drive! The determined pup from the cupboard top was never going to give in easily!

Getting her to stay in the boot of my hatchback when I left the car, was, by contrast, the piece of cake George promised it would be.

"She'll ha' moved for sure. Tak' no notice. Ignore her. Just open the back as usual and make a big fuss of her when, but only when, she's got back where she should be." The third time I did this was the final time. Fern never again made any effort to move about the car.

At home, Marvellous Feet showed the same strong personality and determination. She insisted on trying to leap onto the worktop as I prepared food. In her doggy mind, she was, of course, " rewarded", whenever it happened to be her food I was preparing, so she persisted in the same behaviour for all food preparation.

"Nay problem, Pet, nay problem at all," was George's laughing response.

That day, I had sardines for lunch because I needed a small tin! Afterwards, I washed it out, collected some pebbles from the garden, put them inside, and carefully sellotaped the lid back in position. Then I left some of her food on the worktop, balanced the tin overhanging the edge and left the kitchen. Within seconds, a loud clatter told me the booby trap had been sprung. Sure enough, there was a surprised and chastened puppy sitting at the far end of the kitchen, staring back at the worktop which had just been so horrible to her! Twice more that afternoon I reset the trap, each time in a different guise, for I was becoming ever more aware of Fern's ability to put two and two together. Twice more, the traps were sprung, but the times between setting and springing were lengthening.

When it was time for Fern's feed, I set the trap first, making sure that the tin was invisible from her viewpoint. She sat still, which was a first, but her expectant delight eventually overcame her new wariness and the tin crashed to the floor.

That was Fern's final attempt to steal anything from the worktop, or indeed from anywhere, and because it had been the object that " punished" her, and not me, she could be trusted completely, even when on her own. A bad habit cured in one day!

Fern had long since turned up her nose at the Weetabix and puppy milk breakfast, thank heavens, but the Battle of Grooming raged undiminished!

"Touch her everywhere, Pet. The vet'll thank ye for it," George had said, adding conspiratorially, "even in her private little places."

So I persevered, although she dissolved into rubber the moment the brush was produced, and her needle-sharp puppy teeth were painful! The battle subsided only slowly; another symptom of what I now began to label the Cupboard Top Syndrome.

Her legs were starting to feather nicely, but her tail remained a disaster area! I would brush, then comb the underside and even gently pull down the hair in an attempt to make it look more like the illustration in the Breed Standard. It still resembled a piece of string!

How I longed to take Fern for walks like "a proper dog"! Ringing round all the vets I could find in Yellow Pages, I learned that the vast majority vaccinated puppies at exactly twelve weeks. One of two who would do it earlier, was the vet used and recommended by Jill Saville. He was also the furthest away, but I could always change and re-register afterwards with the local vet, I thought.

So Fern made her first appearance at the Whitegates Veterinary Surgery later that same week and we both thoroughly enjoyed the experience! An old, adapted house, it sat near a roundabout on the main Lincoln-Washingborough road. It really was white and there was a white gate, too, but it appeared to be permanently open, allowing easy access to the car park. And what a car park! Cars crammed like sardines in a tin! Half blocking in the other half!

"Who's the blue Maestro? I've had to go in front."

"Me. S'alright."

"You can have my space. I've just got to pay."

"No worry."

People seemed only too happy to sort out any problem, for their pets' benefits, which was an encouraging sign.

In the waiting room, we met many new people, most of whom wanted to know who Fern was and what she was! At close quarters, Fern herself saw and smelled her first cat, a rabbit and a bird in a cage. She made the acquaintance of her first vet, a slim and attractive redhead named Cathy O'Rourke, who pronounced Fern to be fit and well and injected the cocktail of inactivated microbes.

I paid at the little office window, and then headed for the door, feeling so satisfied and pleased with myself for having protected this wonderful little being, who already meant so very much to me, from all those dreadful diseases!

I closed the door behind me, and paused on the step. The view crossed fields, then a railway line, and rose to distant woods. As I gazed at that wide expanse of green, a secret smile from my heart began to spread its warmth through my entire being. I could feel the promise of the future, a delicious frisson of excitement that tickled my back and reddened my cheeks. I looked down at my lovable, energetic, enthusiastic, determined, oh, so determined companion. Where would we go? What would we do?

I could not know that I would regret forever what I had chosen to do that day.

CHAPTER THREE

"Let's go!"

George wanted to start working with Fern, and his forceful personality was difficult to resist.

"She's strong. She's keen. We're missing the most important time in her life."

I wanted to start, too, and so, only five days after her primary vaccination, we did just that. Now, everything was formalised. I was the client, and George, my paid consultant. He would pick up my dog and me for a weekly lesson for as long as I wanted, or could afford to do so.

The big cream estate drew up to my bungalow for the second time on a sunny and breezy morning. Emblazoned along each side, in green, were the words, "The Talbot Dog Training Centre", and across the back, " The home of good dog training." Fern was dancing with delight as George picked her up, and carried her to the car. Placed in the back with his own three collies, she showed no apprehension at all, and spent the journey playing with So, the good-natured youngest dog. Old Wisp, the pack leader, stared pointedly ahead, while Gus watched the two youngsters with benign aloofness. The car had the same inviting, warm scent that I had breathed before, on my trip with the Airedale, but this time, my own dog was a part of it. My own dog! I could not believe how much Fern had already changed my life. It did matter that I got up in the morning! I had someone who needed me as I needed them, and someone to love who loved me! Yes, you really can buy love!

Our destination was South Common, an area much used and enjoyed by the local community. Along the bottom, were two football pitches. Halfway up the hill, a council owned golf course stretched like a ribbon from side to side, and back again. The top of the common was dotted with mature trees, shrubs and bushes, mostly blackberry. Several springs bubbled to the surface here, and two of them fed large ponds further down the hill. Horses were grazing all over the area, making a golfing hazard

26

with a difference! Golf greens apart, the common was covered in tussocks of thick grass, harebells and, I would think, just about every member there is of the dandelion family! It was into this enormous and strange world that George unhesitatingly placed his small pupil. Then all the pack; two humans, three dogs and one puppy, began to walk.

As we walked, we talked; and I began to learn all about Fern; from the indelible inheritance of her wolf ancestry, to her feeding and appetite, her grooming, her need for play, even her sleeping! He emphasised that I must try to see situations through the eyes of the wolf dog I had chosen to be my companion and not only through the eyes of the human animal that I happened to be. It was both fascinating and a little frightening!

George kept his expert eye on the happily exploring puppy. Should she stray a little too far, or into the proximity of other people, horses or dogs, he would call her name and the moment she turned, begin laughing and cooing and repeating her name, liberally interspersed with such things as, "Good girl, there's clever," and " Oh, yes!" as the delighted pup raced back to him. He didn't care one jot who saw his clownish capers, or overheard his strange noises!

"Light and happy voice all the time, Pet. Only ever use her name wi' a light and happy voice. Never use her name to tell her off.. Now you watch her, and when ye think she should come back, you call her."

Whenever he saw the puppy tiring, George would carry her for a while, all the time continuing to explain what he was doing and why.

During this very first lesson, Fern met the residents of the common at close quarters. Taking many of his clients there, George had learned which horses were placid, and which skittish, so when he spotted a group of the placid kind, he took immediate advantage, and walked the tiny pup right through the middle! With the stoic Gus to her left and George to her right, Fern trotted unconcernedly between those terrifyingly huge and noisily chomping animals! The hour flew by!

"Only socialising this time, Pet," said George as we turned to the car, "but just think what she's started to learn!" He counted on his fingers. "That there's nothing out there to be afraid of. That people and horses and other dogs don't bother you, if you don't bother them, and it's great to come back to Mum when she calls."

Wow! Could it really be this easy?

Now Fern had made her peace with the car, I took her on her first visit. It was to Margaret's and the first time I had been to her home. The presence of a boisterous and inquisitive puppy eased any slight awkwardness. She had been longing to see Fern.

"Ooh! Hasn't she got big paws?"

At once she got down on her knees, soft, greying hair falling over the black pup. She picked up one marvellous foot.

"Ooh, aren't they warm? Aren't they thick?"

It was mutual love at first sight, and our soon to be regular visits to Margaret's were to become the highlight of Fern's life!

Or was that her lessons with George? He was surprised at her desire and capacity for learning. After a lifetime with the reputed brains of the canine world, German Shepherds and Border Collies, he nevertheless pronounced Fern's intelligence as "Second to none." While she would always lack the Collie's inbred ability for pinpoint accuracy, she nevertheless learned to "Come," "Sit," and "Stay," with joyful rapidity. Once she had learned an action, she seemed to know whenever George was going to tell her to perform that action, and she had done it, almost before the command had been completed! Purists might have penalised her for "anticipation", but no one could accuse her of that when I was working her! With me, she often seemed to think about it first, and then execute the action with a bored, "Can't really be bothered, this will have to do," resignation! With hindsight, I believe my total inexperience was to blame. I still felt embarrassed about leaping around and making loud encouraging noises as George did, and I saw Fern as a vulnerable baby, whilst he saw, "A bitch of the very highest calibre". Fern delivered exactly what each expected of her.

I tried to find small comfort in the fact that she might be getting too heavy. She seemed to have developed the strange habit of looking quite fat each evening, but by morning, being slim again!

Another milestone was reached when she accepted that I could leave her, but would always return. This, too, was a grand battle of wills; another symptom from the Cupboard Top! Of course she had been left in the kitchen by herself, but it was a very different matter to be, "home alone". Her protests were long and loud: so long and so loud that even George, from his home just behind us, and with all his vast experience, said he had never known anything quite like it! But I had to persevere, for eventually I would return to work. However, lurking outside, then trying to get back in to praise a silent dog during the short time she paused for breath, was not easy! Eventually, perseverance (or bloody-mindedness!) finally paid off. When the long college holidays ended, she had learned for herself the signs that I was going out without her, and would take

Brenda and Fern

Puppy Fern

Illusion

Fern, Wisp, Gus, So.

Fern and Maddie

Sheer enjoyment, Sandy and Fern

Fern and Louis

Illusion

Rosette!

to her bed with an air of hurt disgust. She forgave me instantly on my return.

There was now a reassuring symmetry in our togetherness; Life had purpose! And how I loved watching this extrovert, gangly, ugly duckling with a tail of string, changing slowly into a beautiful swan! George was more aware of the beginning of the slow transformation than I, and pointed out the narrowing of her face and lengthening of her muzzle long before I noticed. I had seen the growing hair on the underside of her tail however, and always brushed it with great care and enthusiasm to encourage the growth!

Margaret, too, had seen the start of the change from roly-poly puppy into canine supermodel. She could never resist commenting on, or holding one of Fern's great, warm paws! Life had suddenly become so full, so hectic for me, that I ignored a niggling worry about my new friend's health. She was often quite pale and certainly seemed to tire easily, and had not recovered as quickly from the surgery as I had. Selfishly, I put it to the back of my mind. Other concerns were far more fun!

Returning from Margaret's one afternoon, I plucked up the courage to call on the formidable Jill Saville. After all, she'd asked me to keep in touch and I did want to know, from an expert in the breed, that Fern was developing normally.

"You've got plenty of muscle on her."

Sweet relief!

"Coat's good, too."

Absolute delight!

"Not much waist though. Could take just a bit off. Trouble is, she was born greedy. Always was a greedy pup."

I had passed, although not quite with distinction! Eventually, I bade a reluctant goodbye to the shining black whirlwinds of joyous abandon hurtling around the yard outside and headed for the green glass door, accompanied by only one pair of those wonderful laughing eyes. As I reached for the door handle, Jill called after me.

"You do know it's Skipper you've got there, don't you?"

Perhaps it was the "growth spurt" which was to blame for an annoying problem which now arose. Put politely, Fern developed the, "trots" and I began some careful adjustments to her diet.

The majority of her exercise was taken at a locally famous place known as Fen Lane. The whole area of council open space took its name from the roadway which led there. It comprised of two large playing fields, separated by a short, steep slope. These fields were bounded on two sides by smart, detached bungalows, on the long third side by the unadopted part of Fen Lane itself, and along the lower, fourth side, by a public footpath which ran alongside a wide drainage ditch. Both led to the River Witham.

Fern grew to consider that ditch her private swimming pool! Whatever the weather, she would gallop down its steep sides to leap joyfully into the clear water. Then, she would either play around, splashing and stirring up the soft mud, or simply forge along for up to fifty yards or so, before climbing out. I gave up trying to separate her from water. It was more hassle trying to fight her natural instincts than drying her when we landed home. Besides, I told myself, it was good for her!

It was down Fen Lane that I discovered the existence of a whole new sub-culture; that of the Local Responsible Dog Fraternity, or Crazy Owners Who Were Down the Lane Come Rain, Shine, Hell, High Water, Plague or Pestilence!

There was tax-inspector Ruth, with her awesomely built and awesomely obedient German Shepherd, Max. There was something-in-the-city Tony, with Weimaraner, Ross, the only dog never to fall for Fern's beguiling charms: Scottish Bill Binnie, with Golden Retriever, Bracken and a pocket full of treats for every dog he met. There was cricket-mad Fred with fat Beagle, Toby; Alice with explorer Beagle, Wigsley, frequently A.W.O.L. and a very up-market lady who insisted on calling Fern, Fleur, with a standard poodle named Henry. There was Louise and Rottweiler Cleo, who hated all bitches on sight, but made an exception for Fern and Sandra, whose Rough Collie, Benjy, was so laid back as to be almost out of sight! Then Dennis with Big Bob, an amiable travelling hearth rug, Tony with his golden three musketeers, Julie's Weimaraner army of grey ghosts, and another George, with Carly, the G.S.D. he had found on a motorway. So many wonderful, friendly people and their canine alter-egos, with each and every one greatly loved by Fern.

My exuberant, joyful dog seemed to believe that they had come to the field purely to play with her! Perhaps I found that to be the greatest of all Fern's charms: the innocent belief that the world had been created purely for her interest and enjoyment!

Of all these pleasant and indulgent dogs, Max was undoubtedly her favourite. The elderly patriarch was Number One Canine down the Lane, never to be approached by any other dog, except Fern of course. Even from a distance, she would gallop off to greet him, totally ignoring my cries! This generous dog allowed puppy Fern every liberty, even to the extent of stealing his treasured blue ball!

As Fern grew, Ruth became convinced that Max found the attentions of a young and sexy bitch to be most flattering and that she both enhanced his status and enlightened his life during his final months.

Not long after Max's death, Fern came face to face with a newcomer to the Lane, a bitch called Maddie.

They had entered the lower field simultaneously, Fern from the top corner, Maddie diagonally opposite. Both dogs froze instantly, staring across at each other. I felt a sharp pang of anxiety because I had never before seen Fern react in such a manner.

The dog staring back from about three hundred yards, was what I can best describe as bright orange with four flashy white socks. And it was big, very big!

Without warning, the two dogs suddenly began racing towards each other. Then, at some signal, unseen or unheard by a simple human, both abruptly dropped to their bellies, eyes still glued on each other. Fern ignored my calls. The orange dog's owner now appeared, saw what looked like impending trouble, and began calling as well. He, too, was totally ignored. Suddenly, both dogs leapt to their feet simultaneously and resumed their headlong dash. Then Fern dropped to the ground, her action instantly mirrored by the orange stranger. What kind of behaviour was this?

Now I became fearful, for I had seen that the orange dog was not only taller than Fern, but also broader and more heavily built. Dreadful thoughts crowded into my mind. How do you separate fighting dogs? Can you avoid being bitten? If I could just keep my face out of the way...But Fern can't fight! It's not in her nature. She could be seriously hurt. Yet she'd spent hours play-fighting with So! Surely that would that help her when they met? Why, oh why, was she so determined to meet this belligerent looking stranger?

Now Fern was on her feet again, followed immediately by the heavier dog, as both resumed their race. The owner was running as hard as he could after his charge. Forgetting what George had taught me, I did the same, but we were both a long way off when the two dogs finally came eye to eye.

For several seconds, they remained motionless. Then it began! Twisting, turning, rolling on the ground, rearing on their back legs, boxing with their forepaws; they were playing! They were having the most tremendous fun!

What kind of behaviour was this?

The dogs had known. Only we humans, hampered by limitations of logic, had not known. George later identified the bright Maddie as a Rhodesian Ridgeback, in spite of her socks and was able to explain that the lying down had been a sign of submission, each dog signalling to the other, that it had no intention of being dominant. What he could not explain was their instant and simultaneous total understanding of each other's intention and character.

That Fern and Maddie were on the same wavelength was beyond doubt. People of the Dog Fraternity would watch, marvel and laugh at their antics. People not of the Fraternity would give them a very wide berth, unsure as to what was actually happening. Could this be the start of the dogfight that earned drinks in the pub?

Ever afterwards, Maddie's owner, policeman Andrew and I, tried to time our visits to the Lane so they coincided. We would sit on the grass and talk. The dogs would fly around in a whirlwind of canine athleticism and sheer joy.

I remember that after one of these wonderful times, Andy remarked that Fern looked, "A bit podgy."

Although her breed is extremely people-orientated, it was necessary for Fern to meet as many people as possible, so that her behaviour might become socially acceptable by human standards, and she did not launch herself at everyone like an unguided missile, to cover them with enthusiastic and slobbery licks. In dog society, this might promise unending love and devotion, but it's not such a good idea if you're wearing your best clothes! It was to this end, that I screwed up my courage and took her to meet Mary, who had been so opposed to my doggy ambitions. I did not choose my moment well. It was a little too early in Fern's education.

As usual, her confidence and intelligence drove her to explore this new and therefore exciting place, and while I knew she would simply look and sniff, Mary could not accept my assurances. Had Fern been able to satisfy her curiosity, then she would have settled of her own volition, but as it was, I strove to keep her by my side. Normal conversation became impossible. Fern was returned to the car and I left soon after. Mary never asked me to go there again. Although invited, she never came to visit me. Occasionally, I kept in touch by phone.

Now it was time to "adjust" the close bond between Fern and myself.

I wasn't looking forward to it, but I knew that I must. What would happen to her should we ever be parted? This is one of the drawbacks for any dog in a single household, so I had to prepare Fern. I never intended leaving her, but I knew that I must allow her to develop the ability to cope should change become necessary: if I were ill, or in hospital for example.

I put an idea to George. How about if I booked Fern for an overnight stay in kennels, and then, in a week or two, repeated the exercise, but for two nights? He beamed approval.

"Fine idea, Pet! Why not let her spend the day wi' me and the boys first?"

Fern couldn't get in the car fast enough when, after breakfast, George called at seven one morning, as he took his "boys" for their exercise. Apparently, she looked round for Mum just the once, about halfway down the road! A tired and happy dog was returned over the fence that evening, resuming her normal operations with a nonchalance you could package and sell! Excellent! The following morning, I discovered that George's day care also included breakfast; Fern had tucked into that with great glee!

But as the cold hand of winter began to tear away the warmth of summer, so my life with Fern began to change.

It was as I turned around from shutting out one of those cold, foggy autumnal evenings, that I saw what had happened to her. I could not believe what my eyes told me! She was standing with her tail down and her head poked straight out, but had turned up her eyes to focus on me. Her body had changed! Changed! She was wider than she was deep! I stared at her in horror and disbelief! What had happened to her? What was happening to her? As I gazed, dumbfounded, she gingerly took a step towards me, slowly wagging her drooping tail. She looked so sad and so very guilty! Her expression was harrowing to see. How could a dog change shape? How could any living creature change shape? This was insane! It must be me! I must be going mad! No one would ever believe me! What on earth could I do? I wrenched myself back to the moment. It was an ordinary day. I was standing in my own kitchen, my left hand just touching the table. I looked down at its glass top. It looked the same as it always had. I pressed it with my fingers. It felt the same. Slowly, I raised my eyes back to Fern. She did not look the same as she always had.

It was half past seven. The vet's evening surgery closed at seven, but surely someone would still be there! Yet what could I say? That my dog had changed shape? The idea was bizarre, utterly preposterous! She did not seem to be in any pain. She seemed as bemused as I about what was happening. I sank onto the stool. Something was terribly, horribly wrong. As I watched, she wandered away listlessly into the lounge.

"Like a frog," I thought, "she's shaped like a frog."

The whole thing was absolutely outrageous, ludicrous, beyond any logic!

Suddenly, an idea sprang to mind; George would know! I prayed he was at home, and my prayer was answered. The receiver had seemed barely back in place before the door burst open. He ignored me.

"Oho, ma Black Princess, what ye bin up to, eh?"

He ran expert hands over the swollen body of his Black Princess, while continuing to laugh and jolly along an already much happier dog.

"Oho now! We'll away to the garden and get rid of some of that nasty wind, eh? Fern, come." As he disappeared up the dark driveway, he called quietly over his shoulder.

"Just tell the vet you're on your way."

A dreadful empty feeling shot through me. George had not asked if our vet would be open. I did as I was told, then hurried back to the garden. Lit by the overspill from a street lamp and my small outside light, I could see George encouraging Fern to stand with her forepaws on his chest, while he massaged her distended belly. All the time, he made those special, happy sounds she so loved.

"Get your car out of the garage, Pet."

George spoke in the same calm, light tones he reserved for "his" dogs, but they did not match the urgency of his actions. Fern was belching and breaking gales of wind. The horrible, empty feeling in the pit of my stomach grew. As I turned the ignition, I realised my hands were shaking. Why had George come so very quickly? Whatever he had been doing, he must have stopped immediately. Neither could he have come round by road. Somehow, in the damp autumn gloom, he had struggled through trees and bushes to come directly over the fence which separated our two gardens. Why?

I grabbed my jacket from behind the kitchen door and went back into the garden. George and Fern were still playing their hideous, dark game. She gave an almighty belch.

"Oho, there's clever, there's clever! That's ma' girl!"

He caught sight of me.

"She's better, Pet, but your vet must take a look at her. Have you got your door key?"

Dear George! Ever down-to-earth! He watched closely as I locked the door and pocketed the key. Then he lifted Fern into the car.

"Give me a ring when you're back, Pet."

He turned into the darkness of the garden and was gone.

Now I was alone and my fear grew. Whatever was happening, I had to handle it now.

Traffic into the city was light. We made good time by the clock, but it felt like eternity. Now I remembered reading about a dreadful condition known as gastric torsion, in which a dog's stomach becomes so filled with gas that it twists on its axis and interferes with blood circulation. An emergency operation must be performed within the hour, preferably within minutes, of onset. Even so, its victim suffers terrible pain. Should a dog be lucky enough to survive the first onslaught, it invariably recurs with fatal results. Fern had been enormously bloated, but had not seemed to be in real pain, merely discomfort. Was this a torsion? Had George got to her before her stomach began to twist?

We left Lincoln's bright lights and turned along the road to Washingborough village. Other cars were headed in the opposite direction, towards the city, filled with people on their way for a night out. A bright bus loaded with passengers came towards me, and was gone. More cars. Everyone else seemed part of a crowd, purposeful and happy, but I was afraid and so on my own, just as I had been only a few months ago. My life had been back on course; with purpose, goals and above all, love, and now it might all be gone within minutes.

Sometimes, when I looked in the mirror, I could see Fern, sitting up, looking out to the front as she always did. Surely she wouldn't be doing that if she were in worsening pain?

A small roundabout and the sanctuary of the white house took shape through the gloom. A lone BMW sat in the car park. The waiting room was empty. In the strong lights, I saw Fern had deflated still further. A stranger might think she was simply grossly overweight.

Cathy O' Rourke emerged from the office immediately and gestured towards the consulting room. As she examined Fern, I watched her closely, seeking some clue as to the seriousness of Fern's condition, some fleeting change of expression, which would reveal more than any polite veterinary phrases. There were none. I was advised to soak her meal thoroughly for the time being, to be absolutely certain to keep a quiet period immediately after her feeds, and to give her some tablets called Buscopan. Relief flooded over me when she added that this type of incident can happen in puppies and there was no need for her to see us again, unless I wasn't happy.

But I was happy! I was so relieved!. I had thought I had everything, and then I thought I was going to lose everything! But I wasn't! Things were all right again! I smiled and chatted happily to Fern as we joined the evening convoy wending its happy way into the city. I was part of it now, content and unworried.

At home with Fern, everything appeared back to normal.

Happily, I phoned George.

CHAPTER FOUR

I postponed Fern's forthcoming kennel "holiday", just to be on the safe side, but work on the common continued. I mentioned to George that she looked fat each evening, but he put that down to a greedy pup and indulgent owner, so I decided not to say anything again.

Now, for the very first time, George encountered a problem with his Black Princess. She refused to learn the "Down"! He tried two time honoured methods, but neither produced the desired result. "Down" is a very submissive position, and Fern, basically a submissive dog, should not have had any problem with that, yet she refused to go down. She had never shown any tendency to be a Pack Leader, for that role belonged to George (undoubtedly), followed by myself (arguably), then Wisp, who had once nipped her when she overstepped the mark in boisterous puppy play. Next, there was the wonderful and laid-back Gus, then So, and finally, Fern herself. She found her position at the bottom of the hierarchy perfectly acceptable. Bearing all this in mind, add her supreme intelligence and eagerness to learn, and the situation was completely mystifying. George knew that to have shouted and bullied a dog of Fern's sensitivity would have made the situation impossible, as well as threatening the close relationship they had.

"You've nay problem, Pet," he sighed, "neither has she," he added wryly, nodding towards Fern, as she and So resumed their never-ending play-fight. "I've got to think of a new way for next time. All you've got to do, is what I say."

However, we didn't wait the usual week to tackle the Down, because George wanted it sorted before he went abroad. He had been retained by an international oil company to start and supervise their programme of acquiring and training guard dogs for use at their installations, and would be leaving for Nigeria at the weekend, to lay the groundwork and to prepare for a longer visit.

He seemed very pleased with himself as we left the Merc. and headed

41

out onto the common.

"I think I know what the problem was."

I was delighted to hear his use of the past tense.

"I'm sure this'll work."

We walked and talked. We practised all we'd learned. The dogs played and explored, we practised some more, and then it was time to try the Down.

"I've still no idea why she didn'a do it the last time," he murmured. "Y'see, when you do this," he brought his hand once again from beneath Fern's chin, down the front of her chest and along the ground, "it encour-" and Fern went down! I gaped. Fern looked mightily pleased with herself. George launched into fulsome praise, then put her back into Sit and repeated the same action. Again Fern obliged with a smooth and instant Down. He did it once more, praised her, then motioned us to walk He was laughing.

"Did ye see her expression? She was so pleased wi' herself! I canna believe the last time!" He laughed again. "Like she'd deliberately decided she wasna goin' to do it!"

My thoughts exactly! Was it too far-fetched to believe that Fern had decided to play a trick on "Dad"? Could this be the renowned Flatcoat humour allied to Fern's personal Cupboard Top Syndrome?

The loose bowel problem continued to be worrying. George thought he knew the answer, but didn't. His canine nutritionist friend thought she had the answer, but hadn't. Then the vet's pills and potions failed to have all but the minimal effect. So I began a careful, slow and tortuous journey through all the appropriate books, pamphlets and pet foods I could lay my hands on! Fern looked the picture of glowing health and was brimming with energy, so all I had to do, was to keep searching. The answer was out there somewhere!

As the weather grew seasonably colder, it was a pleasure to close the curtains, turn on the lights and curl up in front of the T.V: after I'd taken Non-stop Action for her evening walk around the houses that is! The pavement work helped to keep her nails short, for that was one thing at which I didn't seem to get any better; it was so difficult to gauge how far to clip on Fern's black nails!

It was on one such quiet evening that my new and cosy world began to fall apart.

The very fact that Fern got up slowly from her place, and not in her usual purposeful manner, attracted my attention.

Once again, I saw the dreadful sight of her beautiful body grotesquely distorted. I stared at her in absolute horror. She looked back at me in misery. I wanted to cry out, to scream, to frighten this thing away, but it would have been no use. There was no one to hear me, and this time, neither was there a friendly and knowledgeable Scotsman just over the fence. What should I do? The vet's Surgery might still be open: I could ring to say we were on our way, as George had done. Or should I first attempt to do as he had? I tried to get Fern to put her paws on my chest, but she wouldn't stay. Wasn't she being trained not to jump up? I was certainly no George, who could apparently undo weeks of learning and practice at will. I tried to hold her up with one hand and massage with the other, but that didn't work either. Quarter past eight! Would anyone still be there?

I told the nurse what had happened.

"Mr. Williams is still here. I'll tell him you're coming. How long will it take?"

Forever. Every driver stuck to the speed limit. Each traffic light, every crossing was on red. People vied with each other on who could take longest to drift across. As each minute dragged on, I expected to hear the first cry of a dog in pain and fear. Would it be a whine? Perhaps a howl? Or maybe she'd try to lick the pain away and I wouldn't know. Perhaps that was what she was doing now! Perhaps that was why I couldn't hear anything. I tried to focus on my driving. Maybe, the pain might become so bad that she would growl at it and try to tear it away and hurt herself even more. I had never heard Fern growl.

The road to Washingborough was like a tunnel leading into blackness, away from the lights of Lincoln. It was cold and getting colder. I hadn't turned on the heater, for I wanted to hear any sound from the back, but what could I have done anyway? Driven faster and perhaps been involved in an accident? Who would have known then that my companion needed urgent medical attention? I fumbled with the heater controls. I might feel a little better if I was warmer. But all I got was cold air, and I daren't take my eyes off the road to examine what I was doing, so the heater stayed as it was, churning out an icy wind.

The roundabout, a white house: I was there!

One car and an old Land Rover were in the yard this time. Fern was already standing when I opened the boot. In the darkness, I could not tell how bloated she was. I did not even know if she should, or could, jump out, so I attempted to lift her, and we finished in an untidy heap on the damp concrete.

The waiting room was empty and silent. A sudden movement and a nurse stuck her head through the office hatch.

"Is it Fern?"

I nodded.

"Go straight in," she gestured towards the main consulting room.

I liked Nigel Williams at once. He had a presence that was tangible. Slim and handsome, with dark brown, wavy hair and thick moustache, he looked more like a high ranking army officer, than a hard-working vet whose practice encompassed many farm animals as well as urban pets. He had obviously read Cathy O'Rourke's notes, for he began his examination immediately. Fern was extremely bloated, but not as badly as she had been. I watched in silence as he pressed all along her abdomen. He questioned me intently about the time of Fern's "blowing up", and of her previous meal.

His speech seemed military, too, precise and with an upper class accent, but his tone was gentle and caring. However he asked his question, however he tried to read beyond my words, the answer remained the same; about two hours, and he was not happy with that response.

"Is she still loose?"

Did he think the bowel problem might be connected with this?

He got down to his knees, stethoscope to her abdomen and chest, peering into her mouth, feeling her abdomen again. I could not imagine him missing anything Eventually, he stood.

"She has a great deal of gas inside her, but her stomach's not turning and her colour's excellent." He turned back Fern's silky jowls to check her gums yet again.

"She's not going into a torsion, which is good, but there's certainly something very strange going on."

I suddenly thought of the numerous evenings when Fern had seemed to be fat, and how, by morning, she was always her normal size again. That was strange. Somehow, I knew he wouldn't think me silly or stupid and he did seem to accept this ludicrous tale with keen and serious attention, adding it to Fern's growing notes.

One more careful examination of her abdomen, then he turned towards shelves loaded with medications.

"I'm going to try you with something else, and ask if you would divide her feed into smaller meals for a while. Still soak everything, but feed her three times a day." His dark brown eyes crinkled as he smiled warmly.

"I'll see you in ten days, unless you're at all worried. Tell the nurse your appointment must be with me. She's a lovely dog."

I thanked him, picked up the tablets, and left.

As I drove home, I felt none of the relief of my previous visit. This time, we had been told to return, and to the senior partner, who had openly confessed to being puzzled.

At home, we walked straight into to the dark garden.

"Go wee."

After Fern had obliged, I returned indoors and made myself a hot drink. There was some comfort in the warmth and solid roundness of the mug in my hands. I perched on the kitchen stool, trying to make sense of it all. Why had she bloated again? Had we just escaped another torsion? We didn't know the cause, so presumably, it could happen again, at any time. Did her loose bowels have something to do with the bloating? I wished George were just over the fence, instead of thousands of miles away. Forcing myself to think practically, instead of allowing my imagination to run riot, I carefully weighed one third of Fern's daily food, tipped it into a dish, and covered it with water, ready for tomorrow.

She was surprised and delighted with her extra feed in the middle of the day. Fern ate all the smaller meals with great glee; perhaps thinking she was getting more! In fact she was her usual, happy-go-lucky self. She wanted to eat, play, go for endless walks, do all the normal things we always did. But things were not normal. I could not look at her without estimating her girth. Sometimes, I thought she was her normal size and shape, but at other times, I was equally sure she was fatter. She couldn't be slim one minute, then fat the next! I told myself that I was imagining things, because she was so happy and brimming with energy. Yet there remained a deep, nagging fear that something unknown, but something very real and dangerous, had come to stay.

I phoned Jill Saville. After all, she had asked me to keep in touch, and if there was anything about Flatcoats she didn't know, then it wasn't worth knowing.

I dialled the once so-familiar number to find she already knew of our problem! Of course, Nigel Williams was her vet, too, and Fern "her" dog.

She was very upbeat.

"Magic bloats. Rarely, but every once in a while. Driving in the car always gets her down. She's always been back to normal by the time we've got to Nigel."

I had the impression she thought I worried too much and I had already heard all the advice she gave from Mr. Williams, but I did feel reassured.

The days passed, and now I knew I was not imagining things; Fern's girth did yo-yo. Should we go back before the time was up? Perhaps if I waited until tomorrow, there would be no more unexplained bloating, and we could return with smiles. But tomorrow came and went, then the next tomorrow, and the next. Nothing changed.

Mr. Williams re-examined Fern with all his previous meticulous care. Her weight had dropped, but not significantly. He was mystified at the complete lack of improvement, and incredulous when I reported that Fern belched before food! But he changed the tablets, checked that all her food was thoroughly soaked and that she was not exercised immediately after a feed, and made another appointment one week away.

But this time, I could not wait a week. Fern's bloats began to increase in frequency and severity. She did not reach the gross proportions of the two emergencies, but whatever was wrong, was undoubtedly worsening. And to my horror, I began hearing swilling and popping noises from her belly as she moved.

Nigel Williams could not mask his concern. He examined Fern with all his usual thoroughness, but could not offer any explanation of her condition. Her weight had dropped again, but he made no other comment on her deterioration.

"I'd like to X-ray her. We can do that the day after tomorrow. In the meantime, divide her feed into smaller portions. Make it four a day. Little and often for the time being. I have some food, which will do her good. You can only get it at a vet's," he added, in a slightly embarrassed tone. "It's very easy to digest."

He laughed a small, apologetic laugh.

"And I'd like you to get some gripewater and burp her after each feed. You know, like a baby."

He raised Fern's forelegs onto his chest and massaged her tummy in a manner similar to George. This time, I would have to persevere.

I looked forward to, yet dreaded the passing of those two days. Fern's condition, whatever it might be, was worsening and there was not even any theory to offer an explanation. I wondered if she would be better by Christmas.

The morning of the x-rays came. We went to Whitegates together. I left without her. For the first time in almost four months, I was alone and

I knew at once, it was a state I never wanted to repeat. I had planned to while away the time with coffee in town, do some window shopping, maybe even have lunch out, but all I did was to head home listlessly, and wonder what Fern was doing. Would she miss me? Would they be putting her to sleep now? Was she afraid? Would she come round all right? I tried to distract myself in the garden, but all I saw were signs of Fern: her digging pit behind the garage, a chewed inner tube sprawled, snake-like, across the path, a once lush lawn now pitted with burned brown circles, and an old tennis ball, carried home in triumph from the common. Were these eyesores, spoiling the beauty of the garden? No. These were the symbols of love, fun and a shared happiness. My garden had never looked more beautiful!

I sat on the lawn, hugging my knees. The sun warmed my back and a robin chirruped from the laburnum. Whatever I might have given to Fern, I thought, she had given me more and I blessed the day I decided to have a dog. Fate had drawn me to a Flatcoat named Fern, but Fern was not with me. She was in trouble.

As promised, she was ready to come home at four o' clock. Although still faintly, "under the influence", she bounced around on the end of her lead, and happily followed Mr. Williams back into the surgery, where her X-rays were already on the viewer. He smiled his gentle smile.

"She's forgiven me already."

He wouldn't smile if he had something awful to say, I told myself.

"Her weight's down again. Is she still eating well?"

"Yes."

He switched on the viewer.

"I've never seen anything like this before."

My heart sank. Since our problem began, so many people down the Lane had told me that if anyone could sort it out, Nigel Williams could, and yet here he was, telling me that he'd never seen anything like it before!

"Her entire gut is filled with gas."

He traced a finger along the curves and coils of her digestive system. It was a wild riot of white and black shapes, like bubbles on the top of coffee. He stared at the x-rays.

"She doesn't gulp her food. We've taken out all the gas that's possible."

He spoke very quietly, as if voicing his thoughts and trying to arrive at some conclusion.

"I've tried every medication that I know of," he shook his head, "so where is this lot coming from?"

Was he serious? Was he really asking? Or was it a rhetorical question? He turned to face me.

"I have a friend in Germany who's very good with guts-" he broke off with a sudden grin, realising how incongruous that must sound. "I'll give him a ring to see if he has any ideas. They might know something over there."

But they didn't. Neither did anyone in this country. Appointments came and went. Often, we were there twice in one week and all the time, Fern grew steadily worse. Her meals became smaller. Four per day became five. Five became six and for the first time, an appalling thought began to shape itself in my mind.

But we continued to explore possibilities.

"Could it be an allergy?"

Nigel didn't think so; other signs were absent.

"What about her toys? She does love chewing."

"Chewing won't help, but it couldn't possibly be responsible for the volume of gas in there."

I said I would withdraw all her chew-toys for the time being.

"Would it help if I started a diary? If I noted the times and durations of Fern's bloating? We might spot something."

He nodded agreement.

"Yes, you could do that. It might throw some light on the situation." He smiled and gazed at Fern, who, true to character, looked back at him, happily wagging her tail. He became lost in thought and I waited in silence. Then he turned towards the shelves along the far wall.

"Keep on with those tablets for another week and I'd like to add one more thing."

He rattled a white drum, looking back over his shoulder.

"These are supposed to increase the peristaltic action of the gut. It may help get rid of some of the gas, but," he smiled his apologetic smile, "it could be a little unpleasant for you!"

He counted out the pills, wrote the label and stuck it in place. It was as he held out the bottle for me to take, that looking down at Fern, he spoke words I will never forget.

"You know, I have an idea that this condition in any other dog, would be a far greater problem."

I cherish those words as the greatest compliment ever paid to her.

What was it, I wondered, that made tears burn? Whenever I drove home from Whitegates, I seemed to be blinking away tears. How many appointments was it now? How many tablets? How many changes, suggestions, hopes? But things were worsening steadily. In the mirror, I could see Fern in her usual position, head resting on top of the back seat, facing forward. Not for her the usual doggy position of gazing through the rear window, but looking out to the front, to where she was going, not to where she had been. I had wondered if she would be better by Christmas. Now I began to wonder, would she be with me at Christmas?

The diary began; one day, one page; times in the margin, notes alongside. The book remained permanently open on the kitchen worktop. Every time I noticed the slightest change, I made a note of what it was and the time it happened. Pages filled rapidly.

It had always been a comfort that Fern remained so happy, but now that happiness brought its own anguish. She had no idea anything was wrong, and getting worse. Every morning, her whole being proclaimed that although yesterday had been wonderful, today would be even better! Her innocence and optimism generated a poignancy all of its own, which made her predicament even harder to bear.

But I tried to match that optimism. Every day, we took our walks; down the Lane, on the Common, or through the park, and every time, there would be someone to ask how we were getting on. Many of these doggy friends now seemed to be experts on foods and digestion and would suggest remedies, all of which we'd tried, or which were too outlandish even to consider. But I was grateful for their time and concern. With surprise and pleasure, I realised how many people had grown so very fond of my shining, joyful jet-black whirlwind.

Now I had to time our walks and any rare solitary trips I was forced to make very carefully. Everything, our whole lives, were planned around Fern's feeding times.

But Christmas drew a little nearer.

I didn't feel any embarrassment, only hope, when I passed the book to Nigel Williams. He began to read.

The room fell silent. Traffic rushed past the window. Fern shuffled her feet in impatience. I became aware of my own breathing, as he read every single word. Surely this meant I hadn't written a load of owner-indulgent rubbish and that it was worth reading. He would notice something, I told myself, something which would provide the clue we so desperately needed. A tiny flame of hope flickered into life and I began to play with Fern's ears. She licked my hand, and the flame grew.

"I can't see any common factor."

"Oh."

"Nothing physical....nothing emotional; no particular time..........no trigger ......it just seems to happen."

He passed the open book back to me.

"It's lucky you have some biological knowledge. We're on the same wavelength."

He smiled his slow, crinkly smile. We looked at each other and the silence returned. A single car raced past the bay window and was gone. Inside the surgery, the silence itself grew like a living thing, oppressive and threatening.

What did he want? Should I say something? Could I say anything? Fern was ill, very ill and getting worse and the man whom I expected to know all the answers knew nothing. Yet he had tried! How he had tried! No one could have tried harder and his reputation was beyond reproach.

But might someone else find something? Might a fresh examination reveal something he had missed? How could I suggest that to someone so expert and dedicated and who was so clearly bothered by his lack of progress? Fern's forever wagging tail drew my eye. I knew I must speak.

"Do you think that........ we're so close to all this…its been going on so long….. perhaps we could be…maybe, missing something?"

The words seemed to have been spoken by another voice. Nigel Williams pursed his lips and raised his brows slightly. I struggled on.

"Maybe someone else, if they saw her now…as she is right now…"

"I have no objection at all to your having a second opinion."

He had used the very words I tried so hard to avoid!

"I understand completely how you must feel."

And I knew that he did. I was so relieved and so very grateful! There had been no embarrassment, no resentment, yet his reply filled me with dread. It was the honest reply of a man totally confident of his own abilities, one who knew he had done absolutely everything possible.

"Have you anyone in mind?"

"There's a vet just down the road from where I live, David Ashcroft. I thought I might go there."

David Ashcroft was younger then Nigel Williams. He had trained more recently, his premises were larger and purpose built; there seemed to be more nurses on duty. Perhaps he really might know something!

He was thorough in his examination of Fern and of her X-rays. He read Nigel's notes diligently. He asked numerous questions. He read my diary. He agreed with and even openly admired all that had been done. He was very sorry, but he could not throw any more light on the situation.

I went back to Nigel Williams. My wonderful New Life had fallen apart.

CHAPTER FIVE

"You entering?" Andy nodded at the poster displayed in the Fen Lane pavilion window as we walked past a few days later. I hadn't told him about the second opinion.

"Exemption Dog Show. Pedigree and fun classes. 50p. per class. Rosettes to 6th. Place."

I looked at Fern, tearing around the field, pursued by Maddie. Where her energy came from, I could not imagine! Having a dog of such outstanding pedigree, I had intended to enter her at a "proper" show one day. Perhaps this might be an easy introduction for us both. But an introduction to what? I tried to put bitter thoughts of her illness behind me.

"Maybe.....but I'd be scared stiff."

"What of?"

I had no idea. I just knew for certain that I would be.

"Agility Demonstration by Cardinal's Hill Training Club." That might be worth seeing.

On the way home, we had to pass the bungalow belonging to my new neighbour, the driver of the early morning diesel. He emerged onto his drive from that noisy van to comment on how well and attractive my dog looked, and to learn her name, but was both surprised and dismayed to find she was ill. However, his observations made me think. Perhaps we might give the exemption show a whirl after all.

George was back! Eager to learn how his Black Princess had fared during his absence, he managed to squeeze in a session on the common before his return to Nigeria. Fern had greeted him ecstatically, as she rejoined the most superior pack in the world! Gus licked her face with enthusiasm and even old Wisp deigned to wag his tail, while the never-ending play-fight with So, picked up seamlessly from where it had left off.

When the pack had finished greeting and sniffing, work began. Fern

52

had forgotten nothing, whereas I seemed to have forgotten a great deal! George was not impressed.

"Ye just don't appreciate what ye've got there," he murmured sadly, nodding in Fern's direction.

"Oh, I do, I do!"

But George shook his head. I decided to leave it at that, for it was useless arguing with him, once he had pronounced on something. Of course I appreciated my intelligent, feisty, wonderful companion!

There was something I needed to discuss with him though, and that was the question of Fern's training during his coming three months' absence. She loved to learn and thrived on stimulation, and if her health problems could be resolved, then we would need something. Trying to follow her optimistic example, I asked about the club Andy and I had seen advertising at Fen Lane. Cardinal's Hill apparently ran regular ten-week pet classes, and if one passed the test at the end of the course, then one could join the club proper. George warned me that training methods varied a great deal, but thought the experience would be good for me, and the social interaction good for Fern, so it was agreed we would spend our time there.

I wondered just how many words Fern knew, besides those in her "official" vocabulary, for as I wished George well in his venture, she became listless and even miserable, the one and only time I have seen her other than brimming with happiness in his presence. Did she pick up my apprehension at his impending absence?

Four days later, George left.

We went to Margaret's the next day. I needed cheering up and I knew she would understand perfectly.

That evening, we relaxed in front of her fire. Flicking through the pages of a magazine, I gradually became aware that Margaret was the proverbial miles away. Leaning forward in her chair, chin cupped in her hands, she was gazing at a snoozing Fern.

"Penny for them."

Margaret remained still, but turned her eyes to me. There was a pause.

"You know," she searched for the right words, "I've got this feeling about Fern…."

She straightened, suddenly steeled by the confidence of her certainty.

"She will do something for you… something special. A feeling…I've had it quite a long time… …it's a feeling I've got."

I laughed.

"Oh, yes? Like winning at a real show?"

"No!"

Her response was uncharacteristically sharp.

"No. Well, she might, but this is something else. Something only she can do, only her."

Confidence evaporating, she gave a little shrug, as if embarrassed by her own words.

"It's just a feeling."

At our next visit to Whitegates, Nigel made a dramatic suggestion. What about a laparotomy? This meant an exploratory operation in the hope of discovering something. Of course, it also emphasised that no one had any real idea of what to do, or where to go next. Fern would have her second general anaesthetic within weeks, to enable specimens to be taken from selected sites within her gut and sent to Dr. Edward Hall at the Liverpool University School of Veterinary Science. Fern's condition was worsening. Something had to be done. I agreed.

It was only a block of wood, a big block of painted wood, yet it made feel as I had felt almost a year ago. The door of Whitegates Veterinary Surgery divided the warm, loving world in which I now lived, from the cold and sterile world that had once been my existence. I once again felt vulnerable, conspicuous, different to other people. I pulled it shut, leaving Fern for a second time.

Again, I spent a bleak day of solitary worry, for the laparotomy was very invasive. But once again, at the magic hour of four o' clock, the phone rang and I was told that I could collect her, as soon as I wanted.

Everything had gone well. Bits of my dog were on their way to Liverpool, while the rest of the dog, slightly woozy, but happy as ever, was on her way home.

Relief, and one of Nigel's comments, contributed to my slightly euphoric state. He had told me that a short while after he opened Fern's abdomen, incredibly, her intestine had started to inflate! Slowly, but steadily it had grown, until he began to fear he may never get it all back! He had laughed as he told me, as I laughed now, but at the time, it must have been a total nightmare. Although her gut had looked healthy, Nigel noticed that several small areas, known as Peyer's Patches, were inflamed. This suggested an infection, but Fern's temperature was normal, and prior to her operation, she had been her usual sunny self. He also mentioned he had not noticed the strong, rhythmic squeezes of peristalsis, the muscular contractions which push food through the entire digestive system. Fern's gut had simply fluttered irregularly, but of course, she had been starved and she was under anaesthetic. I was just so relieved and thankful to have her back, I couldn't get home quickly enough!

It was evening time before I looked at Fern's scar. All the newly luxuriant feathering on her underside had been shaved. She was bald! The soft grey of her skin shaded pink towards the scar itself. And what a scar! Crude and livid, it ran the length of her belly. The edges looked as if they'd been dragged together and folded over by a child! Tears sprang into my eyes with their familiar sting. Huge stitches, made with what looked like string, criss-crossed the wound. And this was the handiwork of the man whom I had come to respect and trust implicitly! Surely he was more physician than surgeon?

Yet the trauma barely stopped Fern in her tracks! One quiet day, then she was demanding her usual walk. After only two days of the recommended minimum one week's on-lead exercise, and an increasingly frustrated dog, I decided that to allow her to move as she wished, but to shorten the time of exercise, would be the better option. I watched as she busied herself happily along a hedgerow. Surely such a dog could not be so ill? Surely we would have Christmas together?

But she continued to bloat, she continued to lose weight and she continued to be the happiest dog in the world. I loved her to bits.

It was a relief when the time came to return to Whitegates for the removal of the stitches. The surrounding pinkness had gone, and tiny black bristles of new hair already peppered her soft grey skin.

As usual, Fern behaved impeccably as the stitches came out, and what a transformation that brought! The fold gone, her abdomen flattened and the scar itself was revealed as merely a fine, smooth pink line.

"That'll go eventually," predicted an almost smugly satisfied Nigel.

I was so delighted I could have flung my arms around him! Or confessed my first misplaced horror at the sight of his handiwork! I did neither.

"She's done well," he mused, "you know, she's such a very strong bitch...all this other stuff....so odd."

He consigned the stitches to a small bin, and then began what had become our usual routine. Appetite? Ravenous. Weight? Down again. Happy? Of course. He palpated her abdomen; still filled with gas. Effect of gripe water? Some. Has anything changed? I thought she was bloating just a little more, a little more often.

I made an appointment for one week later, and Nigel promised to ring as soon as he received the results from Liverpool.

The day of the Fen Lane show dawned warm and sunny. It was almost like summer. There was very little wind, so if we did enter, Fern would not be distracted by interesting scents wafting into her ever-inquisitive nostrils. Perhaps I might try our luck.

We had our morning walk a little later than usual. As we crossed the field, I saw that three areas were already roped off, one much larger than the other two. I guessed that must be for the Agility demonstration and the other two would be for the fun and pedigrees classes respectively.

As I watched, two Transit vans drew up. From one of them, two young men began to haul strange items of equipment; brightly striped poles, three huge and heavy wooden planks, and what appeared to be a concertina of canvas covered hoops! And there was more still in the other van! We left the field, turned along the dyke and headed for the river. Should I enter the show? The very thought made my heart pound!

It was a lovely day. The sun was warm on my face. Two ducks waddled across the path in front of us and splashed into the dyke. Why should I want to disrupt this peace and beauty to battle for a tiny prize? Fern bounded along in front, the sun gleaming on her glossy coat. We reached the river and began to walk along its banks. Then, in the distance, I could make out the shadowy figure of a heron standing amongst the reeds. Any moment now, Fern would surely put him to flight! I called softly. She turned at once and the heron was left in peace to catch his dinner.

But we had been forced back on our tracks and back onto the field.

Now it was a hive of activity! I paused by a table to read a list of classes: handsomest dog, prettiest bitch, waggiest tail; all this was new to me! Best condition, best chocolate drop catcher: Fern could win three of those easily, I thought to myself. Suddenly, I realised people were standing behind me. I had started a queue! The die was cast! I handed over my 50pence.

The class I chose was number four, Best Mover. I avoided the pedigree classes because I thought Fern was too thin, and, rightly or wrongly, I could not imagine an exemption judge knowing anything about Flatcoats. Or maybe it was because I already felt nervous and one class was the most I could take. Or perhaps I dare not risk the shattering of any illusions!

I looked around the rapidly growing crowd for a familiar face, but there was none. Andy had said that he might be on duty. We walked towards the Agility ring to while away the time until our debut.

The brief glimpses I had seen on T.V. were no preparation. It was awesome! A young man and woman were erecting a line of jumps. The "concertina " turned out to be a kind of round tunnel, which was curled into a horseshoe, and there was a second possible tunnel that had a large doll's house at one end, the rest being a tarpaulin tube which lay flat under its own weight! Were dogs expected to go into the house and force their way out through the tube? The three planks now formed a roadway in the sky! One was fixed horizontally between two frames each about six feet high with the other two leading up steeply from either end. Then two more men appeared carrying a seesaw!

I tried to imagine what it must be like working a dog in all of this, but Fern's interest lay only in the black and white Border Collies she could see at the opposite end of the ring. Did she think that they too, were already her friends, just like George's pack?

We wandered on, past the pedigree ring. " Any variety, non-sporting"; I wondered how different breeds could be matched against each other. And how could any one person know about all the very different dogs that would be in the ring?

Still no one about that we knew.

On to the Fun ring. Fun? Everyone looked so deadly serious! It was easy to pick out the experienced pairs; hairy dog-statues, intent only on gazing up at their handlers, who were making strange moves, bordering on the occult, with their free hands. To receive their rosettes, the winners were made to stand in front of the unplaced competitors, and what a chasm separated those two lines! Such disappointment in the long faces and drooping shoulders of those left behind! Such sadness! Such a dashing of hopes and the now forlorn expectation that the judge could not fail to see that their dog was the most wonderful, most talented canine in the whole world! (They were wrong, anyway. She was on the end of my lead!)

"Class Four! Best Mover."

Disappointment was the last thing I could bear right now, but I found myself entering the ring, securing a place at its edge and trying to make Fern stand still as I had seen those others do. But Fern didn't want to stand still. This was new! This was exciting! She jigged about and tried to strike up a friendship with the dog on our right.

"Leave it!"

The woman pulled her dog away. I felt annoyed. Fern was not an, "it"! She dived behind me to try her luck on the other side. I spun right round, so that the lead was again in front, and pulled her away. But the Cupboard Top Syndrome struck, as Fern used the momentum to resume her original intention.

"Leave it!"

This was awful! What had happened to everything I had learned with George? I shuddered to think what he would say if he could see us now. I tried to get a grip on the situation, gave Fern a quick jerk on the lead and spoke sharply to her. A semblance of calm descended, but her eyes continued to dart from side to side while her tail wagged with mischievous intent.

One by one, the judge ordered each entrant to parade their dog. First, in a straight line going away from him, then across the top of the ring, and finally, coming back towards him; a triangular route. I became more and more jittery as each contestant finished the run. Then it was our turn.

Now she had something to do, Fern responded. She strode out beautifully. Her long, flowing stride simply ate up the ground! To my surprise and delight, she exuded an authority I had no idea she possessed; an authority which seemed to me as if it proclaimed to everyone, "Look at me! I'm best! I know!" It was as if she did know each and every entry in her glittering pedigree and was absolutely positive she was equal to that heritage. I was so proud of her! But was it also possible that I could be a little prejudiced? Apart from her thinness, no one would ever dream she was ill. We completed the run smoothly, much to my intense relief!

A greyhound won, and a whippet came second. Fair enough, but how anyone could suggest that the stiff-legged, up and down gait of a Golden Retriever to be even acceptable, was beyond me. But we were placed fourth! In the envied front line, we received a silky, green rosette.

I fondled its smooth surface gently, eased my fingers into its welcoming tucks, and felt its friendly roundness. I pocketed it so very carefully, trying vainly to keep the trailing ribbons straight. Our first rosette! It was as if it were made of the purest, most fragile gold! But as we left the ring, dark thoughts began to crowd into my mind that this small, green prize might, one day, also hold another place in my memory. I made a conscious effort to dismiss such thoughts, straightened my back, and held my head high. We had not been passed over! We had made an impression! Satisfied, I turned for home.

As we approached the gateway, Fern suddenly pulled sideways. I couldn't see anything which might have attracted her, but it did remind me that I had totally forgotten the Agility demonstration! Looking at my watch, I saw there was just enough time to stay a little longer before her next feed, and judging by the dogs lined up at one end of the ring, the demo was to start any minute now!

I found a spot and settled onto the grass. Fern stretched out beside me. The air was still, the sun shone and the temperature had risen.

As the first dog, a yellow Labrador, set off, excited barking erupted from the spectator dogs. Fern raised her head to glance around and she saw the Labrador as it slowly mounted the first of those three great planks. In a flash she was on her feet, ears pricked, tail up, mouth agape: totally transfixed! As the Labrador trotted across the top plank, she added her deep voice to the canine chorus. When the dog swung round to pass in front of us, I had to hang on to the lead for dear life to stop her joining in!

A Border Collie set off. They did go into the little house and push through the tube behind it! Then a third dog, but I couldn't watch any longer. All my attention and strength were taken trying to keep a grip on Fern! As more dogs demonstrated their prowess, the accompanying barking diminished as spectator dogs lost interest: but not Fern! She became ever more excited, bouncing up and down on her fore legs! When a large G.S.D. passed, I had to wrap my arms around her chest to stop her charging into the ring! What had started out as funny, was fast becoming a liability! What on earth would happen if I lost my grip on her? Before any other dog could begin, I gathered and tightened her lead.

"Come on you, we'd be better off at home!" I announced loudly, for the benefit of anyone watching our ill-disciplined performance.

"Or take him in there," replied a voice.

I looked round. A man with greying hair smiled down at Fern.

"Likes that, doesn't he? You'd better get him trained."

Taken aback, I muttered a vague kind of agreement. He wasn't to know she couldn't possibly do agility. Running, jumping, climbing, twisting and turning at high speed must demand supreme physical fitness, something Fern did not have. I glanced back into the ring, suddenly envious of owning one of those running, leaping dogs.

"Woo-oof!" bellowed Fern, utterly oblivious to everything except the excitement in the ring. I gave the lead a tug, but she remained still, eyes flicking to and fro as she searched for another climbing, jumping dog. It was the Labrador, back for a second run. This time, Fern's voice was the only herald to his start. I took a firmer grip on the lead and planted my feet wider. She so wanted to be part of this impossible, breakneck world!

Illusion

The familiar sting began to burn my eyes. The Labrador blurred and was transformed. His short, yellow coat darkened and grew longer. The broad head narrowed and the muzzle lengthened. A luxuriant tail streamed behind the gleaming black Flatcoat flowing effortlessly over the jumps. I looked down at Fern, foursquare on the grass, head erect, tail lashing the air, watching every move. Now the tears overflowed and I lowered my head that no one should see. But in that moment, a new resolve began to form, to take shape from the clouds threatening our future and a new determination to face and to defeat the despair that threatened us was born. I bent to whisper in her ear.

"If you want to do this, sweetheart, then you shall. Maybe not now, not tomorrow," I slid my arm around her. Her entire body rocked to the rhythm of her lashing tail.

"But one day, one day."

CHAPTER SIX

"It's a wonder you can see your dog in this light!"

For some reason, I had been unusually late taking Fern for her evening walk that day and as I turned to cross the road to our bungalow, she suddenly pulled in the opposite direction. It was our neighbour, just inside his drive, locking the diesel van which woke me most mornings.

It wasn't all that dark I thought. I jerked Fern back and reprimanded her.

"Oh, no," he protested, "she only wondered who it was! I think I startled her."

I knew Fern better than that, but at least he wasn't annoyed. He came to the end of the drive and for he first time, I really looked at him. Medium height and quite stockily built, he had friendly brown eyes which crinkled in much the same way as Nigel Williams's. They beamed from an open face framed with curly red-brown hair and a full, coarse beard. He bent down to Fern, who got as close to him as she could, aiming great, strong licks at his face, and wagging her entire body! He seemed rather taken aback by her unbridled enthusiasm.

"Ooh. She's very friendly!"

But the evening had grown chilly. I twitched Fern's lead, said my goodbye and crossed the road.

As we reached the door, I saw him turn away and realised he must have been watching us. He seemed a lonely figure and I wondered why, but as usual, my thoughts returned to only one thing. We were still waiting for the laparotomy results.

I began to prepare some supper and put the kettle on to boil.

Fern had come through the operation extremely well. Hadn't Nigel said she was, "Such a very strong bitch?" Surely things were, at last, due to go our way?

The kettle began to sing.

"Doctor Edward Hall, head of the University of Liverpool School of Veterinary Science"; he sounded so important, so skilful. He might have the Answer. Nigel had sung his praises; he was a specialist after all, the top specialist. Yes! He would surely have the Answer!

The kettle boiled. I poured water onto the Horlicks and stirred. A tiny whirlpool circled round and round, generating its own rhythm.

The answer will come, the answer will come,

The mug will be stirred, the answer will come!

Without realising it, I had begun to look forward to the results. At last there would be the explanation, and with it would come the cure. The present may be pretty grim, but the future had begun to beckon once again.

A strident sound disrupted this bout of self-generated optimism.

"Hello, Nigel here. The letter's come from Doctor Hall."

My stomach lurched. I had a mental picture of him standing by the phone in his little office, back to the window, holding the open letter in his hand. I could not see his expression.

"He's examined all the specimens I sent."

Well, of course he had! That's why they were sent! I wished he'd get on with it.

"He took sections of them and put each under the microscope."

Why, oh why didn't he just give me the name of Fern's illness?

"He's got better equipment than we have here of course. And he dyed them, different ones, to show different things...so he could see more clearly; what he was looking for; if there was anything."

I knew that! I'd even done that sort of thing myself! Why was he taking so long? I felt a familiar and terrible hollowness developing in the pit of my stomach.

"Erm..I'll not bother you with all that...." paper rustled. The line became silent.

"Well," Nigel laughed his gentle, apologetic laugh, "he found nothing. Absolutely nothing. Everything was normal. Everything. There was nothing out of the ordinary, nothing unusual. Nothing which could explain the volumes of gas inside her. Oh-" the rustling came again, "-he did find Peyer's Patches to be slightly inflamed, like we did, but all her blood tests and signs show there isn't any active infection. Just like we did. So why there're inflamed...." There was a pause.

"She really is a mystery."

There came another silence. I couldn't break it. Perhaps he knew, for it was a while before he continued.

"So, we can't say any more than that. I'm disappointed, but...well, that's it. He can't offer any more advice. And I do know he's tried. We spoke on the phone this morning. Had a really good talk. Must have been an hour or more. He's seen one or two cases like this, but nothing where there's been this volume of gas."

Still, I couldn't trust myself to speak.

"Actually, he did wonder if spaying her might help a little. It certainly wouldn't be a cure. Nothing like that. He didn't even recommend it, but thought we may like to consider it. Sometime. It'd helped a dog he'd treated before, but who wasn't anything like Fern. Not the same amount of gas. Something to do with hormone levels; even he can't say why it helped. Just that it did. A bit less gas, you know."

He laughed in his apologetic way again.

"We'd be grateful for anything!"

His voice dropped.

"Something like that, anyway."

I wanted to put the phone down. I wanted to be on my own, but he continued.

"There's nothing more we can do. Nothing more than we are doing already...."

His voice droned on. He gave the clinical detail he'd promised to spare me. Detail followed detail.

Terrible words then began to push their way to the forefront of my mind to drown his: words such as sleep and down. But they're harmless words, aren't they?

"Nothing more we can do."

So why not go to sleep? Why not stop fighting? No more watching, or hoping; no more praying, no wishing, no fear, no hurt; only oblivion, and finally, peace.

I realised Nigel had finished when a familiar phrase jolted me back to reality.

"Carry on as we are. I'll see you on Wednesday then."

I managed to thank him and rang off.

I did not move, but stared straight ahead, out of the window. A bus, almost empty, rumbled past towards the city and was gone. A sudden gust stirred the lilac at the end of the drive and made a deep, sad sound as it passed the open window. Fern came in, looking for her supper.

"Carry on as we are."

Carry on getting worse. Automatically, I reached out to close the window.

Sleep. Down. Die. Carry on dying.

Fern's demands to be fed forced me back to something like normality. She ate the tiny supper with her usual gleeful relish.

Old feelings as to the pointlessness of it all began to re-emerge. Feelings which had only been papered over, now burst out to flood my whole being. I ached. I wanted to go to bed, yet how silly it seemed at that hour: pointless again. But only there, might I find a few hours' relief from resurrected misery.

"When Man is lonely, God sends him a dog."

Was God now taking Fern away? Had I basked in the radiance of her unconditional love for long enough? Did He now want that love Himself? Perhaps our life together had been merely a temporary respite, an all too brief glimpse of what it was like to be loved again and needed. It had all been an illusion. Of course! Illusion! I had been living with a beautiful illusion! After all, that was her name wasn't it? "A deceptive impression of reality." A name I had once thought so inappropriate!

But I could get another dog! Of course I could! It was the obvious answer! People did that, didn't they? She was, "only a dog," after all. People said that, didn't they?

I caught my breath, appalled. However could such a thought even have occurred to me? Give up and move on? Give up on Fern, her intelligence, her sensitivity and her joy in life, which was so plain to see? If she were human, would I have thought that? Should she deserve any less because she walked on all four limbs?

Without warning, a strange, ridiculous idea took shape, an idea born perhaps, from the resolve which had first grown at the Agility demonstration and which somehow, even with this news, still flickered in the back of my mind.

I opened a wall cupboard and lifted out a packet of breakfast cereal. Emptying its contents into a plastic container, I split the box with a knife. Then with a thick felt tip, I wrote carefully, in large capitals, on the grey inside. Next, I trimmed and then fixed the cardboard behind the small rails which edged the corner unit, above my head. I stood back to view my handiwork.

Yes, that would do. It would be visible whenever I was in the kitchen. Every time I opened a cupboard, every time I stood at the worktop, and, more importantly, each and every time I entered the bungalow, I would see it. It would remind me never to give in, but, for as long as Fern remained happy, to fight, fight, fight, and to go on fighting! I would not be the one to break the unspoken bond of our triumvirate. I knew that my indomitable Fern wouldn't. I knew the wonderful man who was our vet would never give in. And now I knew with certainty that I, too, would never falter. I licked my lips, and tasted salt. Tears had trickled down to slip into my mouth. Yet I was smiling as I read those words once again. They would be my constant reminder.

"When the going gets tough, the tough get going."

I reached it down again and signed my name. Then I put the pen in my left hand, and carefully printed four large, wobbly letters; FERN. Yes, that looked about right. I put I back.

Strangely, I slept well that night.

Thoughts of spaying were to keep me awake in the following nights. Once, I had thought I might breed from Fern, but that was now out of the question. White Rose puppies would forever remain roly-poly dreams. Was the small chance of only a slight improvement worth the risk? "Something to do with hormone levels," Dr. Hall had said, but he'd also said that no one knew why it may help.

Here we were again, blundering around in a darkness of ignorance, whilst Fern became more and more poorly! Even though it was a run of the mill operation, it would mean a third general anaesthetic for her. And think what had happened during the laparotomy, when Fern's intestine had begun to expand through her open abdominal wall! What if, this time, it did become impossible to get back? And what about having to starve her for twenty-four hours beforehand? Lack of food, as much as food itself, started a bloat!

I broached the idea with Nigel. As always, he listened with grave concentration. He immediately worked out a strategy.

"We can book her in as usual, but don't bring her until I ring you." He shrugged apologetically. "We're often delayed, and the less chance she has to miss you and get upset, the better. When you come, I'll give her the pre-med in the waiting room and you can wait until it starts to take effect. Then I'll take her straight in. I think that'd be best." He seemed satisfied and smiled. "Would that be alright?"

Yet again I was in his debt. He thought nothing of going the proverbial extra mile. How thankful I was that I had not changed vets as I once intended!

So we talked ourselves into it, and a date was fixed. I think we both wanted to seize this chance for Fern, however faint it might be, but at the same time, we each needed the other's approval.

Two days on, when I made my supper, I also put together two marmalade sandwiches and secured them in a plastic bag. Then I made a small flask of tea. I took a tea plate from the cupboard, gathered them all together and headed for the bedroom. The sandwiches went on the plate behind the curtains, onto the cool windowsill. The small flask stood beside the radiator. This strange picnic was my tomorrow's breakfast! I couldn't possibly bring myself to eat, watched by a starving Fern!

With Nigel's approval, I continued to feed her right up to bedtime, and even gave her a drink on the morning of the operation; a totally exceptional practice. But this was a totally exceptional dog and we were between the proverbial devil and the deep blue sea! Don't feed Fern and she would bloat. Feed Fern and she just might not bloat, but could be sick and inhale vomit into her lungs. We were balancing on a tightrope. Poor Nigel! I admired him for his willingness to take on such a risk He quite rightly had confidence in his own ability, but he had never before been in such a situation. No one had. I found comfort in two facts: there wasn't a better vet. and there wasn't a patient with greater fighting spirit!

We took a short walk that morning, as I tried to keep things as normal as possible. Fern, of course, saw through the pretence! We met our bearded neighbour again on our way back and Fern rushed to greet him with enthusiasm. He must have thought me rather rude, for while he was ready to chat, I was just as keen to return indoors, in case Nigel rang early. However, I did learn that his name was Gordon, that he pounded a computer for British Telecom and was at home because he worked an eight-day week, and today was part of his "weekend."

I began to busy myself in housework, always with one ear on the phone. It rang at ten minutes past ten exactly.

"Mr. Williams is ready. Can you bring her now?"

Twenty minutes later, a record, I drove into the car park. The waiting room was devoid of clients, but constantly criss-crossed by nurses hurrying between office, surgery and hospital. The slow, gentle waving of Fern's tail became almost frantic when Cathy O'Rourke passed through. She smiled warmly.

"Hello, Fern."

I took a seat. Fern sat beside me, continuing to look around with interest.

The tallest and bonniest of the nurses, Christine, emerged from the hospital.

"Hello, Fern!"

She came over immediately.

"I was here when we did the other operation. She's a smashing dog. She even let me take her for a little walk." She kneeled to stroke Fern.

"Are you staying now?" I asked.

"I'm here till four. You'll be good again, won't you Fern?"

Fern climbed onto the nurse's knee, covering her with warm, wet, wonderful Flatcoat kisses. I felt glad Christine would be there. She obviously liked Fern and there was every advantage in a little extra T.L.C., I thought selfishly.

Now Nigel himself appeared, carrying a hypodermic syringe. He didn't hang about!

"Hello Fern," and the syringe went home. It may have hurt, but she still greeted her friend with enthusiasm.

"It'll take a few minutes. I'll be back."

Another nurse hurried through. Frances, the senior nurse, had previously seemed a little distant, fiercely efficient, but today, she came across to us, smiling.

"Hello, I think you'll have to bring your bed!"

I raised a smile.

"It'd save on petrol! And Fern wouldn't mind if I did, she's made so many friends."

"Well, she's a lovely dog, so tolerant and cooperative. She's a wonderful patient."

Mentally, I blessed George, for making me persevere at touching Fern all over, "Even in her private little places."

"I can't believe she's Magic's daughter," Frances continued, "she hates it here."

I was grateful for the distraction of conversation, but Fern was beginning to lose interest. She laid down.

"Think it's taking effect," said Frances over her shoulder as she disappeared.

I hoped she would be assisting at the operation. She always seemed so capable. Yes, that would be perfect! Nigel operating, Frances assisting, and Christine with the after-care.

Fern sat up suddenly and looked around. I ruffled her ears, and she lay down again. It had all gone very quiet. I couldn't hear a sound from any of the other rooms; even the traffic on the main road seemed to have stopped. I wished Nigel would return.

Suddenly, Fern scrambled to her feet, turned and looked at me, wagging her tail hard. I stroked her smooth head.

"Down," I whispered.

She obeyed instantly. I think she was glad to have a good reason to lay down! But she was there only a few moments, before she stood again.

"Down."

She obeyed, but no sooner had she gone down, than Nigel returned and she was up again.

"She keeps standing up!"

His dark eyes twinkled.

"She will! She's fighting the effect. Some do, some don't. She'll be alright." He took the lead from my hand. "Come on, Fern."

She set off, back legs plaiting slightly. She never looked back. Now I was alone. Just me, perched on a wooden chair in that cool, silent room. Nigel hadn't told me when to fetch her, or even when to call! I felt a touch of panic and looked round. I didn't know what to do! I made an effort to take a grip on myself. If anyone knew the routine, then surely I did! I was opening the outer door, when Frances reappeared, heading for the surgery.

"See you at four! You can ring earlier, if you'd like, maybe two." A brief smile and she was gone.

Driving home, I was more worried than I had ever been before. This time I knew the dangers which applied specifically to Fern. I thought two o' clock was a long time to wait; they'd know the outcome ages before! But then, that was the norm, and this was a normal operation. Wasn't it?

I made myself work. The garden became tidier, the bungalow cleaner. I tried to cheer myself at lunchtime with a rare fry-up. I prepared two cakes for the oven; one mixture, two different flavourings! Time passed. Eventually two o'clock struggled round.

"She's fine. She's even had a little walk round the yard. You can collect her at four." It was Christine's voice.

Four o' clock! Throughout my life, four o' clock had been a magical hour! For years it had been the time school finished for the day, and now once more, it was the time to be re-united with Fern.

I was there on the dot. Christine, framed in the office hatch, looked up.

"Hello. I'll get her. She's fine. Had a little walk in the yard and she's wee'd, so that's all O.K."

I heard Fern before she appeared. Claws clicking and scraping on the floor, she towed Christine into the waiting room, to throw herself at me in delight.

"She's not supposed to jump!"

I got down on my knees in an effort to greet her, and to keep her still, but with little success. So I took the lead from Christine's hand, and stood, speaking sharply to Fern. She looked up in surprise, and then turned to sit with her back to me: and a most eloquent back it was, too! I felt suitably guilty.

"One or two days' rest, then she can go for walks, on a lead, until she has the stitches out in ten days. Then it's back to normal."

Normal?

"Anything about feeding?"

"Oh, nothing until tomorrow-"Christine stopped short, frowning. "She's different though, isn't she?" Her voice trailed off.

Yes, my beautiful Fern was different.

"I know," was my rueful reply. "I'll play it by ear," I added with a confidence I did not feel. "Nigel knows all about it."

I watched Christine fill in our appointment. Nigel didn't know all about it. Dr. Hall didn't know about it. I didn't know about it. No one knew about it.

"Come back if you're worried at all, or give us a ring. She's been ever so good."

I allowed Fern a small drink of aired water not long after our return home. Then she went to her bed, curled round and slept. An hour later, she was asking for food. Her hopeful requests grew into ever more insistent demands. At half-past nine, I gave her a tiny, tiny feed, then sat up until eleven o' clock to make certain all was well. It was. Neither was there any sign of bloating. I tried hard not to think of a miracle. All that night I tried so hard.

Next morning, Fern greeted me in her usual, enthusiastic way, eager to start a new day. I gave her a smaller version of her small breakfast, which she ate with gusto. Again, there was no sign of bloating. I fought the hope that was growing inside me. It was too early I told myself, much too early. Although she went through the motions of asking for a walk, she accepted our non-departure without demur. Instead, she mooched around the bungalow and the garden, and when the sun came out, found herself a sheltered spot in which to doze. But she was always hungry. Gradually, I began the return to our usual feeding schedule, still without any sign of bloating.

It was as I prepared the intended fifth feed of the day that the dream shattered. Fern had bloated. The feed postponed, much to her horror, I waited for her to subside. Within the hour, I was able to feed her. She didn't blow up again until half an hour later. She subsided in a matter of minutes, only to re-inflate into a bloat which lasted over an hour. She didn't completely return to normal after that, but this was late afternoon, and the later in the day it was, the bigger Fern was likely to be.

We were back to square one and I was angry! Not angry that the slim chance we had grasped with hope had proved a futile and potentially dangerous exercise, but angry at all the contradictions this awful disease threw in our faces. To blow up without any food was utterly, completely preposterous. To blow up before feeding was beyond belief and to inflate and deflate at random totally bizarre. And we knew nothing of the cause! If it were some kind of organism, some parasite, then surely, it could be killed? If it were some dysfunctional organ, surely it could be identified, and a means of coping with it substituted? We would recognise the reason and deal with it. But we knew nothing. We were in a dark tunnel, which was growing darker and ever more steep. A tunnel leading inexorably to only one destination.

Gordon called round that evening after he had finished work to find out how everything had gone. I thought how strange and pessimistic my answers to such kind enquiries must seem, but he showed no disbelief, only concern.

As we talked, we discovered a strange coincidence. Twenty-seven years ago, we had both arrived in Lincoln from Yorkshire within two weeks of each other and had lived with our respective parents about two hundred yards apart! We must have seen each other many, many times before. Perhaps we had even spoken!

"That's a song, isn't it?"

Gordon had seen the cereal packet notice.

I hadn't heard any song. Instead, I simply passed him a pen. Without hesitation, he added his name. I thought it a lovely gesture.

Next day, Fern refused to take no for an answer. It was time to go for a walk. We always went for a walk, so why on earth should Mum think that today was any different? I kept her on a lead, and turned back at the bottom of the playing field, instead of continuing to the river. Fern was thoroughly miffed, and showed it, looking back over her shoulder, then up at me to frown as she always did when things did not go her way. Eventually, I was forced to treat her as I had done after the laparotomy; walks off lead, but shorter ones. However, Fern had learned from experience, and immediately suffered the onset of Selective Deafness!

Or should I call it yet another symptom of the Cupboard Top Syndrome? It was not easy to devise ways of outwitting her! But her recovery, as before, was excellent and when the stitches were removed, it was back to our version of normal.

"Carry on as before."

CHAPTER SEVEN

One week later, we darkened the doors of the Cardinal's Hill Training Club for the first time. Their field was awash with cars, people and dogs, many of which were the black and white Border Collies, so loved by Fern.

Most people were standing around in front of a wooden pavilion, many sipping from steaming plastic cups. I must have arrived at break time. Leaving Fern in the car, I made my way through the throng, towards the pavilion, searching for someone who looked official. A large notice beside the entrance stated, "No dogs allowed inside," yet the first thing I saw as I stepped in, was a dog! A small Border Collie crept towards an opening in the large counter which stretched across the end of the pavilion. None of the people standing around took any notice; either of the dog, or of the stranger in their midst.

Three people were behind the counter; two trying not to burn their fingers as they dispensed hot brews from a large urn, and the third, a quite attractive dark haired woman, at the opposite end, was sifting through some papers. She looked like the official I needed! She was also the object of the little collie's journey. Without a sound, it lay behind her and curled into a tight ball, burying its nose in its tail.

I made my way towards her. Although we were alone at the end of the counter, she seemed unaware of my presence. Not wanting to interrupt her flow, I waited. And waited.

Eventually, I spoke.

"Excuse me, I wonder if you can help? I'm interested in joining the pet classes."

No reaction.

"Hello! I've come to find out about the pet classes. I'd like to join."

She continued to push the cards she was holding into a perfect foursquare pile and replied without raising her head.

"There's a new course starting Sunday. Ten o'clock. You need a vaccination certificate."

"Oh, good."

What luck! I thought there should be more.

"So I just turn up? I don't need to get my name down with someone or anything?"

"Its £10."

The conversation seemed at an end.

"So I just come with my money?"

She looked up for the first time, her exasperated expression suggesting my stupidity bordered on the moronic.

"It's £10, with an up to date vaccination certificate. Sunday."

She returned to her cards and I thanked the top of her head.

Nigel had said Fern's weight loss seemed to have slowed, and she was raring to go as usual and virtually towed me onto the field that Sunday to where she was certain new friends would be waiting, especially for her.

About fourteen people with their pets stood around in front of the pavilion, looking lost. The rest of the field was alive with dogs and their owners, busily engaged in all kinds of strange manoeuvrings. On closer inspection, they seemed to be divided into groups, each following orders shouted by an I'm-in-charge, but what struck me most forcibly, was the noise! George had always said, that as a dog's hearing is so vastly more acute than a human's, there was absolutely no point in shouting and that everything depended on the tone of voice used! Still, there were a great number of bodies in a relatively small space.

Ten o'clock came, and passed.

Peering into the gloom of the pavilion, we could see several people moving about, but as we all had our dogs with us, no one dared to defy the notice, go inside and find out if we were in the right place. So we continued to wait.

Some dogs made friends. Some hung behind their owners' legs, unsure as to what was happening. A few growled their uncertainty. Some barked and distracted the dogs in the nearest class. Everyone grew colder.

At almost ten past ten, the dark haired woman I had spoken to before emerged from the pavilion, strode through our ragged group and into the nearest class. She immediately spoke to their I'm-in-charge, then turned on her heel, and returned towards the pavilion.

"Tie your dogs over there," she called, waving her right arm in the air as she passed, "then come into the hut."

She disappeared inside. So that's what it was; a hut.

Tie them over where? Fourteen pairs of eyes scoured the field to our right. One brave soul walked over, considered carefully, then suggested that the line of small concrete posts along the edge of the field might be where we had to tie our dogs. No one came up with a better idea, so that is what we did. But it wasn't as simple as it sounded! This was new to everyone, and some worried about how their dog would react when apparently abandoned in a strange place, and, worse still, next to a strange dog! But one by one, we managed to tear ourselves away from our canine companions, and to enter the inner sanctum.

Here, we completed forms that not only required name, address, dog's name, age and breed (if known) but our dates of birth and occupations as well! Then we queued to hand the completed forms to the dark-haired lady, now reinstalled behind the long counter. She examined them, and the vaccination certificates, rapidly certified their validity on each form, and managed to do all that with barely a glance, and never a word! It was going up the hill towards eleven as the queue neared its end.

"Are these mine?"

Behind us, a small and bespectacled middle-aged man had entered the hut. Beside him stood an enormous German Shepherd. The dark-haired lady ignored him and continued with the final forms. He looked around at us and smiled.

"You the pet class?"

Heads nodded and a few voices of agreement broke the silence.

"You are mine, then. I'm Harry. Get your dogs and line up beside them. I'll be with you in a minute."

With that, he turned and left the hut. The enormous G.S.D. padded out beside him. Glances were exchanged: impressive, or what?

We trooped out. At least he smiled, I thought to myself, and wondered why the dark haired woman always seemed so grim.

The G.S.D. was alone at the end of the fidgeting, jumping, barking, whining line of tethered pets. No owner, no lead, no anything, just one large, still dog. I longed to go to stroke him, but an excited Fern demanded my attention, even though she was nowhere near as wound-up as some of others.

Then, to my surprise and delight, there, at the end of the line furthest from the hut, I saw a second Flatcoat! Gathering Fern's lead, I headed towards a kindred spirit. Not so! As we approached and Fern showed her eagerness to meet a cousin, this Flatcoat tucked down its tail and cowered behind the concrete post. The owner, an older lady with beautifully coiffured grey hair, explained.

"She's so timid; always has been. That's why I've brought her; to try to get her out of her shell a bit. I wish she was more like yours."

I looked at Fern, mouth slightly agape, eyes sparkling, tail straight out wagging furiously in hopeful greeting, then thought of Jill Saville's boisterous, loving mob, racing to greet a potential friend. What a stark contrast this lovely little Flattie was! Whoever heard of a timid Flatcoat? I sat Fern, then crouched to make myself smaller and less intimidating, and held out a hand. The Flatcoat sniffed from a distance, then began to wag its tail. Fern took this as a personal invitation and lunged forward in delight to make friends. But the "friend" leapt upwards and backwards in alarm. I picked myself up from the wet grass.

"Oh dear," said the beautifully coiffured lady, again adding wistfully, "I do wish she was more like yours."

I pulled bits of grass off my coat.

"I'll take Fern away. It's all these dogs that're upsetting yours. She'll be alright when she's more used to it. She's gorgeous."

Small Harry appeared from behind the hut. He walked straight past his dog and took up a position about four yards in front of us.

"Right? I'm Harry."

Conversations ceased abruptly. Heads swivelled round.

"I'm going to take you through this pet class. After ten classes, you all take the test. That's with another trainer. Then, if you pass, you can join the club and do proper obedience. Or you can do Agility if you want," he added as an afterthought. Then a third suggestion; "Or Man Work, if any of you have the right sort of dog, or are given that way." He looked along the line, which included a few retrievers and one G.S.D. "Not many of you do. Ah well, we shall see what we shall see. Nothing spectacular, just plain, simple obedience, like you taking the dog for a walk, instead of the other way round."

Guilty and apologetic titters fluttered along the line.

"Right! Get your dog sitting on your left. If you can't do that, I'll show you."

He uttered a short, sharp sound. With sad expression, the huge G.S.D. padded silently across to sit by his left leg.

"Stand!"

Although not exactly a shout, he must have been audible well down the field. Bending over, he seized the hapless dog by the thick fur and skin at the sides of its neck, and pulled it around in front of him.

"Sit!"

The dog obeyed instantly.

"Heel!"

The dog stood, moved to the right side of small Harry, around the back, and sat with a resigned air alongside his left leg, where it had been originally.

Harry grinned.

"Sometimes, they get too bloody clever! That's called anticipation. They get to think they know it all. Can't let 'em do that! You've got to be the boss!"

He glanced up and down the line.

"Now, where was I? Ah, yes! The Sit."

And so began what was left of Lesson one at the Cardinal Hill's Training Club.

We were back home, a little later than I would have liked, for Fern's third feed of the day.

Autumn fogs now began to accompany our evening walks, and having learned from recent experience, Fern took full advantage of the new opportunities this offered! Sometimes, a thick, white mist would materialise magically a few inches above the water in the dyke at Fen Lane, to creep eerily over the lower reaches of the bottom field. Rising no more than three or four feet above ground level, Fern could melt into its invisibility at will. She often did!

On one such late afternoon, we emerged from its damp clutches to meet up with Maddie on the top field, but this time, we were joined by a stranger, a beautiful black and white Great Dane bitch. Solo stood alone, gentle breath wisping into the cold air, watching in apparent envy, as the two friends whirled and galloped across the wet grass.

Fern was first to invite the newcomer to join in, reaching up to lick her face with enthusiasm. Maddie's lowered tail wagged agreement. After hesitating, the huge dog took the plunge. She was ungainly and slow compared to the two smaller bitches, but she enjoyed herself enormously, much to her owner's delight.

"She's so big, most dogs are frightened of her!"

We promised to keep an eye open for our new friend in future, and then went our separate ways, driven home by the creeping mist and failing light.

At our next appointment, things remained much the same, except that Nigel suggested I cut down an old jumper to fashion a coat which might slow Fern's weight loss during the cold weather.

Back home, I found such a jumper, cut and fiddled with it, and tried to make a neater fit, but on our walks, it rapidly became a cold and wet mass hanging beneath her belly. So it was off to Perky's, our local pet shop for an early Christmas present!

Fern looked a picture in the green waxed jacket; and so she ought, for it cost exactly as much as my pretend Barbour had done!

The following Sunday saw us back at Cardinal's Hill for a full lesson.

"Dogs and handlers, forward!" bawled small Harry.

We set off, a ragged army of nervy recruits.

"Right turn! Give 'em a good yank. Halt! Make 'em sit. Sit! Dogs and handlers, forward!"

We tried.

"Right turn! Keep going, don't stop, make 'em keep up with you!"

Lessons with George were never like this.

"Halt!"

Harry surveyed his motley crew with a resigned air.

"You're the boss, not your dog. Give one quick, firm jerk on the lead, then it goes slack. Whenever he pulls, jerk him back. Go forward when he's not pulling. Don't drag your dog about! Dogs and handlers, forward!"

How this would ever make the timid Flatcoat more confident, I couldn't imagine.

"Right turn! Jerk on that lead, one jerk! Don't strangle the dog! Halt! That was better, at least, some of you were. Dogs and handlers, forward!"

I struggled to keep Fern with me, but the dog who was far more advanced than any of her classmates, was rapidly becoming one of the worst.

"Jerk that lead! Once, don't pull it, then let it go slack, slack! Right turn!"

I was thankful when a break interrupted our marching, and those of us who had remembered to bring fifty pence, could warm ourselves with hot tea or coffee. I worried about leaving Fern in the cold, even though she was, conspicuously, the only one wearing a coat, so I returned her to the car, trying to ignore the curious looks which followed my action. This meant we joined the re-start a little late, and therefore gained Harry's attention.

"Let me have her."

Harry demonstrated his one jerk technique on Fern. She was having none of it. The dog who walked perfectly to heel for George, with or without any lead, simply threw herself around, pulling in all directions! Harry jerked the lead constantly.

"Like this! Don't let her have her own way. She'll learn."

Harry shoved his spectacles back up his nose and returned a very excited pupil to me, without the success he had expected, and, I thought, rather thankfully! Fern had been bad enough with me that morning, but I was sure she had been even worse with Harry.

With the benefit of hindsight, I realise I should never have gone back, for those regimented, repetitive techniques were utterly wrong for a dog of Fern's intelligence and sensitivity. After a very few forward marches, and right turns, the Cupboard Top Syndrome struck with a vengeance! She was bored stiff, and showed it. But I didn't like being beaten! I knew Fern could do all of this very easily, so I persevered. I didn't want to leave, allowing everyone to think that this very basic stuff was beyond the capabilities of my wonderful dog. They, of course, knew nothing of the fact that each day she survived was a triumph in itself.

So we continued, Sunday after Sunday, and we made no progress at all.

But the time dreaded by so many animal owners was now here: November fifth. I had done my best, but just how "bomb proof" was Fern? As her first Bonfire Night drew nearer, I hoped this might be one of my rare successes, not one of my more usual failures.

The master plan began in the morning; we got up earlier! Fern ate her breakfast earlier, and in the evening, her dinner would be earlier too, so that she would be safely indoors before any firework parties began and hopefully not notice that the day was different to any other.

All was quiet when her dinner bowl had, as usual, been cleared. Foolishly, I let her out alone before going into the bedroom to fetch my coat. From a nearby garden, there came the sharp reports of a firecracker, and before they had finished, a great, roaring swoosh as a large rocket hurtled skywards!

I dropped my coat, tore out of the bedroom, and back through the lounge. As I reached the kitchen, a second rocket soared upwards. How could I have been so stupid? Why, oh why hadn't I gone out with her? I raced up the drive, round the corner of the bungalow – and froze.

Perhaps it was her superb gun dog breeding. Perhaps it had been the manner of dealing with the thunderstorm. Fern was sitting quietly, plum centre of the lawn, staring upwards. A large Roman candle began throwing its brilliant globes into the dark sky, their glowing colours flashing through the near-leafless trees. Her head followed each glowing ball, until the delighted shrieks of children, two gardens away drew her attention. As she looked round, her eye fell on me for the first time. But I wasn't worth a second glance! A fountain of crackling golden sparks glittered through the bare branches and she turned back to look. She was watching! She was enjoying herself! And enjoying herself hugely! Tonight was exciting and beautiful beyond belief! Tonight brimmed with colour and sound, far, far better than the usual darkness, with entertainment provided only by the occasional cat, or wandering hedgehog! We stayed and watched together, until driven indoors by the cold.

The next evening brought another avalanche of cracks, booms and sparks, again watched by one enthralled dog.

The following night, after dinner, Fern expectantly took up the same position, in the centre of the lawn, waiting for the action to begin. But this time, there was only disappointment. A few sporadic bangs in the distance and an occasional rocket bursting overhead did little to break the dark stillness of the garden.

She hurried out again after dinner the next night, once more full of happy optimism. Sitting on her haunches, head up, she scoured the night sky. Absolutely nothing. After a few moments, she began to wander around, sniffing the grass, but glancing up occasionally. Eventually, she wee'd and made her way back to the door, looking quite miserable.

Was this dog bomb proof? I hugged and cuddled her in delight. Fern cheered up immediately, then fetched her plastic bone, imperiously demanding that I provide the entertainment that night!

Wearing a coat had certainly slowed her weight loss, but I feared her bloats were becoming more frequent, even with our after-feed gripe water burping sessions. Sometimes, when I touched her, her body sounded dreadfully hollow and tight, like a drum, and I wondered how long this could go on. Getting food into her was a problem of ever-increasing complexity. Feeds were often postponed because she was too bloated. How much more could she take, I wondered, before her stomach twisted into a fatal torsion? It seemed inevitable. Where would we be if it did happen? Would we be close enough to get to Nigel?

I tried to put such fearful thoughts from my mind and concentrate only on the present with the tantalising goal of Christmas together creeping ever nearer.

Nigel now introduced a steroid, prednisolone, in the hope of reducing the mysterious inflammation which had been noted in certain areas of Fern's gut. Perhaps that might have an effect on her bloating. Of course, I trusted his judgement implicitly, but I was still unhappy about this development. I knew that Fern could not live a normal span of life on regular doses of steroid and that it would eventually have adverse side effects. But could she live at all without such treatment? Nigel must already have waited as long as he dared. One good thing was that he agreed wearing a winter coat had slowed her weight loss.

But as Christmas drew ever closer, there came more devastating news. I think, maybe, that Nigel had been waiting for what he considered to be a suitable time, but just as easily, in the whirlpool of ignorance, deterioration, and experiment, he may simply have forgotten. His stethoscope was placed low on Fern's chest and he had been listening intently, as he always did. He removed the earpieces and straightened.

"You do know she has a heart murmur?"

No, I did not know. It was like a physical blow! My own heart began pounding and the breath caught in my throat.

"It's very definite, and quite loud."

My legs began to shake. What more could Fate throw at us? How much more? Why us? Why Fern? Why did she deserve such a raw deal? What had she ever done, but love and laugh and play?

"What can we do about it?"

I heard the edge to my voice. I knew it was a stupid question, but still went ahead and asked.

"We'll worry about that when all this other is sorted," he replied quietly. "It doesn't seem to be affecting her."

We drove home. As I turned into the drive, I suddenly realised I needed the proverbial shoulder to cry on and that I would have liked to tell Gordon this latest awful news. But why? He was only the man from across the road. Anyway, he wouldn't be home from work yet and he might not be all that interested.

So I sat in the kitchen instead and read the cereal packet notice over and over again.

Nigel's revelation hadn't actually changed anything I told myself. It was just that I was now aware of it.

An idea stuck me! Taking down the notice, I added another name: Nigel. I knew he would have signed if I'd taken it and asked him. I felt a bit better after that.

Now there were only two weeks to Christmas! Last year, I hadn't bothered with anything; no decorations, no special meals, nothing. To have done so, would merely have emphasised my lonely state, and made the so-called festive season even more of an ordeal. But now, I had Fern! I was trying harder than ever to mimic her relentless optimism, and although I fell far short of her joyful zest for life, I did at least try! Fern may not understand what all the special Christmassy things were, but she would certainly pick up the atmosphere, enjoy it hugely and that in turn, would reflect on me. Perhaps we could both have fun. So I set about getting ready, and fetched the old tree and box of trimmings down from the loft.

Fern had broken my glass prison. Once again I lived in the Real World with all its fancies, and foibles. We began decorating for Christmas.

CHAPTER EIGHT

Kneeling on the floor, I opened the large and battered box, so loved from my childhood. "F.J.Batchelor, Costumier and Furrier", proclaimed large black capitals on its lid, but who had worn the costume, or the fur, I did not know. Fern was sitting as close to the box as she could, peering beneath the layers of tissue paper as I removed them, her wide, black nostrils flaring and relaxing, trying to make sense of something she had not encountered before.

I sat back on my heels and as I gazed into that box, memories from years gone by danced out to fill the room. A pillowcase, stuffed full and wondrous lumpy, Auntie Connie in a red cape as "Mother Christmas", tiny Uncle Fred with the husky voice making his annual pilgrimage to visit us on Christmas morning, and Dad, clattering cutlery and laughing as he laid the table to accommodate the reality of delicious scents, wafting in from the kitchen.

These glittering tokens, many older than me, snug in their cotton wool beds, were the treasured symbols of all of this. Fern turned her head to look at me, wondering why I had stopped. Perhaps she thought my stillness a signal that she should delve into the box, or maybe, just maybe, the magic of Christmas had already begun?

Carefully, I pulled out the lights. I stood, wound them into the tree, held my breath and plugged in. Yes! Fern sat bolt upright in surprise. She glanced at me, and then gazed back at the tree, orbs of bright colour glowing in her dark eyes. Was she reminded of the fireworks she had so enjoyed a few weeks ago?

I considered the other inhabitants of the box. I would hate to see these icons of a bygone happiness broken. Would it be asking for trouble to take them from their soft cocoons? Yet Fern never touched anything that wasn't her own, and always seemed to know the whereabouts of her ever-wagging tail. She hadn't damaged a thing; not after leaving the teething puppy stage, that is! And hadn't the two of us something to celebrate? I began hanging them on the tree.

Time for a feed! Time for the gripe water dance!

Later that evening, I finished the decorating. Could I now say that we had made it to Christmas? A teacher had once criticised me for counting my chickens before they hatched. No, I wouldn't do the same this time.

The following day, we visited Margaret. Her small end-of-terrace house lay tucked in the corner of a cul-de-sac on a large council estate. Every house boasted its own garden, but most were ignored, used as the preferred site for rubbish collection or as an open-air garage, sporting some old banger, usually in a stage of dismantlement or rust. But Beauty was also to be found in this road. It was Margaret's garden.

Small, and with the disadvantage of facing northwest, it was nevertheless, an oasis of calm and sanctuary for the wildlife that somehow survived the urban rigours of a rented population. Throughout summer, flowering shrubs jostled to provide food for bees and other insects, which in turn encouraged the many birds who unceasingly voiced their gratitude, and drowned the hum of city traffic. In winter they remained to feast on food scraps lovingly saved and "bird cake" specially cooked.

That year, Margaret's tiny pond had been filled to overflowing with frogspawn, the happy result of hours of work, laying and arranging stones and pebbles brought home in her pockets one by one, from wherever she chanced across them. They provided a safe haven for frogs from the predatory cat next door, whose favourite sport was to bite off their heads and leave the headless bodies to adorn the garden path.

I never allowed Fern into the garden without first making sure it was a cat-free zone, not because of any ill will she might bear, but because I didn't fancy her chances of remaining unscathed in a confrontation with the feline Hannibal Lecter!

"Go wee."

It was safe for Fern to go in the garden.

Margaret was preparing tea, and we always did it together. Today however, she seemed determined to busy herself alone. She kept her back to me as she fiddled with plates and cutlery, arranging and rearranging, only to be dissatisfied with her efforts and to start again. I watched her, uneasily. Something was wrong; it was in the angle of her shoulders, the tilt of her head. Then I realised she was weeping silently.

With my hands on her shoulders, I gently turned her round. She felt so small and fragile. Now there was no point in her pretence and the tears flowed freely.

"She's so thin!"

Margaret raised her head to look out of the window, and I realised Fern was the cause of her distress.

"Every time I see her, she's thinner. She doesn't know. She's so happy!"

And now I wanted to cry with her, to give vent to my feelings, and to tell her how utterly desolate I would be without Fern, for I knew she would understand. I knew she would not find my grief, for what others might see as "only a dog", better reserved for only a human.

But I couldn't see Margaret so upset. I hugged her.

"Look again."

Fern was engrossed in sniffing her way along the flower border.

"She is happy! You said so yourself. Does she think anything's going to happen? She knows it isn't! She wouldn't be like this if she did. She thinks life's a ball. She'll be fine. I know she will."

"You really think so?"

"I do. So does George! There's nothin' that bitch canna do!" I added, drawing on one of his comments and imitating his Scots accent.

Quite suddenly, our roles had reversed. Now I was the strong one, shrugging off pain and grabbing at vague hope with both hands. Margaret could pass her fears to me and I would shoulder them with my own, because I could.

She wiped her eyes with the end of her apron and her gesture wiped away the moment.

"I hope you like your tea. It's nothing much really."

Margaret always said that.

Driving home later, guilt gnawed at my conscience, for I had actually felt a tinge of gladness in some perverse way because Margaret was upset. I no longer felt so alone with my worries. Her tears were my comfort: a dreadful admission to make! How could I feel anything but concern and sympathy that my closest friend had been so distressed over something I had brought to her? But it had further strengthened my resolve and I was grateful for that.

Test Day at Cardinal's Hill was the Sunday before Christmas. Our struggle there had continued. We could do everything at home beautifully. We could do it at Fen Lane. We could do it on the Common. We could even do it on a roadside grassy verge, to the accompaniment of passing traffic, but at Cardinal's Hill, we were hopeless. It was all so deadly serious, but Fern refused to take any of it seriously and I worried lest others think these simple exercises beyond what I knew to be her seemingly limitless capabilities. It was there I first heard the expression, "Scatty Flattie", but Fern's fooling about was quite deliberate. She never behaved in this fashion with George! For him, she had love and respect and therefore wanted to please him. She had neither for those who tried to bully her. As would be expected of her breed, she showed not the slightest aggression towards them, but instead, pretended she did not understand what was wanted. I had seen all this before. To use George's words she was, quite plainly, "Putting two fingers up."

Nigel laughed when I told him, but knowing Fern as well as he did, he readily agreed that it was very likely!

Test Day dawned, cold and grey, with icy showers hustled in on a bitter wind. One by one, in front of a pleasant young man whom we had not seen before, we performed our soldier-like routines: or not soldier-like, according to the pair under test! I thought we were just a little below the average for the group, but I knew with absolute certainty that George would have been thoroughly disgusted with me.

Poor Fern! None of the excitement of learning with him! None of the joy of doing something properly, and knowing she had done so. None of the confidence and pleasure gained in earning the approval of a loved and respected pack-leader, only boring repetition and a handler whose lack of confidence and irrational nervousness were sending all the wrong signals straight down the lead to make matters even worse. Fern's heelwork had certainly deteriorated during our time at the club, but her "Stay", in both sitting and down positions, remained sound. Here, my confidence never wavered, so why couldn't I bring the same approach to her heelwork? The truth was dawning. I was a born-awful handler who had a superb dog. I knew it, but seemed incapable of doing anything about it. Kind people explained it away by putting it down to the constant worry over her health. Certainly, I always had one eye on her girth and the other on the clock, and should we have even one appointment in a day, then that entire day had to be planned very carefully, with all eventualities covered.

Test day, for example; a virtually unknown quantity. How long would it take? We could still be there when it became time for a feed. In this case, I had decided the best course of action would be to get up earlier, which would allow Fern not only to have her breakfast, but to get in a second feed, with a rest afterwards, and build up some energy, before Cardinal's Hill. To be on the safe side, I would also take along a plastic container with a third feed, already soaking of course and a small flask of warm water to top it up if necessary. Then if we were delayed, I could feed her at the club and she would rest afterwards in the car, before we set off home. There the fourth feed would be waiting, weighed and already partially soaked. With us, one small task claimed an entire day!

But we passed! Everyone passed. We had been promised a rosette and certificate, but there weren't any. These would be ready next week, when we could return to collect them and also join the club as full members. Fern and I hadn't deserved to pass. Our rosette and certificate would lay unclaimed. They have remained so.

Now there was only one day to go before Christmas! On Christmas Eve, I battled my way round the local supermarket. This year, should anyone have bothered to look in my trolley, they would probably have been mightily impressed, or on second thoughts, perhaps not. There was more than one way of looking at the half dozen bottles of gripe water standing across the front!

If I took the car, I would leave Fern inside, but whenever I walked, I tied her as near the entrance as possible. On such occasions, she invariably generated an audience to keep herself company. Most often, it was children who would be stroking or even hugging her, but today, I returned to find her holding court with only one middle-aged couple.

"Is it a kind of black red setter?"

"No, a Flatcoated retriever."

"Oh. I've never heard of them."

"Not many have. Only the Golden and Labrador."

"She's beautiful. What's her name? It is a girl?"

"Yes. Fern."

"I knew! She looks like a girl, sort of feminine. She's beautiful."

"Yes, she really is. Beautiful."

"Thank you."

A few more strokes and tickles then, with reluctance, they picked up their plastic carriers and moved on. As I watched, I wondered how many other people had continued on their way, feeling just that bit better for having met the loving, ingenuous being with whom I was lucky to share my life. A little more happy, a little more relaxed because of friendship which had been so freely offered and which asked for nothing more in return than a kindly look. Perhaps this was why she had survived; to pass on a little of her joie-de-vivre, to "Spread a little happiness."

It was growing dark. We left the crowds and headed home.

Like a child, I decided we'd go to bed early that Christmas Eve. If we were asleep, then Christmas would come more quickly, and we would have reached our goal.

And so it was! I really did jump up that morning and hurried for the kitchen. Fern was already standing in her bed, yawning hugely. Christmas was here, and we were together! We had made it! Today, it didn't matter what the future held. Today was a day to savour, to celebrate, a day of happiness. We had come further than anyone expected, and we would pat ourselves on the back, and enjoy it!

Surprise! An unexpected card had been pushed quietly through the door:

"To Brenda and Fern. Happy Christmas from Gordon."
Oh, dear, and I hadn't even got a spare!

After breakfast, Fern mooched around in the garden, wondering why we hadn't set off for a walk, but I was preparing a chicken and vegetables, making gravy and sauce mixes, and readying everything as much as I could, so that there would be as little as possible to do on our return.

Time now for her second feed, her second "burping," have a coffee, set the oven timer and tie a piece of red tinsel into her collar: red, not only because it looked so dramatic against the gleaming blackness of her fur, but because red is the colour of winning, and hadn't this indomitable spirit already won against the greatest of all odds?

The weather was dry and sunny with a brisk northeasterly crackling the bare branches of the trees; perfect for a winter walk! Hartsholme Park had never looked more inviting! We threaded our way beneath those trees, past bare blackberry bushes, and then set off down the broad main path between the pines and the lakes. Canada and Brent geese swam about noisily, perhaps hoping for some food, but I never brought them any, much as I would liked to have done. Had I thrown food into the water, the outcome would simply have been many upset geese and one soaked retriever, eating things she shouldn't!

I was surprised at the number of people out and about. Many were dogless, a sight which, oddly, always worried Fern. Lone people on a city street were perfectly acceptable, but not so in the country. She was always uneasy, sometimes to the point of voicing her apprehension by barking at their approach. But today was different. Everyone wished us "Merry Christmas", or "Season's Greetings", or complimented Fern on her appearance and proffered friendship. And she did look attractive too: shining black fur, dark green "Barbour" jacket, topped off with a sparkling red Christmas bow!

Illusion

How different this was to last year! I breathed in the icy air and tasted its coldness, kicked frosted leaves like a child, and felt my mouth crease up into a smile of its own accord. We walked around one lake, and headed for the playing field. Here, we did a spot of heelwork, then played ball. Fern's coat often twisted to one side as a result of her running and jumping and she repeatedly burst open its front fastening!

Then it was back around the other side of the lake and home in time for the third of Fern's feeds, which today would include freshly cooked and chopped giblets; Christmas dinner!

After we'd eaten, I ignored pot washing and did something, which I had not done ever since Fern came: watch afternoon television!

Then it was time for another feed and another gripe water burping-dance.

I believe Time to be a great measure of happiness. The happier one is, the more quickly time passes and I was taken by surprise when daylight started to fade. We took our evening walk around the houses. So many brightly lit, crowded rooms, but that night no one was happier than I!

I realised I could squeeze in another feed at eleven o' clock, but it was hard work, staying awake until midnight, watching for the safety of my gently snoring companion.

I suppose many people would have found my Christmas Day to be lonely, or boring, perhaps even both. But not me! It had been a beautiful, wonderful day. It didn't take much to make me happy!

Boxing Day dawned fine and sunny, but our walk was shorter than usual, because I wanted to conserve Fern's limited energy for later that day, when we were to visit her favourite place. As the sun sank towards the rooftops, I packed the presents, Fern's "tea," plus the usual emergency feed, and then we drove off across the city.

Turning the corner of Lindum Hill, I looked expectantly in the mirror, and sure enough, Fern stood and whined softly. She knew her destination. Through Newport Arch, along the main Nettleham road, turn right, follow the estate road, first left and down to the end of the cul-de-sac. Margaret's only son, David, would be there too, home from college and temporarily deserting his friends.

Dearest, gentlest Margaret, who had survived a hard life beset by many problems, knew how to make things special. She did not have the money to splash out on lavish entertaining, but neither did she need it. Her cakes sometimes sank, a sauce might be too runny or contain a few lumps, her pastry too hard, or soft in the middle, but everything was prepared with such love, that it all, invariably, tasted delicious. Today was no different. We giggled and struggled to eat by the light of one large red candle and the overspill glow from the Christmas tree. David cracked wicked jokes about "Mother's cooking." Fern, having already eaten, lay beneath the tree, her eyes following our every move, ears pricking at each burst of laughter, tail thumping the floor.

Then, it was time to exchange presents. Margaret insisted we did so one at a time, for she loved to watch each person's surprise and pleasure. Eventually, only one present was left beneath the tree. Margaret picked it up.

"It's for Fern. It's nothing really. I made it. Just some old stuff I had. It's a dolly."

It had been months since Fern played with a dolly! I thought she had outgrown such puppy pursuits!

Margaret solemnly presented the wrapped parcel to Fern, who stood to accept it with all the graciousness of her heritage and the gentleness of her breed.

"Does she know it's for her?"

"What's she going to do with it?"

"She'll eat the paper!"

"Can she tell there's something inside?"

To our astonishment, Fern simply laid down. With the dexterity of a cat, she manoeuvred the parcel between her front paws, until it was vertical, then bent her head forward, and carefully took the tip of the paper between her front teeth. She pulled upwards, but her teeth lost their grip and the parcel slid from her mouth. She tried again, but this time, the parcel escaped from between her paws. Pulling and pushing, she manoeuvred it back into its original position.

The incongruousness of the situation suddenly struck me. There we were, three full-grown adults, watching in silent concentration as a dog opened her Christmas present! Fern again gripped the top of the paper between her front teeth, but this time, instead of pulling steadily, she jerked her head downwards and sideways. A strip of paper tore away. In the glowing red Christmas light, we stood, mesmerized.

She repeated the action. As each succeeding strip came away, she flicked her head and spat the paper aside.

A shiver ran down my spine. Some "experts" would have us believe that all dogs are incapable of reasoning, that it is impossible for them to think in the abstract or foresee the consequences of their actions. What would they have made of this? "Pure imitation," might be a cynical reply. But what degree of intelligence was needed for that alone? And imitation could not explain why Fern had changed the direction in which she pulled the paper.

Even though the contents of the parcel were now clearly visible, she continued to strip off the wrapping, until all that was left was a shallow paper collar. Then she stood to extract her present. Turning aside from the confetti she had made, she laid down again and set about playing with her dolly, rolling onto her back, raising it in the air and holding up it to chew.

Margaret was first to break the silence.

"Oh! Ooh, that was fantastic! That was marvellous!"

Her face glowed in the lights of the tree.

"How did she know what to do? She'd watched us!" she added, answering herself.

"Impressive," murmured David, eyes still glued on Fern, "very impressive."

Margaret knelt beside her.

"That's been the very best thing this Christmas," she said, taking one of Fern's great warm paws in her hand, "I'll never forget it! I can't wait to give her another present! I'll wrap that one up, too."

She looked at me, her face alive with pleasure.

"I know! I'll get her some kind of Easter egg!"

Margaret and David continued to watch Fern, but my thoughts stayed with Easter. It was such a long, long time away. Fern had known Christmas. Could she possibly know Easter, so very far beyond the horizon? Too far to become our next target, but there was my birthday first, and that was only six weeks away. Weeks? When we lived on a knife-edge of minutes? But it was the nearest special day, so there and then, I set our next target. It would be my birthday. We would be together on my birthday!

CHAPTER NINE

One week later, a New Year dawned. Now I could say that I'd had Fern since last year! That way made it sound longer. Gradually, the six weeks, the forty-two days, to my birthday struggled past. Six weeks of constant awareness, clock-watching, food soaking, suddenly readjusted feeding times, gripe-water massaging, veterinary appointments, weighing, renewed prescriptions, disappointments and hope, all came and went. It was a strange birthday: more a celebration that Fern had reached another target and not one of any minor longevity on my part. But we had made it.

I studied the calendar. The time for Margaret's Easter egg was next month. But for how much longer could we continue this fraught existence, lurching from day to day? Beyond Easter, in the far distance, lay a date I tried in vain to keep from my mind: the twenty-ninth of April.

Ridiculously flushed with success after the Exemption at Fen Lane, I had sent away for the Real Thing, a Kennel Club Open Show schedule. I think I completed the entry form more as an act of bravado than anything else. I was daring this dreadful disease without a name to take away my beautiful Fern before she had been given any opportunity to prove her worth amongst her peers.

I entered her in the junior Flatcoat class, which was for both sexes between six and eighteen months of age. I worried about her thinness and the state of bloat she would be in, but she did have wonderful movement, her coat shone, and I knew now that she could assume such an imperious air of confidence. Considering the marvellous pedigree she had, surely the only way we could make fools of ourselves was if I fell flat on my face, or did something like that! (Which, knowing me, was quite possible) Besides, the venue was only eleven miles from home, just down the A46, at Newark, and we wouldn't have the crack-of-dawn start, or marathon journey of some competitors, which would be an advantage. I convinced myself it was worth a try.

But as soon as I'd squeezed into a parking space, I was already questioning my sanity. Absolutely everyone there had several dogs. Their cars, or Transits, were specially adapted with metal cages and hooks for umpteen leads of different styles. Many cages were draped with the glories of past rosettes! Everyone looked so focused, so experienced. What on earth was I doing here?

Illusion

Where to go? After a wee walk (literally!) in the designated area, I left Fern in the car and went to explore. Several huge halls of galvanised metal seemed to be in use, which I guessed would be for farm animals at the agricultural shows. I followed some people through a small door into the nearest hall and my baptism began.

The hall was heaving! The scents overpowering! Dogs, people, leather, damp wool, dog food, people food, and, strangely, something akin to talcum! But all the dogs were small! Every shape and colour, a few on the floor, but most in their owners' arms, they were all small. I couldn't have the wrong date, could I? Or maybe I was in the wrong place?

Along one long side of the hall there were market stalls, but they sold products connected only with dogs. I eased my way into the throng.

The first stall displayed pictures and portraits. I looked in vain for a Flatcoat. The entire stock of the next stall was aimed at the care of a dog's coat. Shampoos for every type, to enhance every colour, and for every condition. The same, too, for conditioners; an array which put Boots to shame! Then there were the specialized preparations: creams, gels and lotions to prevent or combat dryness, to de-tangle, to promote weather-resistance. I thought of what I had at home for Fern; one bottle of the cheaper Co-op version of Johnson's baby shampoo, and I winced inwardly.

The third stall sold grooming equipment: brushes in a vast selection of sizes and styles, with and without handles, long or short bristles, soft or hard, and brushes like gloves with short spikes which seemed to be made of a kind of metal! And then there were the combs! Such an immense variety of lengths, of teeth, of materials!

Fern had two small, metal combs with wooden handles and one second-hand brush intended for a horse.

Apprehension began to gnaw away the little confidence I had left. I should be using some of these things on Fern! How could we compete on equal terms if I hadn't taken proper care of her coat? I moved along the line. There were stalls selling bedding, vitamin and mineral supplements, country style clothing, and even more coat and skin care preparations, each with their own customers, examining, questioning, commenting, buying. I was both fascinated and frightened! I should know about all these wonderful things. I should have learned what to use on Fern, and be using it! We were grossly unprepared!

Then a trolley clipped my ankle, adding bloody scratches to my already battered ego. It was rather like the trolleys in a garden centre, but at the bottom there was a cage, and at the top, a tray with slightly raised edges. This particular tray held two plastic boxes, beside which were three different brushes and several combs, and alongside them was what looked like a tin of talcum powder. In the cage below, sat an orange Pekingese, staring with baleful expression at the forest of human legs. As I stared around at all this frantic activity, I realised there were more of these vehicles, a few with two or even three dogs riding in them, but many had their lower decks shrouded in some kind of sheeting, to hide what lurked beneath.

The centre of the hall was occupied by four large rectangles, marked out with low, wooden trestles. Across one corner of each rectangle, was a table with three chairs behind, facing into what I reasoned must be the show ring. A large placard hung from the front of each table, bearing a number. This end was number four. These must surely be ring numbers, so that competitors knew where to go- which was more than I did! The schedule told me that Flatcoats were to be judged in ring twelve, but where on earth was ring twelve? In one of the other halls! And time was going on! I had spent far too long gazing around and doing nothing.

The third hall turned out to be the right one. Brimful of wagging tails, this was the Gundog hall. Judging had already begun here and all four rings were full. There seemed to be an enormous number of Golden Retrievers and almost as many Labradors, yellow, black and a few chocolate. There were all types of Pointers, Spaniels, Weimaraners, and there, at the end, Flatcoats!

I picked my way through the crowd. All the Flatcoats had glossy coats, and all seemed incredibly nosey and overwhelmingly friendly; just like Fern, in fact! Plucking up courage, I asked a bystander which class was being judged.

"Twenty-five."

Panic! Our class was twenty-six! I rushed back to the car.

Getting Fern out of the boot, my eye fell on the grooming equipment I had brought with me: the horse brush and an old towel. It occurred to me then, to drive off. No one would know; only Margaret, and she would understand. What did I hope to achieve, taking on the "professionals" at their own game, my solitary pet and I, hoping that the judge might not notice her thinness, and that she wouldn't be bloated? This was madness!

I looked down at Fern. Wondering why we were doing nothing, she looked up at me, enquiringly. Eyes sparkling, tail wagging, she was excited and happy. This was new and she wanted to know all about it! I grabbed the horse brush, made a few sweeps along her back and through her tail, tossed it back into the boot, then headed for ring twelve before I could change my mind.

If I'd been nervous at the exemption show, I can't think of a word strong enough to describe my feeling now, except perhaps, terror. My stomach felt horribly empty, my knees really did shake and my heart pounded. I could actually see my blouse twitching! I pulled my jacket round so that others wouldn't see.

Class twenty-five was nearing its end. The judge, a young lady, wore a smart suit and shoes with quite high heels. A huge rosette on her right lapel proclaimed, "Judge". Wherever she moved, she was followed by an older man, also smartly dressed, who didn't have a rosette, but who carried a clipboard stacked with papers, a pen on a chain around his neck, and another pen which he was using to write on papers on the clipboard. Behind the table, a large huntin'-shootin'-fishin' woman in classic twin-set with pearls was seated on her own, presiding over more papers, four piles of single coloured rosettes, and several much larger, more elaborate ones.

The competitors were standing in a line that stretched along one side of the ring and most of the way down the next. Some of the dogs maintained their statuesque show poses, whilst others were more relaxed. This seemed to be because the judge wasn't looking. She and her helper were deep in earnest conversation. There was an air of expectancy. The people in the ring appeared to be more interested in each other's dogs, than in their own. Everyone seemed to be waiting.

Suddenly, the helper wheeled from the judge, hurried to the table, and held out a hand. The huntin'-shootin'-fishin' woman passed him four rosettes, one of each colour, whilst the judge's gaze once more swept to and fro along the line. Competitors and dogs alike responded, jerking to attention. One more, stern gaze, then the judge extended her left arm, palm upwards, to point at the pairing third from the right. She nodded once and smiled a brief smile. Bringing her arm down, she gestured at a spot on the floor immediately in front and to her left. A round of applause greeted the pair as they rushed forward, to take their places, centre stage. The owner's face was wreathed in smiles and even the dog was bouncing about in apparent delight! These must be the winners!

The judge repeated her action until there was a line of four competitors with their dogs, in the centre of the ring. Applause had muted steadily as each was called forward, but the smiles of the owners were just as bright. Each competitor received his or her reward; a card, which the helper had filled in, and a rosette; green for fourth place, yellow for third, blue for second and brilliant red for the winner. How wonderful any of these colours would look against Fern's black, gleaming fur! As the winners received their prizes, the man called out each entry number and dog's name. Then the unplaced competitors trouped from the ring, most with the same shoulder- drooping disappointment that I had seen at Fen Lane, but a few with an air of resignation that appeared to border acute boredom. The successful foursome took one turn around the ring, and then made their exits.

"Class twenty-six! Junior! Class twenty-six."

Us! Our turn! Should I leave now? Should I go home? Fern had been somewhere new, she had enjoyed what she had seen. I could still go away! No one would know!

Go away? Run away! Shortening Fern's lead, I pushed my way to the ring entrance, and I was in! I was in a real Show Ring and there was no turning back.

I took a place on the perimeter. There were about twenty other dogs, including one of the more unusual liver colour. To my delight and relief, Fern settled by my side at once. Then I realised she was the only dog sitting! Perhaps I ought to make her stand, but before I could do that, I noticed the Judge's helper working his way along the line and towards me, noting something on his clipboard as he passed each competitor.

A stab of horror burned down my back, and I felt my cheeks flush. My entry number! The card was still in my pocket! I rushed to pin it on, but my fingers refused to obey. I tried to manipulate Fern's lead, the card and pin all at the same time. It was virtually impossible. When I did get them sorted, I couldn't force the safety pin through my jacket! And then the card tore! My head held down in embarrassment, I continued to fumble.

"Your number?"

I knew the helper was waiting for me, because Fern had stepped forward, tail wagging, ready to greet a new friend.

I kept my head down.

"Number please."

"Er...it's torn."

The entire length of my back prickled hot in shame. I daren't look up.

"I'm sorry," I added pointlessly and pathetically.

"Just tell me your number," the voice intoned.

"Two-five-six."

He consulted his list.

"Tilsley. Fossdyke Illusion."

"Yes. I'm sorry."

He moved on.

Fern took several steps after him, watching his retreating figure with disappointment.

It was as I reined her back that I saw several people at the far end of the line looking across. Staring might be a better description. Hastily, I tugged Fern in to my side, where she promptly sat again. This was dreadful! Squaring my shoulders, I tried to pull myself together, only to notice two more, nearer the corner, gazing across at us. Had I already been found out? Did they realise I was totally out of my depth, the misplaced owner of one pet?

She must be an obedience dog, that's why she sits; I tried desperately to convince myself that's what they were thinking. Then thoughts of Fern's pedigree sprang into my mind. Why should they stare? I had every right to be in that ring! But I wished I wasn't. I wished I were anywhere but there. And then I felt so sorry for Fern! Heaven knows what fears and conflicts I was sending down the lead to her! I so wanted her to shine, to stride out in that wonderfully flowing, authoritive manner I now knew she had. Yet here I was, worrying and apologising and looking forward only to the time when it might all be over.

"Class twenty-six!"

The helper called to establish order. The judge stepped forward. The other handlers and dogs sprang into their poses and I cringed.

Eighth in line, I had time to watch what happened. First, the dog was simply viewed from a short distance away: sideways, then from the rear, and finally head-on. Next came the close inspection; head, including eyes, ears and teeth, then neck, back, brisket, front legs, belly, and hind legs. Like an idiot, I tried to keep Fern "disciplined", and in what I believed to be show pose, instead of allowing her to relax, and it seemed an age before the judge reached us.

"How old is she?"

"Nine months."

She looked at Fern from the side, the back, and then the front. She gazed at her head for such a long, long time, that I marvelled at Fern's restraint, with a potential new friend only a lick away.

Then the judge bent forward, gently taking Fern's head into her hands.

"Hello, you," she whispered, then straightened, looking down at a still and quiet dog. Giving Fern a single stroke, she took one ear and measured it alongside her muzzle. Next, she pulled down one corner of each eye in turn. Then it was on to her jaw: so far, so good.

She lifted one side of Fern's jowls to inspect her teeth, and the honeymoon was over! Fern pranced to one side, puppy-bowed, then licked the judge's hand. But she didn't seem to mind! Flatcoats were supposed to show confidence and bonhomie, after all! She straightened, and then tried again. Fern attempted a full frontal assault.

"Oho! You're just full of yourself, aren't you?"

I grabbed Fern's head and tried to hold it still.

"I'm sorry."

The judge managed to part Fern's lips. A rosy tongue shot out as Fern twisted sideways in order to land her tongue more effectively on its objective.

I pulled the collar further up on her neck. This was awful. Everyone must be watching. I wanted them to know it was me who was useless, not my dog. She's never like this at the vet's, I thought to myself.

"I'm sorry."

Somehow, between licks, jumps, pushing, pulling and sorries, Fern had her teeth inspected. She retained a reasonable demeanour until the judge began to feel her rump, which became the cue for another joyful dance. I wondered if I should say this was our first time, but then thought it would sound totally pathetic, so all I did was to mutter yet another sorry, fuss around, and make things worse.

So convinced was Fern that this was a new game, she continued to prance sideways as we set off on the first leg of our, " triangle", but as we turned the corner, she suddenly settled. Now I really did want everyone to look! She was no longer my pet, my companion. She was a Queen, striding imperiously through her subjects, telling them that she was the finest of them all, and should they dare to disagree, then it was they who were wrong! Now I knew they could see it was I who was the idiot, and not my dog. Turn again, back towards the judge. Fern suddenly spotted the lady who had started the new game for her, the queen abdicated and my pet galloped the rest of the way, leaping up to greet her new friend. The judge stepped back swiftly.

"I'm sorry."

She moved to the next competitor and it was over.

I was breathless and so very hot! I could feel sweat trickling between my shoulder blades. My legs felt like jelly. I didn't watch anyone else. I can't even recall what Fern did, or didn't do. I was so thankful it was over. All I wanted to do was to crawl out of that ring, go away and hide! I would never, ever do this again! My breathing gradually slowed and the loud thumping of my heart faded. Eventually, I became aware that the helper had fetched the rosettes, and that the judge had begun the presentation; red, blue, yellow:

"Two five six!"

No one moved. Someone else here, as well as me, must be pretty stupid I thought to myself.

"Two five six!"

Fern! Me! Us! In spite of my appalling handling, we had been placed!

How Fern behaved during the presentation, I have absolutely no idea! I walked forward as if in a trance and held out my hand. The judge shook it, and then brought up her other hand to sandwich mine firmly. She looked intently into my face.

"You must get more body on her, a lot more, and work hard. She has great potential." Then the judge turned away. We trouped our lap of honour, and left the ring.

Now it really was over.

Fern still wanted her usual walk that evening, but I shortened it. As we returned, Gordon was just parking his car in his drive: why one man should need both car and van, I couldn't imagine.

"If you want to see a real rosette, next time you're not busy, I'll show you," I said, beaming with pride. "She came fourth today in her first proper show!"

Fern made her usual great fuss of him, even though she was tired, wouldn't admit it and had no idea of what she had achieved that day. In spite of the most inept handling (it would be years before I really appreciated how truly awful I had been) and being underweight, she had been placed in her first Open Show.

What was it the judge had said? "She has great potential." Was that why she had stood in silence for so long, simply looking? "Hello, you;" words which had been spoken so softly, and to Fern alone. What had the judge seen? Had she seen the sparkle and self-belief of a true champion? I thought Fern's movement to be her best attribute, but the judge had seen precious little of that. Then I remembered how some of the other handlers had stared and the thought stopped me in my tracks! A shiver ran down my spine. What if their stares hadn't been derision? What if they had not been looking at me, but at Fern? Looking at her, and envying me? Had they seen the same as the judge? My imagination took flight. Jill's pick-of-the-litter, George's bitch of the very highest calibre; what if Fern did have what it took to become a champion? I knew little of the long road to such exalted status, but had heard something about three Challenge Certificates from three different judges. If Fern could win just one Challenge Certificate, then that would be wonderful, beyond my wildest dreams! But if one, then why not two? And if we had two, there would be only one more to go and we'd be there! We'd have done it! Champion! Champion Fossdyke Illusion! It rolled off the tongue! It sounded right, as if it were meant to be!

"Work hard", the judge had said. Of course I would! Somehow I would become a decent handler; I wouldn't let Fern down! I would do whatever it took to enable her to fulfil her potential. Champion Fossdyke Illusion! Glowing with pride, I gazed at her, estimating her girth as a matter of course and the dream shattered at a single stroke.

How could I be so utterly foolish? How could I let my imagination run away like that? How could I dream of a possible championship years away, when today we lived in hours and minutes, and I targeted Fern's lifespan in hope? All the pleasure, all the dreams which flourished so happily only a moment ago, died in that instant.

I went into the kitchen and looked up at the cereal packet notice, which I had read so many times before. I read it again and again. I read it more slowly. Then I spoke each word out loud, but this time, its magic did not work.

I must have been the only rosette winner that night who cried herself to sleep.

CHAPTER TEN

"Yesterday was wonderful, but today will be even better!"

Every morning, Fern's wagging tail and sparkling, laughing eyes proclaimed her unshakable belief. I tried to match that spirit, but it became increasingly difficult, for I could see her condition slowly, but inexorably, deteriorating. Her feeds were now every two to one and a half hours, depending on her state of bloat. If things were good, I often stayed up beyond midnight in order to get in another feed and to wait until I was certain it was safe for me to go to bed. How long could this go on? How long could she survive? I had no idea where her energy came from!

The weeks leading to Easter were peppered with our usual veterinary visits, but Target Easter did arrive! I bought an egg filled with chocolates for Margaret, a Cadbury crème egg for myself, and the smallest bag of doggy choc-drops I could find, for Fern. It was not meanness, for they would have to be strictly rationed. It was her first taste of "chocolate", and how she loved it! Maybe some would keep for the birthday I tried hard not to think about.

One afternoon, her excited and insistent bark drew me out into the garden. She was right up at the far end, facing George's house, tail wagging her body. She glanced round at me, laughing with delight and I knew George was back.

Sure enough, that evening, the phone rang and I heard a familiar voice. George had heard his welcome earlier and now enquired about the progress of his Black Princess. I didn't think he ever fully appreciated the seriousness of Fern's condition. He knew there was a big problem certainly, but he seemed more concerned with Fern's training and the fact that my ability, if I dared endow it with that name, in no way matched hers. A lesson was arranged in three days' time, for George would very soon return to Nigeria.

"Show me what ye've learned then."

He stood back, legs spread, arms folded high on his chest, piercing blue eyes narrowed against the fleeting sun and waited. A sudden breeze whirled down the hillside, caught a wisp of his thinning hair and twirled it into his face. He made no attempt to draw it back. Nor did he clarify his instructions. In fact, he looked thoroughly belligerent.

"Do you mean heelwork? And turns? Things like that?"

"Just show me what you've been doing, pet."

This was George at his intimidating best. Why had he adopted such an attitude? But I'd show him! I gathered Fern on a short lead, gave her a firm jerk, almost shouted "Heel!" and marched off. Today, I didn't care if people were watching. About turn! Right turn! Left turn! Back and forth we marched, with a few sits and downs thrown in. Eventually, I stopped in front of him. He had not moved. A golfer picked up his stray ball, glanced enquiringly at us, and headed back onto the course. Gus wandered over, staring up at George. Still he did not move.

"Is that what you wanted?"

In reply, he got down on one knee, and spread his arms wide to Fern. I released her and she went forward, tail wagging, head down. George put his arms around her.

"Oh, Fern, Fern, ma poor Fern, what have they done to you?"

He cuddled her to his chest and made those soft, happy sounds she had so loved when a puppy.

I was taken aback. I had expected criticism, not this. He continued to stroke and hug Fern. Then he stood and faced me, his expression grim and accusing.

"I never want to see this bitch as dour and introverted again."

Shocked and mystified, I looked at Fern. This attitude certainly was different. Whilst her behaviour with George had always been impeccable, there was now none of the sparkle, none of the sheer fun of their previous relationship.

"Did you no see what was happening?" He waved an arm in the air. " She loved t'work! Now look at her! Wondering if she's right, no confidence, no..." he searched for a suitable word, "no attack!"

He glared at me, and in that moment, I hated him. His arrogant stance and his biting criticism made me feel like a stupid child. I hated him because, appallingly, I knew he was right. He must have seen the change in Fern the moment he set eyes on her.

Suddenly, his attitude softened a little.

"I suppose it's easier for me. I've no seen Fern for a long time."

He motioned us to walk. We did so in silence. Wisp had long vanished over the top of the hill, but Gus stayed alongside. So and Fern each made their separate explorations. We threaded our way past horses and more golfers. The wind had picked up. Of course, George was right. The different method of training had undoubtedly been detrimental to Fern. I had been unhappy with what we were doing at Cardinal's Hill, and yet I had stuck with it. Why couldn't I see what was happening? Why had I been so lacking in confidence to admit that it was wrong for us? Why did I always worry so much about what others thought?

I didn't know what to say. How could I make everything right again? It didn't matter one iota to George whether or not I admitted any mistake; his only concern was for Fern, but I thought an open admission of my stupidity would bring down more even criticism on my head. I couldn't face that. But the way forward was decided for me. Perhaps George reasoned that I'd had time enough to squirm, and to think.

"We're no working today, pet. I want you just to play wi' her. Don't do any work. Don't put her in any position where you might have to correct her. Just try and relax and play wi' her."

He turned his head, but continued speaking in the same tones. "Fern come!"

She came, tail straight out and wagging, her head raised this time.

He gave a short, sharp whistle.

"So!"

So turned back.

"Gus."

Gus edged closer.

He looked around, growling, as he always did when assuming mock anger.

"Now where's that black-hearted, no-good rubbish, Wisp?"

From the far side of the common, a black and white bullet was already hurtling towards us, skimming the ground. Wisp, winner of almost every top competition in Open Agility, was on his way. The lesson was over. It was perhaps, one of the hardest of my life.

Nigel had obviously been giving our situation a lot of thought, for on our next appointment, he broached an idea.

"There is one thing we might do; something called a fluoroscopy. It's not curative, but it would show us what's actually going on in Fern's gut. They're given a barium meal and everything that happens in the gut is filmed. It's followed through the whole digestive system."

He smiled his crinkly smile, then continued the explanation.

"Dr. Edward Hall would do it at Liverpool University; he's Head of the veterinary school there. It can only be done on dogs of very sound temperament, because they can't be put to sleep; anaesthetic would interfere with the results. It takes a day. They're starved the night before, then fed there. It might give us a better idea of how to treat her, but it's not a treatment in itself."

He paused, holding my gaze.

"Actually, I've spoken to him already. I think I could get him to accept Fern. I said her temperament was good." The smile came again. "There's none better," he added.

I liked the idea that we might find out something concrete, but didn't like the idea of Fern being put through a process which appeared to be a protracted ordeal and neither did I fancy the idea of starving her.

"But if she's starved, she blows up!"

This was the greatest anomaly in Fern's condition: she blew up after food, she blew up before food, and she blew up without any food at all!

"I'd speak to him about that. Probably missing the morning feeds would be enough. Anyway, think about it. Let me know what you decide."

That was one of the things I so liked about Nigel. It was never "I say this", or, "I will do that". It was always "We", always suggestions and listening. We may be battling an unknown enemy, but we were doing it side by side.

"What actually happens?"

"Well," there was a moment's hesitation, "she'd be laid on a table, then strapped to it, and the table is rotated so that the gut can be x-rayed. The process is repeated as the barium travels along."

It sounded horrific.

I went away and thought. How many times would she suffer the ordeal of being tied down? Tied down! It made me shudder. And being revolved? She could be terrified! It might damage her beautiful nature forever. Neither would it treat her condition.

But was there a chance it could point us in the right direction? A chance! Our life together had been a series of chances. Why should we not take just one more?

And so it was arranged. It would be on April the twenty-eighth.

I wasn't looking forward to driving over the Pennines twice in one day, but I would face it. Margaret had been quite unwell recently and I could not expect her to come with us, even though I knew she would if asked, so I didn't tell her of the plan. Salvation came from a totally unexpected quarter.

"I'll come with you, if you like."

"But you're working."

"I can take the day off."

It was Gordon making this out-of-the-blue offer.

"We could share the driving. If you don't mind me driving your car, that is. Some people mind. Or we could go in mine. That way you'd be there and back in a day. It's a long way when you're worried."

He seemed determined to come, and had already thought everything through. Fern would be delighted of course, although would I fancy his company for an entire day? But dogs are supposed to know about people, aren't they? With this comforting thought, I accepted his offer.

Nigel discussed the case with Dr. Hall, who agreed to our special circumstances. Fern was to be fed right up to the previous evening, and then starved only on the day of the test.

A very strange way to spend a first date, I thought to myself as I packed a bag for the day. But then, it wasn't a date, was it? Yet I found myself deliberately preparing a rather upmarket picnic that I thought might be somewhat impressive, high on the Pennines! Perhaps I needed something else to focus on.

A thick, wet mist shrouded those bleak hills that Thursday morning, and I was glad of Gordon's company. He took over the driving as we reached the Liverpudlian outskirts. Experience had taught me that it is quite acceptable for a man driving a car with "foreign" number plates, to find himself in the wrong lane, but should that happen to a woman, then it is because she is a woman and therefore, at best unobservant, or more likely, brainless. I took the opportunity to chicken out!

We found the Small Animal Hospital easily, by heading for the Roman Catholic Cathedral, "Paddy's Wigwam", as instructed. In one of the many university car parks, we readily found a parking space and were careful to lock up and leave nothing on show, as notices on almost every lamp standard instructed! The surrounding buildings were pleasant and modern, but we noticed that every single ground floor window had bars! Around the corner, was the hospital itself. An old, Victorian building, with new bits incongruously tacked on, it was dwarfed by the surrounding modernity. Here, too, all the lower windows were heavily barred. Inside, the contrast was startling: everything seemed like an up to date general hospital, complete with its antiseptic odours!

The waiting room was pleasant enough. It was also quite full! Who had all these other people come to see? I resolved to make a big fuss should any attempt be made to palm me off with anyone less than Dr. Hall himself. I had come too far for a minion!

Eventually, a friendly looking young man in a long white coat came through from the back. Holding the door open, he gazed round the room until his eye fell on us.

"Miss Tilsley? Fern? I'm ready for you now."

This man looked too young to be anything other than a student.

Not likely, I thought grimly, as we went through the door. I followed him along a corridor lined with similar doors. He stopped outside one and held it open. Perhaps he'd just come to fetch us to Dr. Hall's room.

No. Inside two more young men in short white coats waited, one standing, the other perched on the edge of the windowsill. I turned my back on them and drew breath to protest to the young man who had fetched us. It was then I saw his name-tag. It read simply, Ed Hall.

He was wonderful. He made me feel as if Fern was his only patient. He explained what would happen, said she would remain there most of the day, and that I was to return for her at five o' clock. Part of me never left that hospital.

Gordon and I drove down to the refurbished tourist area of the Albert Dock. It was a lovely, sunny day, with a stiff breeze blowing across the brown, oily waters of the Mersey. As we walked along the promenade, I thought only of Fern. Was she missing me? Was she being the wonderful patient Nigel had promised? Was she afraid? Might she think I had left her there forever? Gordon sensed how I felt, and seemed content to walk along with me in silence. The wind whipped up the sea, cracked the flags on their poles, and provided safe background sound, so I didn't feel the need to make bright conversation.

Eventually, we reached the Maritime Museum. We examined models and photographs, artefacts and souvenirs from famous Cunard and White Star ships. Later, we drank tea and ate scones in the café. Somehow, time passed. I wouldn't mind going back there one day.

Five o' clock, and I was in the waiting room. This time, there was no one else there, so I sat down, wishing I had been asked to collect Fern at four. Things had always worked out when I collected her at four. I must have been noticed, for within a few moments, I heard the patter of paws, the doors were pushed open and there was a nurse, with Fern. Delighted to see me, she looked none the worse for her ordeal. The nurse escorted us back to the consulting room. Dr. Hall and the same two students were already there. He was seated behind the desk and it looked very formal this time. I took my invited seat, telling myself that whatever he said would change nothing. Fern would still be in the same condition. It would be like the heart murmur; I'd just know.

"Everything went well. We saw what we needed."

In spite of my resolve, that familiar, horrible emptiness shot through me like the blade of a knife. Dr. Hall looked at Fern.

"Never stops, does she?"

Was this a compliment or a criticism? Had she not lived up to her reputation?

He grinned.

"All the cages are at one end. Most dogs watch what we're doing for a while, then they get bored and lie down. Some go to sleep. Not her! She was always watching. Every time anyone went remotely near her cage, she got up, and wagged her tail. I think she's very intelligent."

I liked hearing that.

"I've been told so before, but I don't really know. She's my first dog."

"Oh."

A brief silence.

"A real baptism of fire!"

Now, where had I heard that before? I wished he'd get on with it.

"Well, as I'm sure Mr. Williams said, today hasn't been a treatment. It can only tell us something and we have to decide then, if that something is relevant; and for us, it was. It's told us quite a lot."

I couldn't take my eyes from his face. I tried to discern what might be coming. I wanted, so badly to know, yet was so very afraid of knowing.

"We can think of the digestive system as one long tube. It's made of muscle, and muscle is what makes us move."

I wondered if I should tell him I taught biology, but that might seem rude. And now he had begun his explanation, now that I would know the truth, I wanted to put it off for as long as possible. I wanted to keep myself in the dark, to bury my head in the sand, for in that way at least, I would keep the comfort of hope. When the answer finally came, I might have that taken away.

"We've found that Fern's digestive system doesn't move as it should. Normally, food is pushed along by waves of contraction-"

"Peristalsis!"

He looked slightly surprised, then nodded agreement.

"Yes, peristalsis. Peristalsis is very feeble in Fern's gut: in fact it's non-existent at times. There just aren't any strong contractions like there should be."

He paused, to allow me time to take this in.

"What contractions there are, are very weak, and they are irregular."

Since entering the room, Fern had been gazing at the two students, and, whenever their eyes met, wagging her tail ever harder. Now she could bear it no longer. She jumped up and fussed around the feet of the nearest student. Dr. Hall looked round at him.

"Go on then, you can talk to her, you know!"

The student crouched to return Fern's favours. The doctor continued.

"As her gut empties, the contractions virtually stop. All her gut wall does, is to flutter spasmodically. I think you see what I mean."

I nodded, remembering Nigel's comment on the lack of strong peristalsis during her operation. I remembered the first symptom of diarrhoea. Her gut wouldn't have been able to absorb water if it wasn't moving properly.

"Do you know what's causing it? There aren't any other puppies like this."

"There might not be. It seems to be a nerve defect. It's in those nerves which lie in the gut wall and tell the brain what's going on in there, like how full it is. We can't tell, in Fern's case, if those nerves just aren't there, or if they do exist, then for some reason, they don't tell the brain what's going on. The brain doesn't know the gut is there, so it doesn't tell the gut to contract and digest food."

I sat back in my chair. The student continued to fondle Fern. So that was it. Nerves that didn't work and nerves can't be repaired. If they could, there wouldn't be anyone left paralysed. But Fern's nerves must exist, for there had been no problem during the first months of her life. Something had interfered with the working of those nerves. I might understand the explanation, but not the reason why this devastating thing had struck. I dared not think of the prognosis. Dr. Hall continued.

"Food is digested very slowly. When we expected it to have reached her intestine, there was nothing there. Nothing had even left her stomach."

He paused again. Perhaps he thought this was all too much. Perhaps he didn't like what he was having to say.

"Although the contractions are very weak and irregular, they're at their best when she has just eaten. As food is digested and passes out of the stomach, then it simply relaxes. This happens all through the system. As food passes along, instead of keeping muscle tone, the whole thing just...relaxes."

He spread his hands on the desk.

"All that gas in there is simply air. Air has free entry into her gut."

Now I remembered how Nigel had watched as Fern's exposed intestine slowly inflated. Of course! Under anaesthetic, she would be totally relaxed.

The silence of absolute stillness filled the room. Head resting on outstretched paws, now even Fern was still

"With every breath, air enters her gut."

He picked up a pen from his desk, and began to twirl it round and round in his fingers.

"Have you ever heard of mega-oesophagus?"

I nodded. He replaced the pen in a pot.

"It's a bit like that, but throughout the entire digestive system."

Conversation died a second time. The student who had played with Fern stared at the floor, whilst the other gazed through the barred window at a brick wall beyond.

Dr. Hall read my thoughts.

"There isn't any cure."

I looked right at him, willing him to be truthful and to tell me everything.

"So even as she breathes, air can get in?"

"There's nothing to prevent it."

"What caused it?"

He shook his head slightly, staring at his desk.

"What do you think caused it?"

I wanted an answer. I wanted to apportion blame.

"I would love to know," he replied gravely, looking up. "Are the nerves actually present? Are they fewer in number? Have they been damaged somehow?"

He lowered his head again and spoke very quietly.

"Only Fern could tell us."

The world stood still. Then suddenly, I felt calm. Nothing had changed after all.

"What's it called?"

Again the slight shake of his head.

"I'd call it Intestinal Motility Disorder. I've seen a few dogs with something like this before, but not one so severely affected. Her stomach's already been distorted by the constant bloating. It's shaped like a J, instead of a C."

He closed the folder of notes.

"One thing I can say," he added with a slight smile, "is that the longer she survives, the better her chances of survival become."
He could not miss the tears brimming in my eyes.

"I'm so sorry I can't tell you anything better. She really is a good-natured dog. I'll be writing to Mr. Williams. You won't need to come to see us again. She's a lovely dog. Exactly the right personality to cope."

He came around the desk, smiling and held out his hand. He shook mine firmly.

"Just remember, you've come this far."

Gordon drove most of the way back.

I was still sitting in the lounge when it became the twenty-ninth of April.

CHAPTER ELEVEN

Another milestone had been reached.Fern was one year old. Her age could now be measured in years rather than months, so it must have been a milestone. We had reached yet another target in our life of targets. As each had been reached, I'd always set a new one, but this time I didn't. I had begun to expect the target would be reached. That was dangerous.

Regular vet visits continued, with a few unscheduled ones in between, and now Nigel allowed me to see his growing concern. It was becoming increasingly difficult to get any food at all into Fern, because she was always bloated to some degree. Yet she was invariably hungry and always cleared her bowl!

But in the middle of May, Fern ate her final solid food. Now, she could take only liquids. Nigel gave me a recipe which I had to make fresh several times each day.

It was a strange concoction, but Fern loved her two tablespoons of sunshine yellow cream made with Farex baby cereal, cottage cheese, honey, eggs and vitamin supplements. The "feeds" came as often as every hour, depending on her state of bloat. Sometimes, I could get as many as ten or even eleven feeds per day into her, but the lack of real food was beginning to tell its tale. She remained an extrovert, happy individual, but her relentless drive was becoming muted. Content now to stay beside me on our walks, she strayed only a few yards in order to investigate a particular interest. No longer did my glossy black beauty spend most of our walk as a dot on the horizon, racing the wind, in sheer joy.

"Settling down, eh?"

"Quieter, I see."

"Growing up at last?"

Remarks like these tore into me and threatened to destroy the tattered remnants of any resolve I had left. More than once, I held back a bitter reply. Would I have felt any better for shocking a well-meaning friend? But I thought that reply. I saw that reply. It was written across the sky, along the green fields, written in huge, black letters.

"No, dying,"

"No, slowly dying."

Or even a casual, "Just dying."

Because that's what was happening. I was watching my beautiful, feisty companion, whose love of Life was so strong, gradually losing her grip on that life; having it prised away little by little by a relentless disease with no textbook name and no cure, and I couldn't do a thing about it.

Almost one year ago, my life had been rekindled by the love, excitement, and fun generated by the fire that burned within Fern. Was I purely selfish in fighting for a life which now seemed doomed? Did I strive to keep her alive just for my own benefit? She was quieter certainly, but still happy. Did she not deserve to live for as long as possible?

But those thoughts would not go away. Was I the "tough" person of my cereal packet notice, or was I selfish and stupid, in fighting the inevitable? Was I too stupid to acknowledge defeat and to accept it?

One afternoon we were sitting beside the river. The sun shone warmly, a gentle breeze stirred the growing grasses and it was so beautiful, so new and fresh, yet here was I, struggling in the turmoil of what I perceived to be the End. It was that appalling dilemma which faces so many pet owners; would I have to decide the moment of Fern's death? Would I have to play God? How could I give myself that right?

I looked at Fern. Stretched out on her side, long legs extended as if she were running, the sun imbued the still glossy blackness of her coat with a deep, steely blue shine. She must have known I was looking, for she lifted up her head to look back at me, and thumped the ground with her tail. I knew in that moment I would never give up. She was thinner than ever, her stamina almost non-existent, yet her eyes sparkled and she tackled everything with the same zest as she always had. I looked at her and I knew I could never forfeit the determination and unshakable optimism of her spirit whilst ever the faintest hope remained.

But back in the quietness of home, I did acknowledge the day might come when it must all be over. I even got as far as considering how: at home, and not by Nigel. Much as I would need his kindness and understanding, I could not ask him to do that. He had fought too long and too hard to be the one to end it all. I would spare him that.

But right now was not the time. We would keep fighting.

I rang Jill. Perhaps it was with the vague hope that, even at this stage, she might know someone, or someone who knew someone else, or someone who had heard…. It was a well-trodden path. Yet I knew that if she'd even the faintest of ideas, she would have called at once.

Within seconds, I knew it had been the wrong thing to do. Her manner was careful, guarded, as she tried to find suitable words. Eventually, she let me know the worst possible news. Magic was dead. She had been put to sleep after several weeks of diminishing appetite, and then days of not eating at all. Endless investigation during her illness had not revealed any trace of disease, but Jill had wanted an answer. An autopsy showed Magic's entire digestive system to be atrophied: hardened, shrunken, dead. She was almost three and a half.

I couldn't bear to be with Fern. Leaving her in the lounge, I fled to my bedroom and waited for the tears to come. None did. I sat on the edge of my bed. It was very quiet and the room felt cold. Poor, sweet, gentle Magic, vibrant and alive whilst part of her died. I tried to imagine what a dead gut inside a living body might look like, and shuddered. Not pink, not moving, but grey, wizened and still; above all, very, very still. How the rest of her beautiful body must have cried out for the nourishment it so desperately needed! Was this what was happening now to Magic's tenth baby?

Still no tears came. I tried to think logically. Could this be an inherited problem, something which Magic had passed on to her daughter? But if that were the case, then some of the other puppies would also have the condition. Jill had already followed this up, and none did. I saw no reason whatever to doubt her word. But if the problem were inherited, then surely it would have been apparent from birth? It would not have developed in late puppy hood, nor would its onset have been gradual. Those nerves, which Dr. Hall had found to be the cause of the problem in Fern, had once functioned perfectly. And Fern had never been a fussy eater! She ate everything put in front of her! So something must have happened to damage those nerves, but what? Such a devastating thing, surely I would have known! I would have known there was something wrong!

But none of this wondering, questioning, supposing, changed a thing. Magic was dead. What chance was there now for Magic's daughter?

Tears would not come, nor would they have relieved the despair I felt at that moment.

I shivered. I had been in the bedroom long enough. It was time to feed Fern.

If she had been able to speak, she could not have made it any more clear that she regarded her feed as inexcusably late! At first sight of me, she hurried to her feeding place, stared up at me wagging her tail vigorously, and frowned! Any unfortunate person who believes a dog's expression incapable of change, has either never lived with one, is arrogant, unobservant, unintelligent or any combination of any two or more! She forgave me the instant I began to prepare her food, watching in gleeful anticipation, then lapping it up within seconds. This wasn't like her mother!

As Fern disappeared into the garden, I thought of other ways in which the two were different. Fern was altogether a more ebullient character, an extrovert who believed the world was there for her, purely for her enjoyment and interest. In her guileless innocence, she expected to love everyone she met, and to be loved by them in return, and so it had been, with the sole exception of Mary, but that was not personal. Mary would have disliked any pet of mine. There was Fern's great determination too, which I had named the Cupboard Top Syndrome. How determined was that seven week old pup not to stand on the cupboard top! How determined not to allow me to take her away from her home, or to let me groom her, or leave her, to insist on doing all her usual things immediately after her operations, and to resist those people who tried to bully her with regimented training methods. Fern had always known what she wanted, and more than anything else, she wanted to live.

"She has exactly the right personality to cope," Dr. Hall had said. "You've come this far."

Was this as far as it went? But it was not in Fern's nature to give up. How could I?

So now we drove to our walks down the Lane, on the common, or into the park. We still went shopping. We visited Margaret. We worked and played in the garden, and all the time, I strove to get as much food as possible into her.

That Monday morning, Fern had been her normal exuberant self. Mondays meant that we went to the common in order to meet the Dobis, another "pack" with whom we had become firm friends: on Fern's initiative of course! I marvelled that Fern could still find the strength and vitality needed for play. At times, I wondered if I should avoid these situations and keep her quiet, but quiet was not for Fern. Life was for living!

Sandi, a pretty, bubbly American, had married her merchant sailor husband and lived in the U.K. for many years. She bred and showed prize winning Dobermanns. Number one dog Toby was the stuff of criminal nightmare! Black and brown, all teeth and pointed ears, he lunged around on the end of his lead, oblivious to Sandi's plaintive cries of, "Toby, behave yourself for mama!" or "Toby, you'll have mama's arm out!" But this was a huge dog acting out his fearsome reputation, for he was the proverbial big softie to those he knew, and in the show ring, he was a perfect gentleman, honed to immaculate statuary. He would dearly have loved to forge a different relationship, other than that of playmate with Fern, but she was able to keep him in what she considered to be his place, with ease. Sandi's younger bitch, Indi, also ruled Toby with a rod of iron! The bond between the two Dobermanns was unbreakable, but it was usually Indi and Fern who played and explored together. Much of that morning, for instance, Toby had watched from the sidelines as Indi and Fern sought out as many puddles as they could in which to compete for wettest, dirtiest dog, Sandi encouraging them both with loud American fervour.

"Atta girl, Fern! Atta girl! Go, Indi!"

It was a very tired and muddy Flatcoat who returned home, so when she merely raised her head to watch as I prepared her feed, I wasn't unduly surprised. The worry began when she did not eat all that feed. It was the first time ever Fern had not cleared her bowl and licked it with a vigour which threatened to remove the stainless from the steel. Perhaps I hadn't added enough sugar, or maybe the egg was "off". I threw it all away.

Fern didn't want much of her next feed either, although she drank readily enough, then wanted to go for a walk. She wouldn't do that if she were ill, I told myself.

When we set off, she appeared her usual self: brisk, swinging gait, tail out, head up, but nevertheless, I shortened the already short walk.

She refused most of her next feed. Two tablespoons of "cream", and it was too much? Three feeds had now been only partially eaten and she couldn't afford to miss any food at all! I looked at the clock. We could make the vets if the traffic was kind to us. Yet she had wanted a walk and the lack of food had not produced more bloating than usual. Why was she so full of contradictions? I decided not to go. But when her next feed came round, Fern refused to eat at all and the worry grew. The surgery had long since closed. Was this an emergency? For a normal dog, of course not, but how I wished I had taken the opportunity to go earlier!

She was still drinking, and I even got her to drink more, by making her a sweet cup of tea. Jill had told me how much Flatcoats enjoyed a cuppa!

The lack of anything in her stomach was the most worrying part, for it could trigger larger and more frequent bloats, and there was a very long night to get through.

So I slept on a sun lounger, alongside the open kitchen door. Twice during the night, I heard her moving about, and found she had left her bed to lie on the floor. She would be cold! Each time, I insisted she returned to bed, despite her reluctance and reproachful gaze.

It was such a long night! The lounger was hard and the pillow had a mind of its own. I hated the yellow street lighting, sneaking around and above the curtains. I wanted it to turn grey; to tell me that the new day had come. How I wished and wished we had gone to the vets!

When day did come, Fern would not drink. She would not even go into the garden. I virtually pushed her outside for she must want to relieve herself! But she simply stood in the drive, looking up, the picture of misery, imploring me with sad eyes to leave her alone. But I didn't, I continued to command! Hadn't George said I was not firm enough? Hadn't they said the same thing at Cardinal's Hill? But Fern would not move. The very sight of her with tail right down and head lowered spurred me to greater effort. She had to relieve herself! I forgot what I had been taught and my voice grew louder. Fern raised her head to look at me, dark eyes pleading for me to stop. She was defying me! It was that Cupboard Top Syndrome again! Now, I really shouted, but even that had no effect.

The fact that I continued to berate her haunts me to this day. Eventually, I gave up. She followed me indoors very slowly, and immediately returned to her bed.

Only Frances was at Whitegates when we arrived. I explained I could not persuade Fern to leave the car. Lying right up to the back of the rear seat, she had not moved when I called her out, and when I reached in to her, she had growled! Frances stopped work at once, and hurried outside. I lifted the hatchback. Her reaction was immediate.

"You lift that side of the blanket. I'll take this."

Together, we lifted Fern on the blanket I used to line the car boot, and carried her into Nigel's surgery.

"Wait here with her."

She bustled away to continue preparations for the morning's surgery.

I sat on the floor next to Fern. Gone were my attempts to command, to dominate. I was ashamed and very afraid. Stroking her gently, I promised that "Uncle Nigel" would soon be here to make her better. I'd never said anything like that before. That was what foolish, pretentious people said.

Illusion

But I said it. And I said it again. Somehow, that word strengthened the bond between the three of us. Uncles were family. They were obliged to make everything all right again, weren't they?

Fern seemed unaware of my caresses; she seemed unaware of my presence. Frances had said nothing, but her response had been so very swift. The seriousness of Fern's condition must have been immediately apparent to her, or perhaps, I tried to reassure myself, Frances would have reacted like that anyway. She always seemed surrounded by an aura of brisk and clinical efficiency.

Rush hour traffic surged past the bay window, and the phone began to ring. Every car I heard, I wanted to be Nigel's. Paws tapped their way into the waiting room and a chair scraped along the floor. People were starting to arrive. At last I heard a familiar voice and Frances's muffled response. The door was flung open. Nigel dumped his case and a load of files on the table, and was on his knees beside Fern before I'd chance to complete the courtesy good morning. Frances followed and stood in the open doorway.

"Tell me what happened."

As I did so, Nigel began his examination. When he lifted Fern's jowls, I saw the inside of her cheeks, normally rosy pink, was almost white. Her gums, too, showed the same ghastly hue.

"Get the lamps ready," Nigel ordered over his shoulder. Frances disappeared. Somehow, he picked up Fern from the floor, to follow Frances across the waiting room and into his hospital. I knew I shouldn't follow. I just stood there, numbed with shock and feeling utterly useless. After a moment or two, I moved into the doorway, where I could be seen, for I felt ill at ease, left alone in the surgery surrounded by drugs and specialist equipment. But I became the focus of curious stares from those waiting with their pets. I couldn't tell what they were thinking. Was it sympathy, or accusation? Could they tell I should have come earlier? Did they sense I'd shouted at her? I shrank back. Fern's blanket lay on the floor so I picked it up. I hugged it to myself, smelling her gentle scent.

She was obviously very ill. I went over and over the previous day's events. I should have seen more. I should have brought Fern in, when I'd first thought about it. I should never have shouted at her when she had stood so forlornly in the drive. How could I have thought she was being defiant? How could I not have seen she was ill?

I began to fold the blanket slowly, very slowly, so that I might have something to fill in the time. Two, then four, the folds grew with geometric precision.

116

Nigel returned.

"She'll have to stay in. She has some kind of infection."

Infection! It was almost a relief! It wasn't anything to do with her gut problem! The right sort of tablets and she would soon be well!

"When can I find out how she is?"

Nigel hesitated. His brow furrowed.

"Give me a ring this afternoon," he said slowly, measuring out each word. He seemed to reach a decision. "Yes, ring about four."

I didn't loiter, for I expected he would want to begin surgery: the waiting room was already crowded and I could hear others in the car park. I thanked him and left. As I turned, I noticed he went back immediately through the hospital door.

The drive back into Lincoln had an air of unreality about it. There was a stillness behind me, an emptiness I could feel. I hadn't expected to be alone. At least, I told myself, this time there was no operation, no general anaesthetic. It was an infection. Just an infection.

The day dragged. When the magic hour came around, I was surprised when the nurse, whose voice I didn't recognise, said she would fetch Nigel. As I heard his footsteps cross the tiled floor, my expectation of a happy outcome began to drain away into that dreadful, familiar hollowness, and the louder the footfalls became, the more my heart raced.

"Hello, Nigel here. She's better-"

Such sweet relief! I felt a smile widen its way across my face. So typical of my lovely, feisty Fern!

"But she must stay in tonight. She's on a drip."

A bolt from the blue, totally unexpected, and it knocked me sideways!

Afterwards, I sat by the phone, staring unseeingly, at the wall. Fern must be very ill indeed, far, far, worse than I ever imagined. But she was getting better! Hadn't he had said so? Hadn't she already come further than anyone expected? She would fight her way back again: there was no doubt!

But there must be doubt, because she had to stay in. Then I began to worry about how she would fare during the night. Was there a nurse on duty? Did someone live upstairs at the house? I had heard footsteps up there. Surely Fern would be lonely and afraid? There might be other animals in there, and they would be some company for her, but it wouldn't be like being at home. I would willingly stay up all night to watch her! How I wished I could watch her all night.

Next morning, I rang so early that the emergency system began to operate. Hastily, I rang off. I sat staring at the fingers of the clock as they crawled on. They reminded me of when I learned to tell the time.

"The big finger's at four, and the little finger's between eight and nine."

"That's twenty past eight:" Mum's voice.

Fern stayed away the whole of that day, and the next night. I thought of her all the time. I was so used to living by Fern's clock that I found I couldn't overcome my constant awareness of the passage of time. And how it dragged!

On the third day, I was advised to ring again later, in the afternoon, because by then, Fern might be well enough to come home. Time passed more slowly than ever. I thought that if I waited until the magic hour of four o'clock, then surely, I would have the answer I so desperately wanted.

And the charm worked! Once again I could fetch her! Less than half an hour later, I was standing in the waiting room, listening to sounds coming from the hospital: Cathy O'Rourke opening the cage door, talking to Fern, putting on the lead, and bringing her to me.

Fern knew I had come. She rushed into the waiting room, to fling herself up at me. Covered in warm, wet, wonderful Flatcoat kisses, I hugged her, until she slipped through my arms, and onto the floor! She lay there, panting. Alarmed, I shot a glance at Cathy. She was watching Fern, but caught my eye, and smiled. Fern scrambled up to restart her ecstatic greeting, only to fall back once more. Something was wrong! I looked at Cathy again. Her mouth still smiled but now I saw that her eyes did not. I didn't understand what was happening. I had been told that Fern could come home! This must mean she was well enough. She was recovering! She renewed her onslaught of joyful reunion, only to sink once again onto the tiles. I went down on my knees to fondle her, so she didn't have to get up.

"You can see how exhausted she is."

The vet's voice seemed a long way away.

"The least thing......"

Fern regained her feet to stand, licking my face. To think that I had shouted at her for being ill! She licked away a tear as it escaped down my cheek.

"...she's exhausted."

Fern continued to lick my face. I stroked her soft neck. Cathy watched.

The time I knew so intimately seemed suddenly to have stopped. I wanted this moment to last because I had become afraid of what would happen next.

Cathy broke the spell. She spoke slowly, allowing time for the full significance of her words to sink in.

"But she can go home. Take her home and enjoy the weekend together. I'm so very sorry, but I can't see much future for Fern."

CHAPTER TWELVE.

We spent that weekend together. Each day, I relished her company. From the exuberant tail wagging of morning hello, to the kiss on top of her smooth head at night, these were times to remember. I needed memories I could hold on to; memories I could store in the depths of my mind, warm and safe, ready to conjure up for whenever the world became too harsh in its reality; a bitter-sweet treasure trove to cherish forever.

That precious weekend slid by. A new week began.

We went by car to Fen Lane for our walk once again and there we found souvenirs of this time. A green plastic frog lost by its owner and wrested with delight from dense undergrowth; the deflated and battered football dragged from beneath a blackberry bush and carried to the car in triumph. She had never looked better than on that day; sun gleaming on her black coat, forelegs stepping high, tail held out, neck arched with pride, sneaking tiny sideways glances to make certain that she and her wonderful prize had been noticed.

She looked forward to everything: her tiny meals, her walks, playtime, meeting friends, turning strangers into friends: her spirit was irrepressible.

At night, I would sit on the kitchen stool, gazing at my alter-ego, as she lay curled in her bed, one marvellous foot laid protectively over the top of her nose, and wondered how such a big dog could occupy so little space. I would stare at her, long and unblinking, then close my eyes and try to conjure up the image I had just seen; each curve, every line, every angle, then I'd look back to see if I had it right. It was practice for the future.

A second weekend came and went. Some of Fern's tablets were now almost gone, but our regular appointment had not been made. I rang the surgery.

It was with a kind of dread that I faced Nigel, almost as if he were a stranger. What would he say? Might he withdraw Fern's medication?

He welcomed us, as always, with the warmth of a friend. He showed no surprise at seeing us, made no comment. Watching him kneel to examine her with all his customary care, I imagined there was a little more grey streaking the thick waves of his dark hair. Perhaps we had put it there.

"I'm sorry about all these little bald patches."

He looked up, dark eyes crinkling into an apologetic smile. All? I had noticed three but dismissed them as insignificant.

"That's me trying to get a line in. All her veins were collapsed. See that one there?"

He pointed to a spot I hadn't noticed, on her rear left hock.

"That's the one which saved her."

All I could do was to stare, open mouthed, at the top of his head.

No, my revered doctor, you're the one who saved her.

"We're supposed to use a vein here," he explained with a gentle laugh, holding up one of Fern's front legs.

For a moment, my sorrow and pain were transferred to him. He had worked tirelessly, right from the start, was still doing so, and what had he to show for his unending efforts?

He stood to face me, but now the laughter was gone from his eyes.

"It was touch and go, you know," he confessed. "Her liver and kidneys have taken one hell of a beating."

Then, for the one and only time, he dropped his eyes.

"In fact I actually got as far as picking up the phone that first afternoon, then I put it down and went to take another look at her. She was no better, but something made me decide to wait just a bit longer; something. I don't know what. When I next went in, she looked up and managed to wag her tail."

He ruffled Fern's ears and laughed ruefully.

"Then she chewed off her drip! Some dogs just won't have it, you know. Came in to give her a drink at two 'o clock. She needed the fluid. Now! You came for some tablets, didn't you?"

I pulled out the piece of paper listing all Fern's tablets and how many of each was left. Nigel took it and turned to his shelves to organise their renewal.

As he counted them out, I tried to take in all I had learned, not the least being that Nigel must have left home and driven to his surgery in the early hours to give Fern the fluid she needed. Yet wasn't it pointless? Wasn't she now on what people called borrowed time? If Nigel had made that phone call, if the "something" hadn't stopped him, then it would all be over right now. He had done so much. Was there any point in struggling on? He turned back to face me. Was now The Time?

Tentatively, I began to voice the awful thought which had begun to pursue me relentlessly.

He stood perfectly still, listening intently, bottles of pills clasped in each hand. Perhaps he wanted me to say it.

I took a deep breath and tried to stifle the feelings that made my voice tremble and break.

"There's nothing more we can do, is there? Its all been done."

It was as if someone else spoke.

"It is going to come to a decision, isn't it?"

He knew the decision I meant. He watched me gravely as I struggled on.

"I can do it, you know. I can decide."

It was not necessary to explain further. Silence was a bond between us.

"Fern mustn't suffer."

Nigel transferred his gaze to her. She knew at once and looked up, wagging her tail. Suddenly, I knew what he was thinking.

"She's still happy, isn't she."

It was not a question. Looking back at me, his gravity melted into a smile.

"She's a fighter. As long as she's fighting, so will I."

He held out the pills.

It was not the Time.

We returned home. Our routines continued. In the garden, down the Lane, on the common, in the park, Fern enjoyed every minute. The outings were shorter. She tired more quickly, but after a rest, would bounce back, ready for another onslaught at Life. Each day was a bonus.

Margaret was ever supportive. She lived my fears and hopes as if they were her own. It was there I first voiced an idea born from the desperation of our plight.

"What do you think about homoeopathy?"

Margaret knew the implications of what I meant at once.

"Ooh, yes, a good idea! I like natural things. You've done everything else. Where would you go?"

I had no idea.

"Well, there's homoeopathic doctors; so there must be homoeopathic vets."

My own G.P., whom I dearly loved and respected, had retired from the

N.H.S. three months before Mum died, then studied homoeopathy and set up a practice locally. Cambridge trained, and with a lifetime's so-called traditional experience, if he thought there was something worthwhile in homoeopathy, then that was good enough for me.

"Would he treat a dog?"

"I'd ask. I'd try to find out about vets. But I'm sure he'd help me. Even if it was supposed to be unethical, he'd find a way."

"What about Nigel? Would he mind? Would you tell him?"

Of course I would! I made an immediate appointment, but I knew I wouldn't be asking for his approval. This time I could, and would, be willing to oppose this brilliant man of skill and dedication. I would be telling him of my intention.

"Is there such a thing as homoeopathic vets?"

He looked surprised, then grinned.

"Oh, yes. Why? Are you thinking of going that way?"

I nodded.

"I'd like to try."

Nigel's grin widened, and his eyes twinkled.

"Do you know anything about it? It's crazy! They use medicines that the weaker they get, the more effect they have! I can't understand it. Makes no sense at all!"

His grin vanished and he became serious.

"I don't really see how it can work, but we can try. We've nothing to lose."

He had said "we".

He found some kind of directory and leafed through it. He told a nurse to search through another. Yes, there were homoeopathic vets, and some not too far away either. Then an idea struck him, and he began to search the book more purposefully. He found what he was looking for.

"Would you go down to Oxford?"

He didn't wait. He knew the answer.

"There's a vet down there. Actually, he's quite famous: written books, lectures at universities. Gets a hard time too, from some of the students sometimes! Treats animals from all over the world. Perhaps you've heard of him? His name's Christopher Day. Would you like me to refer you there?"

And so it was arranged. Once again, I felt my heart quicken and a sharp excitement stab into the pit of my stomach. Once again, a tiny shaft of light gleamed from the future, to brighten today with Hope.

Illusion

One long week later, a large brown envelope dropped through the letterbox. Inside was everything I could possibly need to know about finalising a consultation at the Alternative Veterinary Medical Centre, although there would be a wait of at least three weeks before any appointment could be made. Three more weeks! Another three more long weeks!

There were warnings about being on time laced with pre-emptive apologies should appointments run late, because "Mr. Day does not hurry the case if there is more to do than expected." Another warning told owners to "Be prepared to answer many questions about the animal's life-style, behaviour, character and habits," because "alternative medicine requires a deep knowledge of the patient." There were maps of how to get there, including maps of the exact locale, and even suggestions of where to stay overnight should that be necessary.

"Two For The Price Of One," proclaimed the enclosed handbill from the Crown Hotel in nearby Faringdon. I could ask Margaret! I would not otherwise have done so, for it would have been an expense she could ill afford and she would never have allowed me to pay for her. This was the perfect solution. It must be a sign that things were at last going right! I chuckled at the ridiculousness of that idea. But it was the first time in weeks I had laughed and it felt good. I wasn't only ready to grasp at straws: I could make the straws! It sounded so exciting! Could this be the Answer for which we had searched so long and so hard?

My joy was short-lived. When I phoned the Alternative Veterinary Medical Centre to make the appointment, I was informed that the patient must be off all conventional medication! Muttering something about not realising that and having to think about it, I rang off in confusion. Of course I should have known! Treatment may be alleviating a condition and its symptoms would be altered correspondingly. Neither do synthetic chemicals and homoeopathy mix.

I opened the cupboard to stare at all Fern's medication: pills with enzyme-like chemicals to aid digestion, pills to help release wind, pills to increase peristalsis, pills with steroids which were supposed to do all manner of wonderful things. How could I deliberately stop giving Fern these drugs? They were necessary! They were keeping her alive! Nigel had renewed her prescriptions when I thought he might stop them, and now here I was, with a different vet, who had never even set eyes on Fern, telling me that I must stop giving them to her! How on earth could I possibly withdraw what might be her only hold on life? I could be killing Fern, killing her deliberately! What was it the Police said, "With malice aforethought"?

I tried to keep a grip on my feelings. I tried to be sensible, logical, but it was no use. That tiny flicker of Hope, which I had grasped and held onto so fervently, was gone and in its place, there was nothing, absolutely nothing. In rage and frustration I screwed up the letter then flung it into the cupboard.

"You stupid, stupid man! I can't do that! I can't!"

There was no one to hear me of course. Tears were pointless, the gesture futile. The paper missile merely made contact with the empty shelf, dropped to the worktop, and began to straighten itself out, mocking my anguish. Hot and angry tears burned my cheeks and a lump, which threatened to choke, grew in my throat. I simply stood there, raging helplessly. Once again, Hope had shone from the future, and once again, it had been extinguished.

I did little of consequence the rest of that day or in the days following.

On our walks, I pretended I hadn't seen approaching friends and turned away, endlessly wrestling with the same thoughts. How could I risk watching Fern die as the result of my deliberate act? How she was fighting to live! How Nigel had striven to do more than anyone could ever ask! How could I throw all that away? Yet it was his words that drummed ceaselessly in my mind.

"We've nothing to lose."

Perhaps this was the very worst time of all, the time when Hope finally died, the time there really was nothing left.

"We've nothing to lose."

Hadn't we already lost?

It was dull and drizzly for most of that day. Darkness came unnaturally early, so I closed the curtains. With my legs curled round, I sat at one end of the sofa, and gazed at Fern as she lay stretched out on the hearthrug, dozing. The T.V. played to an unseeing audience. Maybe if I withdrew the medication very, very slowly, then her body might not notice too much. Perhaps if I halved one of the tablets at one dose for a day or two, and then did the same for two doses, maybe we'd get away with it. Then I'd do the same with a second kind of tablet, and so on. I could always reintroduce them immediately if things began to go wrong, couldn't I?

With a start, I realised where my thoughts were taking me and tried to obliterate them. I turned up the T.V. and stared hard at the screen, trying to concentrate on its flickering pretence.

Illusion

It was no use. Reality was too strong. Was I willing to risk being directly responsible for Fern's death? But equally, was I ready to shoulder the responsibility of denying her the final chance she had to live?

We took our short evening walk around the houses. I don't remember which way we went.

I couldn't fall asleep. Twice the brilliant light from George's garden glared into my bedroom, reminding me that there was a world out there. I usually found the light reassuring and friendly, but that night, it was offensive. I curled up into a childish, miserable ball, and wanted to stay there forever, warm and safe, with no decisions to make, no worries to fret over, nothing but a blissful limbo of unreality.

This was what I had thought about in my decision to have a dog wasn't it? How dangerous it might be to take on the responsibility for another life. That danger had never been more acute than it was now.

I must have slept, for when I awoke the following morning, I knew with absolute certainty what I must do.

I made Fern her breakfast. We began the daily tablet routine. We danced the gripe water dance. I ate my breakfast and we took our usual drive and walk.

Back home, I took all Fern's bottles from the cupboard and set them in a row on the worktop. "Ten green bottles, standing in a row", except that there weren't ten, but five and the bottles were plastic and brown which made the pills click instead of rattle. I needed paper and a pen, a ruler, too, if I could find one. Returning with my tools, I pulled up the stool and set to work. Starting at the left hand side, I ruled out three vertical columns, heading them Tablet, Normal Dose and Time respectively. I filled the rest of the page with narrower vertical columns, heading them Day 1, Day 2, and so on. Next, I ruled in five horizontal lines to divide the page equally. Carefully, I copied the name of a tablet into the first box which had been formed in the left hand column. In the second column, I filled in its normal dosage, and in the third, the time each dose was administered. I filled the remaining left hand boxes with the names of the other tablets, their dosages and times respectively and the chart was ready.

Fern trotted in from the garden, wondering what I was doing. She looked up, sniffed the air, decided I was being supremely boring and returned to the garden. I watched her go.

"Yes, my little warrior, you shall have your chance," I whispered after her departing figure. How could I ever have thought the Cupboard Top Kid would want it any other way?

126

CHAPTER THIRTEEN

The Plan began. Fern's pill regimen reduced slowly. Pills were halved then quartered and reduced in number. I kept a detailed record of her state of bloating, watching intently for any sign that my decision could be the wrong one. There didn't seem to be any difference. I explained to the friendly Oxford voice on the phone, the reason for the delay, but a date was set; Saturday, July 20th at 9-45 am.

On Friday, the nineteenth, Margaret and I set off.

There are always difficulties in travelling with any dog, but with Fern, those difficulties were compounded. I still needed to get as much food into her as possible, which meant packing a whole series of tailor-made "picnics", and making frequent stops, each lengthened by the need to allow her to rest afterwards. And all this on the longest journey she had ever undertaken!

The planned route was the sum of time spent pouring over various maps, and with no thanks to the A.A. or R.A.C., who don't do dog-friendly routes. In the end however, it turned out to be intuition, a sense of direction and more intuition, when my plans were scuppered by the appearance of an unknown roundabout and a diversion due to road works. Where I had planned for our main picnic didn't materialise and then the heavens opened! Margaret and I ate parked in the gateway to a field with rain hammering on the roof, hoping the farmer wouldn't appear and I became soaked walking Fern around the field's edge! It was a tired and bedraggled pair who arrived at the Crown reception desk, late in the evening.

The hotel was an old black and white building nestling on one side of the market square, its warm golden lights reflected invitingly in the day's puddles. Leaving Fern in the car, Margaret and I traipsed through the foyer to register and found ourselves in the final thrashes of a most upmarket wedding reception. I felt so out of place, a real member of the proletariat, a country bumpkin and a disreputable one!

Illusion

"I can take my dog into our room, can't I?" (Although I'd like to have seen anyone refuse me when it had been already promised!)

"Of course, Madam. Actually," the receptionist leaned forward, eyeing the group of morning suited young men propping themselves and their drinks on the banisters of the wide staircase, "we find dogs to be less trouble than many of our other guests!"

Feeling much better, I fetched Fern. As we neared the stairs, one well oiled young man turned to stare at us. I imagined him to be wondering what on earth we were doing there; drenched woman, hair plastered to her head, jeans and anorak, muddy shoes, with an elegant, gleaming dog. He hung over the banister, and waved his glass at us as we mounted the stairs.

"I say! Rather fine young gundog, what?"

"Thank you. I think so."

Stifling giggles, Margaret and I, with Fern, raced up the rest of the stairs and through the doors at the top, before collapsing with laughter. People didn't really speak like that, did they? Yes, they did!

Fern took to her temporary home immediately and Margaret thoroughly enjoyed her night away, luxuriating in our bathroom until she turned pink. The beds were soft, warm and bouncy, but I heard the church clock strike the hour many times.

What on earth was I doing here? What did I expect? How could this strange vet, who had wanted all Fern's medication withdrawn, have any answer at all?

We found the Alternative Veterinary Medical Centre so easily the following morning that we were over half an hour early! An old, grey house, foursquare to the narrow road, it looked rather forbidding and unloved. It was the kind of house to have History. A short driveway led into a small yard with a prefabricated building to one side. A large sign beside its door ordered, " Please Enter.".

After I'd completed the formalities, there was still time to spare, so we set out to explore the small village. The previous day's downpour had been replaced with sunshine, but Margaret's feet soon became wet as we sauntered through a small park, avoiding the grazing sheep, and on into the churchyard. She told me then that she wouldn't be coming in with us to see Mr. Day, but would wait in the church.

"I think you'll be better on your own. I'll be warm enough and out of the breeze here."

I knew the real reason. Margaret would believe she could do more

128

for us with prayer and the fine old village church had given her the opportunity. I wanted to hug and thank her so much, but I was too tense. I feared I might break down: everything depended on the next hour. So all I did was to agree casually and say I'd see her soon. God may not listen to me, I thought, He may not grant my dearest wish, but He would surely listen to the pleas of Margaret, who always put others first and from whom I had never heard a cross word or hurtful comment. Surely He would grant Margaret's wish? Fern and I crossed the road together and she ate a tiny meal in the back of the car.

The waiting room was similar in size to Nigel's: a small hatch revealed an office and opposite that, a door led to what I assumed must be the consulting room. No chairs, but a bench of bare wooden slats was fixed to the wall on three sides. There were the usual posters, some magazines on a large coffee table, and one oddity. To the right of the open office hatch, there hung an enormous, framed mirror!

The bench was hard. I gazed at Fern as she lay on the floor, one forepaw curled under, the other leg elegantly stretched across in front. Time slowed. Yet again, I began to wonder if I was doing the right thing. What did I expect here?

The office phone kept ringing, and a keyboard clicked monotonously.

It was time for our appointment. I couldn't hear a sound from behind the door of what I believed to be the consulting room; no voices, no movement, so where was the man we had come all this way to see? Fern started to fidget. I wondered what Margaret was doing, and if she was in the church. Fern was bored, so I practised two Downs and she became even more bored. Time crawled.

Now it was past our appointment. Margaret would surely be in the church. She would be praying for us, for her Ferny-pup, but her prayers would be too early. Would God know whom she meant, I thought ridiculously?

"Mr. Day will see you now."

I had neither seen, nor heard, the secretary come into the room.

"I'll take you across."

Across? She opened the outer door, leading the way through the yard and into the forbidding house itself!

A tiny square hall led into a narrow passage. As we turned left, I noticed the right hand side was cluttered with children's toys and there were two pet water bowls. A big, heavily furred brindled cat, disturbed by our entry, rose disdainfully to its feet and padded out of sight. The scene was so homely and friendly, not what the exterior of the house suggested at all and certainly not what one might expect when visiting a consultant of worldwide reputation who bristled with learned degrees! The secretary ushered us through the only door into a room of medium size. She suggested I took a seat, promised Mr. Day would be along in a moment and left, closing the door behind her.

I looked around. This was unlike any vet's surgery I had ever seen! Directly opposite the door, a long sash window looked out onto a beautiful English garden. In front of the window, an antique kneehole desk dominated the room. Papers, files and books jostled untidily for attention and a beautiful tooled leather blotter of darkest green waited elegantly for its user. Dark oak cupboards, topped with a cream, marbled work surface, lined two sides of the room, while above them, matching cupboards hung on the old, uneven walls. Then I noticed the washing machine. It was a kitchen! No, there wasn't cooker; and with a desk? On the far wall, hundreds of books were held in check by the glass doors of a floor to ceiling cupboard, and in front of that, two antique chairs waited, presumably, for clients. I sat on the edge of one. Fern sat beside me on a wonderful floor of lovely, uneven flagstones that betrayed the age of the property.

Such a strange room! Like a kitchen, but with furniture from an elegant period lounge; used as a surgery, but with none of the antiseptic smells. A room of some untidiness, yet which betrayed the good taste of its owner: a very strange room.

Almost ten minutes of our scheduled forty-minute consultation had already passed. I made Fern sit by my left leg and held the lead short. Birds sang in the sunny garden outside and a second cat ambled slowly across the lawn. The short lead had probably been a good idea.

Suddenly, brisk and heavy footsteps sounded in the hall and the door almost burst open. A tall, broad shouldered man in a long white coat strode into the room, light brown hair flapping in a breeze of his own making. Behind him bustled the secretary, laden with folders of all kinds.

"Good morning."

"Good morning."

A brief smile flickered across Christopher Day's face as he seated himself at the desk to accept the folders. There followed a brief conversation about promised phone calls and the rest of the day's appointments, and then the secretary hurried away.

He pulled the topmost folder onto his blotter, opened it up, scanned the contents, then turned to me.

"Will you let her off that lead?"

I was shocked: a dog loose in a vet's surgery? Did he expect that Fern would remain as she was, sitting quietly by my side?

"Well," I began doubtfully, "I can, but-"

"Then let her off, please."

I did as I was told. Fern promptly got up to go exploring. Christopher Day watched her in silence for some considerable time before turning back to me.

"I've spoken to Mr. Williams on the phone and he's sent me all the details of her case and the treatment so far."

He shuffled several papers from the folder, and began to read, refreshing his memory.

I watched Fern. Unlike me, she was enjoying herself! She sniffed her way along the cupboards, examined the floor, and occasionally looked up at the worktop, scenting the air.

"Now, I want you to tell me exactly what's been going on, with as much detail as you can. When did all this begin?"

Prompted by the notes I had brought giving various dates, and the hour-by-hour diary, I recounted the ghastly story. Christopher Day wrote swiftly, as if taking dictation, but I noticed he glanced frequently at Fern. If he was afraid she might damage something, why had he wanted her off lead? At one time, I was on tenterhooks as she gazed through the window, in case one of the cats reappeared, but all she did was to take a step back in order to gain a better view, satisfy herself, then move on.

"Has she been vaccinated?"

"Oh, yes!" That was the one definite, indisputable factor in this entire, outrageous story, and something I was proud of. I had not left Fern open to preventable diseases. Yet Mr. Day did not seem impressed. He inhaled noisily between clenched teeth. Fern finished exploring then lay down, not beside me, but across the kneehole of the desk, and within inches of Mr. Day's feet.

"Do you know when?"

"July 14th."

As he wrote, he shook his head. His expression seemed resigned, almost weary.

"I see many animals with a chronic condition that developed within three months of primary vaccination; a great many."

There was another silence. I did not know what to say, or even if I should say anything at all. The moment passed.

"Now tell me about her life style, her normal day. Tell me what you do."

I knew that homoeopaths needed to know their patient as well as possible, but even so, I was unprepared for the thorough probing that followed.

Finally, he finished writing, stood, and then moved round the far side of his desk. As he stood, so did Fern. She looked back at him over her shoulder and began to wag her tail.

"She knows its her turn now," he commented matter-of-factly.
The examination began.

Christopher Day had large, capable hands. His nails were well manicured. I noticed his thumbs did not bend out at the tip, but, like mine, were absolutely straight. The hands moved with care and deliberation over Fern's body, while she remained perfectly still, a lovely ebony statue. There was none of the playful fooling of the Show ring, none of the defiant twisting about of the Cardinal's Hill obedience classes. She was calm and relaxed, as if appreciative of the gravity of the situation and wanting to do everything she could to help him find the answer.

It became so silent in that room, I hardly dared to breathe. A gentle breeze stirred the trees in the garden and once, I heard footsteps crossing the yard. They simply intensified the silence within the room.

So this was it. This was the greatest "It" of all. This was the End. After this, there could be no more "its". There was nothing else, nowhere left to go. I watched in hope and fear, as months of trial and error, of tears and disappointment, built to their climax in this strange room in the Oxfordshire countryside. Here was the culmination of Fern's indomitable spirit, of Nigel's tireless efforts, and perhaps of my strengths, too, such as any might be. Perhaps Margaret was still in the church. I added my prayer to hers.

He finished. Christopher Day returned to his desk without a word, and began to write. Fern sauntered back to me this time and resumed her place by my side. I had lost count of the times I'd waited like this; mouth dry, heart thumping, stomach hollow and empty. What would he tell me? How would he tell me? How would I react if he could not help us? Would I break down and cry? Would I make a fool of myself and embarrass us both? Could I stay calm and accept the verdict?

He finished writing. For a moment, he checked his notes, then swung his chair round to face me. I could never have foreseen his words.

"Firstly, I want you to know that you owe this dog nothing," he paused, holding my astonished gaze, "whereas she owes you everything."

He watched for my reaction, but I was too stunned to utter a sound. I struggled to understand. It was Nigel she owed everything, or maybe even George, but not me. I had simply gone along with things. And what of Fern herself? What of her valiant spirit and incurable optimism? What of her courage?

I felt implied criticism and shifted awkwardly on my chair, but Christopher Day's grey eyes remained fixed, unblinking, on me. Suddenly, he relented a little, and smiled briefly.

"I want you to distance yourself from this dog. She is picking up on your worry and this is worsening the situation."

Worsening? I grabbed at the word. Did that mean the situation could be improved? Once more, I felt that tiny flutter of hope.

"In order to treat her, I need to know as much as possible. You told me as much as you could, but that was from your point of view. I needed hers. That's why I wanted her off lead, to see her true behaviour."

Years later, I would discover the reason for that huge mirror in the waiting room. It was two-way! It also explained how Christopher Day had followed me into his consulting room. He explained further.

"She could have been afraid and stayed by you. She could have been equally afraid but rushed to the door to get out, or charged around in here like a mad thing. She could have tried to hide from me, or even gone for me or made a fuss of me, but she did none of those things. She was calm but curious, so she explored, and when she'd satisfied herself, she just sat down, between us, quite content to wait."

The smile came again.

"Then when I'd examined her, she went back to sit with you. She was telling me in the nicest possible way, but quite definitely, that there were two of you; two of you and only one of me, so I'd better bear that in mind!" The smile warmed. "She is extremely sensitive, highly intelligent and very intuitive."

He looked down at her and the smile widened.

"Yes, Fern, you are that rarity; a sane Flatcoat!"

Fern interpreted this as an invitation. She crossed to him and sat between his knees, gazing up at him. Then he spoke words I had only dreamed of, words which were spoken to Fern herself.

"Yes, I can help you. But then you knew that, didn't you?"

CHAPTER FOURTEEN

We arrived home as it was growing dark. Earlier, I'd dropped Margaret, and we'd drunk mugs of tea whilst mulling over the day's events. I had showed her Fern's new pills, lining them up as I had done once before. Together, we had peered at them in silence; small, brown glass bottles, labelled with exotic names, lycopodium, gaertner, phosphorus, like symbols of alchemy from an era long past. Would these tiny shining spheres barely two millimetres across, be the miracle workers we so desperately needed? Collectively, they were known as pilules, never to be touched by hand and to be given at different and inter-related times, as far away from meals as possible. I was also to send in regular reports, at least once a week.

The new diet would take very careful planning too, and even more careful introduction, for it was solid food! It seemed preposterous that Fern could or should eat such things! Right now, all these new foods would have to be liquidised.

The only concession to dogdom was green tripe, the rest of the protein being chicken, white fish, cottage cheese and an occasional lightly scrambled egg. Boiled brown rice and jacket potatoes were to be the mainstays of her carbohydrate, but other delicious things such as milk puddings, vegetables and plain wholemeal biscuits could eventually be included. All this was so very far removed from everything I had learned! Yet this was our last chance. It was a chance I must take.

I had been told there would be no sudden improvement; that it would be a slow, steady haul and while he did not expect to cure Fern, Christopher Day believed he could improve the situation, and "teach" her to live with her disability. Even so, he had not said why her digestive system behaved in its bizarre fashion. Neither had I liked what he said about distancing myself from Fern, and I was perturbed by his strange comment that I "owed her nothing". I'd also found his manner cool and intimidating, with none of the warmth and sympathy of Nigel. Years later, when I met him again, I had long appreciated the truth of his comments about my attitude at that time, and I was able to see the real Christopher Day, a man of great understanding, sensitivity and humour, with the courage of his convictions and the ability to see things as they really were.

He had been so matter-of-fact, so quietly confident, that I believed this strange regime just might work! Or was that simply blind Hope? We had nothing else.

I rang Nigel to tell him how we had fared and to let him know that the clinical details would follow directly to him. Fern's new diet was worth a chuckle and he found the untouchable medicines to be highly amusing, but he was very proud of his knowledge of the word "pilules"! Although his training and experience shrieked against what some might term mumbo-jumbo, he was willing the treatment to work. I thought he had grown very fond of the dog who had caused him so much worry, got him out of bed in the early hours and had most likely greyed his hair! Mr. Day wanted close liaison with Nigel, and had asked me to arrange a check-up with him in three weeks' time.

Oddly, I felt a little more relaxed, more at ease with our fragile status quo. Perhaps it was because I remained ever aware of the "distance from this dog" thereby doing exactly as Christopher Day had wanted. I fully accepted the relationship between Fern and myself could never be the usual dog-owner relationship, and that if she survived, it would be on very different terms to the norm. But Fern had taught me well. A little of her boundless optimism, determination and ability to see good in everything had filtered into me and if I were to lose her now, within the next few days or weeks, I knew I would be strong enough to cope, to go out and to live again, even though, right now, I could not imagine life without her. My beautiful companion had brought me more tears than laughter, yet I did not regret for one second, accepting the Cupboard Top Kid.

Trevor thought we could be on fire! One hand tickling beneath Fern's ear, he leaned over the gate and tried to peer through the open kitchen door. The Geordie postman had learned he must always greet Fern, whether he had mail for me or not. Should he continue straight along the road, then a loud and peremptory bark would demand his instant return and back he would come, pretend-grumbling about all the time he was wasting!

The "smoke" was steam from the large pan of boiling brown rice, for this was how every other morning now began! I'd be up early enough to boil the rice on Economy Seven and to bake the potatoes, too. Trevor listened to the story of our meeting with Christopher Day without his usual regard for passing time, for he had known Fern from the very beginning and forged a genuine friendship with this particular member of the Postmen's Nemesis clan. He stroked her with more deliberation than usual, wished us luck, and went on his way.

The days were passing. Using metal forceps, five times each day I would count Fern's pilules onto a saucer from where she licked them into her mouth. Never once did she refuse to accept them! After just three days, I began to think those dreadful swilling sounds from her gut seemed a little quieter, but no sooner had I dared to think such wonderful thoughts than they were back again. But I did think I was giving Fern slightly larger helpings of food. How she loved those new foods! "What's in my bowl this time?" She could hardly contain her excitement! I noted every little thing and included it all into my first report to Mr. Day at the end of week one. George faxed it to him. Should the need be urgent, then one could phone and speak directly to him, or his secretary would relay the answer. My relayed answer was to continue as now but he sent us new pilules to be used in place of the phosphorous and he wanted another report in seven days. One thing was certain; I was cutting down on the amount of liquidising, because that was easily measurable.

We still went to our walks by car, but perhaps we walked a little further.

Was it my imagination again, or did Fern really look a little less "fat" in the evenings?

Now I was certain that I was feeding her increasingly larger amounts and, although the foods certainly couldn't be called solids, neither were they any longer completely "cream."

But I tried not to form any opinion on the treatment. I did not allow myself to think those observations through. I was too afraid to do so. In my mind, I passed that responsibility to Nigel. He would know. There had been too many dashed hopes, too many false dawns.

I continued the reports to Mr. Day. I tried to keep them purely factual, unclouded by emotion. I thought I succeeded in obliterating any "opinion" I might have had on the treatment. He substituted one of the pilules and adjusted the times of giving the others. I kept writing. Then he returned to the original prescription with one further new addition.

The three weeks were gone.

"How is she?"

Nigel's manner radiated its usual warmth.

"I think you'll know better than me."

He did not press for a reply, but knelt to begin his examination. He took even longer than usual. Was he trying to convince himself of a non-existent improvement? Or was he trying to mask his disappointment?

Suddenly, he looked up.

"What do you think?" he demanded.

Perhaps he did not believe what he found.

The familiar sting of tears began to blur my vision. All those first marvellous vagaries of unformed ideas, all the measuring, all the estimating, all the hope, and prayer rushed back to taunt me. I was so afraid of what Nigel would find. He did not wait for a reply, but returned to his examination.

"There's still a lot of gas in there......"

He continued feeling along her abdomen. Suddenly, he jumped to his feet.

"I don't know what he's doing, but it's working!"

Nigel's expression was that of a child unwrapping the present of his dreams! I had been right.

I closed the door of Whitegates behind me, and stood perfectly still on the old step worn by so many feet and so many paws This was the very first time there had ever been any improvement in Fern's condition. A Scottish voice suddenly echoed from the past: "There's nothin' this bitch canna do!"

The weeks continued to pass. The dreadful swilling noise from Fern's gut was the first symptom to subside, until it virtually disappeared. (It would always return whenever she'd been swimming, but vanish again within the hour) The mechanical liquidising of all her foods lessened as the feeds grew in amount and decreased in number. Her bloats slowly decreased in volume and then in frequency. I continued to write long, long reports as Mr. Day requested. Sometimes we spoke on the phone. He continued to juggle the pilules. Slowly, steadily, he pushed back the barriers.

Eventually, the liquidising stopped completely. Food may be fully soaked and fall-apart soft, but it could perhaps be called solid. Fern was back on "solid" food!

We were on four feeds per day when Christopher Day judged we had reached our plateau; we had come as far as we could and further treatment would be pointless. Fern would always need accurately timed, regular, small soft feeds, but four per day was as nothing compared to our record of eleven! I ate four times per day after all!

Slowly, her weight began to creep up. Her energy levels rose to meet the demands placed on them by her insatiable curiosity and desire to learn. Check-ups with Nigel grew less and less frequent; however much she might enjoy them!

The car remained garaged and we walked the whole of our walks again. Once more Fern met regularly with Maddie. Andy summed up the situation most graphically when he observed, during one of their lunatic sessions together,

"That's the old Fern!"

How delighted I was! How thrilled! I loved that comment. I couldn't wait to write to Christopher Day to tell him and to explain its significance!

Now I looked ahead with more certainty than I had ever felt before. Leaving Nigel after a check-up, I had the glowing confidence to set a new goal for us. Not the weekend, not Christmas, not anyone's birthday, this goal was years away! Life would never be easy. Fern would always need extra vigilance. We would always be in the shadow of a sudden and catastrophic torsion, but we were going to make it! This goal was double figures. Fern would reach double figures!

George, too, back from another trip abroad, was relieved and pleased, although he never knew just how desperate things had become, perhaps because he had been away during most of our trauma. But he still hit the proverbial nail on the head during one of our resumed lessons, when I was proving to be particularly inept.

"There are only three sorts of dog in this world, Pet. Those that hav'na got what it takes, those that have got what it takes, and then there's a few who know they've got what it takes."

He leaned forward, accusing my stupidity with his stare.

"And Fern's one of those!"

I didn't mind his implication at all, for I knew better than anyone, Fern had got what it takes and she most certainly knew that. She had always known.

Now I became aware of a remarkable change in my life; I had Time! Although Fern's four feeds and particularly their preparation, were time consuming, I no longer had to watch the clock creep between minutes. I no longer needed to estimate her girth constantly. I could look upwards and outwards!

We needed something to do. I had no interest in competitive obedience. Fern had little interest in Showing. What on earth could we do? Training for field trials was apparently expensive and I had been told that one could enter a competition and not even get a run! (Later, I very much regretted never bothering to find out for myself, for this, I'm certain, would have been the perfect outlet for Fern's outstanding qualities of intelligence, boldness and determination.)

So, poor Fern; we were off down the road for another stab at showing! Perhaps she might grow to enjoy it.

I tried to stifle my nerves. I tried to remain calm. I tried to think positive. I tried and I failed. But I pinned on my number before we even left home, and I must have handled Fern better, because to my amazement and joy, we were second!

Now I had three beautiful rosettes; two green, one royal blue and I was ridiculously proud of them! The following day, it was off to the local D.I.Y. to purchase one of those cork notice boards so that I might pin them up for all to see. Disappointment! The only ones in stock were huge. But I had to have a board, and I had to have it now! I could fill the space with a calendar, shopping lists, reminders and stuff like that, couldn't I? Or perhaps, maybe, more rosettes?

I hung the board in the kitchen, directly opposite the outer door: blue rosette in pride of place right at the top, with the two green rosettes either side, slightly lower. Then came the space for "Stuff like that", and near the bottom, I added an old notice made from a cereal packet.

I thought I had long since reached my limit in dog training, but continued lessons with George whenever he was available, because Fern loved them so. On one such occasion, we returned home via a field he had begun to rent and on which he was to establish his training school. He would continue private individual training, and the school would begin by concentrating on the sport of Agility.

"There will be different classes for different levels of ability. Mrs. Sandy Long will be taking the beginners' classes."

George could sometimes sound as if he were reading from a script.

"I shall be doing classes for those who're supposed to know what they're doin' and for those who've got problems, because they only imagine they know what they're doin'."

Gradually, over casual meetings by the garden fence, details of his career in the sport began to emerge. He had taken not only one dog, nor even two, but three, to the very top, and had won everything, with the notable exception of Olympia. Mrs. Long had been his doubles partner and their friendship went back many years.

One day, over the fence, came a surprise invitation.

"Would you like to come down before we open, Pet, just as soon as the equipment arrives? Mrs. Long's starting her own young collie. I think she'd like the company."

Sitting quietly in the lounge after tea that night, I pondered George's invitation. It was something I would love to try, but was Fern fit enough? She had been through such tremendous trauma and the amount of leeway between her feeds was relatively short. Would I be asking too much, expecting her to join the running, jumping, racing world we had seen at Fen Lane?

My mind went back to the time we had watched that demonstration. How she had loved the Agility! How excited she had been!

Then I remembered the vow I'd made. "One day," I had promised, "one day."

I looked down at the Cupboard Top Kid.

The Day had come.

CHAPTER FIFTEEN.

The field could be reached from either of two entrances and I chose the wrong one. Fern thought it great sport as we slithered through the deepest, most glutinous mud it had ever been my Flatcoated misfortune to meet, as we made towards George's new Training Centre. Eventually, I slid into the gatepost and hung there, gazing down the grassy expanse towards the river.

The field sloped gently from its entrance, but levelled out about halfway down, until it reached the steep flood bank alongside the river Witham. A large steel container, the sort used on board ships, stood gaunt at the end of the level area. I guessed the opening must be on the far side, facing the river. The surrounding fallow fields were empty, except for a solitary, grazing horse. There was nothing else, and no one, to be seen.

Although the field was securely fenced, I kept Fern on her lead and began to walk forward, looking for any clue that I might be in the right place and at the right time.

As we drew nearer the container, several loud thumps suddenly rang from inside. Fern pricked her ears and wagged her tail expectantly. We were alongside when a red and white striped pole, about a metre long, sailed out through the far end to land with a thud on the soft ground. Gingerly, I came round to the opening.

"Hello?"

"Hello!"

A cheery figure with bright red hair and an armful of similar red and white poles emerged from its gloomy depths.

"Mrs. Long?"

"Sandy."

She dumped the poles.

"You must be Brenda and you want to do agility. George told me about you and the problems you've got with your dog."

She turned towards Fern, swiftly running her hands over Fern's shoulders, back and thighs, and somehow managing to avoid most of an enthusiastic tongue lashing.

"She's fine, and she's bold. That's good."

Perhaps Sandy sensed my nervousness, for she immediately told me to walk Fern over the single pole. Fern tried to go round, but I pushed her back with my knee, and she stepped over very carefully.

141

"Praise her! Oh, that was good! What a good girl!"

Hands on hips, she looked me straight in the eye.

"Go on, then, praise her!"

This woman was over the top I told myself, as I dutifully praised Fern, who seemed pleased as punch.

"Bring her back over the pole, and this time, say over, as she gets near."

I was surprised. "Over" was what I had heard at the agility demonstration. Had the lesson already begun?

"Over."

This time, Fern walked over the pole without any hesitation

Sandy bent to hug her.

"What a super dog! Good girl!" Then to me: "Don't just stand there! You should praise her! She's done exactly what you told her."

She dropped to her knees, and began play-fighting with Fern. It was quite difficult to hang on to the lead!

"You've got to praise her," she repeated, pushing, stroking and tickling a gleeful dog. "Really let yourself go. Let her know you're thrilled to bits with what she's done. Now do it again, both ways. Don't forget over and stop and really praise her both times."

We did as we were told and Fern reaped fulsome reward from the both of us.

Sandy Long straightened then spoke seriously.

"You've just done your first round of agility, and you went clear."

This woman really was totally over the top! Perhaps she read my thoughts.

"The course was one pole," she explained. "Fern went over it. She did exactly what was asked of her. That's all any dog can do."

I just nodded in agreement. This woman took my breath away!

"Tea! I've brought a flask. You can bring some biscuits next week. We've got to get properly organised!"

I had scarcely drawn breath at this sudden switch of conversation when she turned back into the container and began to drag out one of those large wooden picnic tables with attached benches. I rushed to help her. The legs made a firm anchorage for Fern's lead and as we sat there in the warm sun, I began to relax.

I suppose Victorians would have described Sandy Long as buxom. She wore not a trace of make-up and her jeans and jacket were practical, not designer. She seemed so much larger than life, almost flamboyant, yet at the same time, had an air of down to earth conviction and authority.

I learned she had spent many years in South Africa and there, apart from dogs, had loved horses and riding. Returning to the U.K., she had established a breeding kennel of quality Boxers, married for the second time and quite deliberately turned to Agility when she wanted something new and challenging. Compared to Sandy, I felt very boring and parochial!

She asked about Fern's illness and I also mentioned the heart murmur. We agreed that any effect would have been apparent months ago, and that agility would strengthen her heart. Looking back now, I'm amazed this problem hardly ever worried me at all! After the initial shock, I dismissed the noisy heart as of little importance. Fern had always brimmed with energy, which proved it did not impact on her and if she could do agility, then her heart would become so strong, I reasoned, it wouldn't matter at all if a valve didn't shut completely!

After the break, we repeated the pole exercise once more, but in a different part of the field. Then Sandy fetched two "wings" from what she called the hut. Now I felt I really was learning! All pavilions, sheds or any structure whatsoever on a dog training field, is known as the hut. The wings normally held the poles at any of three jumping heights, but we were to use them on their own.

"Just walk her straight up between them and praise her when she's gone through. You stay on the outside."

Twice we did this, then the pole was brought in to lie on the ground between the wings.

"Over!"

Fern walked through the obstacle without the slightest hesitation, then danced in delight at her achievement.

"Praise her, go on, put some welly into it!"

Sandy was pleased with Fern, but not with me!

"She's going through there like she's been doing it all her life! Some dogs take weeks to do it like that."

Rightly or wrongly, I took this with the proverbial pinch of salt, but I thought Sandy's delight at Fern's attitude and progress seemed genuine. I resolved to try harder. Then I caught Fern's eye. Was it my imagination, or could she really be thinking, "Is this all I have to do to drive these two nuts and to get all this attention? O.K., I'll have more of this!"

I didn't appreciate it then, but that was indeed the very object of Sandy's method. She hugged Fern.

"So you think you're smart, eh? You really think you're that smart! We'll see how smart you are, gal! Brenda, put the pole in the bottom cups."

Sandy stood behind the jump, encouraging Fern as we ran up.

"Over!"

Finding her way blocked, Fern stopped dead, the pole across her chest. Sandy was unconcerned.

"Try again, but this time, you keep going. Just keep going."

"How can I, when Fern stops?"

"She won't. Not this time. Just run up, and give the command. She knows what it means, and keep going."

I wasn't convinced, but I took Fern back for a second attempt. Sandy crouched, arms spread wide, yelling encouragement.

"Over!"

Fern stopped, but I kept going. Then, in that split second, I remembered Fern had never, ever jumped! Jill had warned me not to encourage this in a young puppy and then other considerations had taken over. Fern had no idea at all that four feet could be off the ground at once! The lead tightened. Fern gazed longingly at her new friend, separated from her by a gaudy barrier. She tried to step over it, but it was too high. Suddenly, she jumped. Her forelegs and head seemed to go in three different directions at once! She had to scramble her back legs over the pole, because the jump had no length, but somehow, it stayed up and Fern pulled me gleefully towards her new friend.

Sandy's praises soared off the Richter scale.

We tried the jump twice more after that, and each time Fern cleared the pole with a little more coordination.

"That's it! Always finish with the dog wanting more. She's done brilliantly. She likes learning. See you next week! Don't forget the biscuits!"

As suddenly as it had begun, the lesson was over. I walked back up that field on air! Fern had not only survived her first attempts at Agility, but had loved every minute. After lunch, most unusually, she slept soundly for almost an hour. By tea-time, she was raring to go for her walk.

Life was now assured. A warm, contented feeling filled me inside and lasted from the moment I got up until I went to bed. I had things to do, appointments to keep, responsibilities to shoulder; I had Fern. Two years had now passed since Mum died and so much had happened! I felt I had left a grey world of foggy misery to bask in blue skies and glorious sunshine. All the heartache, all the tears, had been worth every single minute! Some people began to congratulate me for never giving up, but I could not, nor indeed ever will, understand them. It was not something I decided to do. I wasn't being clever, or some kind of martyr. It wasn't a matter of choice. There simply was never any other option. Fern was my responsibility, a living, breathing, sensitive responsibility that I had chosen to take on. That responsibility was not to be "switched off" because it had become inconvenient, because it had become too much trouble, and was not what I had expected. We were together and we both had to make the best of it!

It was our second spring, something which no one had anticipated; no-one that is, except Christopher Day, and perhaps Nigel Williams! Spring, the traditional time of renewal and I began to feel the need for a physical break with the past. More prosaically, it might have been the weekly arrival on the doormat of the freebie newspaper, "Property Echo!" Houses and bungalows galore! The world was my oyster! Fern and I could do anything, go anywhere!

I could return to my hometown of Sheffield. A childhood of happy memories flooded back; my home next to a broad-leaved wood; aunts, uncles and cousins, Wednesday football every Saturday with Marsden's special pork pie brought home for tea to celebrate victory. (I can't remember what happened when the unthinkable occurred!) Sunday cricket at Hallam with tomato sandwiches turning deliciously soft in a green tin marked Sandwiches; magical, sweaty nights up in the Lyceum gallery during the visits of ballet companies and shopping in the many splendid department stores, even though it was of the window variety! But these were only memories. There was nothing tangible, no threads left for me to pick up and weave into a new fabric of life. Our lives were here in Lincoln, or perhaps elsewhere.

So I began to trawl the estate agents. I contacted the embassy of "elsewhere": the land of magical splendour and midnight sun, Norway. Yes, it seemed they would accept a British teacher in good health. I thought long and hard. Five visits and Norway had never lost any of its original thrill. I knew I could make a go of it there, but emigrating would be an enormous task on my own. Perhaps that meant I wasn't really committed if I allowed such technicalities to worry me. But none of the properties I viewed was ever quite right; not enough garden, nowhere to exercise a dog off lead, too much work needed. Perhaps I should take the plunge?

Illusion

At our second Agility lesson, we met Daisy, Sandy's Border Collie who was a few months younger than Fern but much more proficient at jumping. However, Sandy remained delighted with Fern's progress, and she did seem to have the more retentive memory of the two dogs. When both had done some jumping, Sandy returned to the hut, taking Fern with her and "winding her up" with laughter and fuss. Today, the rigid tunnel made its first appearance. Concertinaed as tightly as it could be, it was easy to encourage both dogs through: Sandy calling at the exit for Daisy and me at the exit for Fern. Then the tunnel was pulled out a little, then a little more. Next, a gentle curve was introduced. By the end of the lesson, both dogs were happily running through, even though they couldn't see daylight at the far end when they entered!

In the third lesson, we strung together a "course" of three jumps and the tunnel. Then we introduced one pole into the next, higher set of cups, and Fern began to show her real mettle. She had the true gun dog's eye for judging height and distance, always clearing the bar, but only just! Everything was going so well!

"Exclusive small development of eleven bungalows in Philip Court." The advert seemed to leap out from the paper. Now, a brand new place would be a real financial investment, and perhaps, if the garden was big enough, I could have fun adapting the architect's plans a little! It was barely one mile away!

We walked there on a dull, warm and damp Sunday afternoon. Philip Court itself seemed to be the modern equivalent of terraced houses, reduced to one storey, and built around a series of tiny, paved courtyards, with raised flower beds and plenty of large, mature trees. Presumably, these dwellings were for elderly people, so where was the "Exclusive development"?

The sun came out for the first time as we walked further to a large, five-barred gate that stretched across the end of the narrow road. Beyond, a recently cleared area, about 200yards square, was bounded on one side by the back gardens of existing houses on the main road and bungalows on the other sides. About three quarters of the way along the left, rose the gaunt, half finished shell of a large bungalow, whilst opposite were the foundations of a smaller, semi-detached pair. This must be it!

I leaned on the gate. A gentle breeze disturbed the tree above my head and shafts of sunlight beamed through its leaves to weave intricate patterns on the rough soil. It was so peaceful. Fern poked her head through the lower bars of the gate and sniffed the air.

"Would you like to live here, Fern?"

Two days later, I went back to find a rather elegant notice erected beside the gate, promising the opening of a site office in two weeks' time. A map showed the positions of all the intended housing. There was to be only one pair of the cheaper, semi-detached bungalows, and the one at the south side, strangely, had much the largest garden of the entire development! That bungalow began to look like home.

I asked Margaret what she thought. She had been very preoccupied recently, trailing backwards and forwards between doctor and hospital as they tried to find the reason for her constant feeling of being unwell and the vague pains and general discomfort she had been experiencing. Her brown eyes lit up as I unfolded my idea. She listened with her usual care and concern and thought that it was about the right time for me to make a change. My life was settled, I was happy and I should be able to make the right decisions. By the time I reached home that evening, I had decided.

My deposit was the first and I got a huge discount! Number 57 went up for sale, and I began clearing out and packing. The only thought to dampen my enthusiasm was that I would be moving away from Gordon. Somehow, I'd begun to feel reassured and happy that he was just across the road. I told myself not to be so silly. The entire process flowed through painlessly until almost the very end, when my buyer suddenly decided he must have the bungalow right now! I mentioned this sudden need for speed when I happened to bump into Gordon and he turned up trumps yet again, helping me transport the many plants I had potted, to their new home. It occurred to me that I really would miss him. Fern certainly would.

"You'll come down and visit us sometime, won't you?"

He promised to do so.

Then it became a matter of dovetailing newly-plastered walls, laying carpets and immediately moving in! The plasterers were behind schedule, but the redoubtable Shanti Shah started on the carpets the very next day as promised, finishing in his usual immaculate style and in record time.

The following day, the hottest of the year, we moved. Fern thought the whole thing huge fun, until she realised her home was vanishing in front of her eyes! Poor Fern! She grew ever more agitated, until, just as we were ready to leave, she rushed into the drive and threw up.

Margaret and David came along to help unpack in our new home which cheered her, but as the sun began to set on our efforts, she kept going to the door, or to the garden gate, which clearly meant she thought it was time for us to go home. She repeated the behaviour for almost a week, even though she seemed perfectly happy during the day. She dreamed a lot too, during those first nights.

I spent three weeks as the sole occupier of Philip Court. Waking in my new bedroom each day, it felt as if I were on permanent holiday! Fern made friends with the builders, especially Richard, who always brought his working pointer, Tiffin. Before the joiner had my garden gate in place, Tiff would leap over whatever barrier I had erected to keep Fern in and the two of them would hurtle around the garden in high spirits until someone noticed.

"Oi, Richard! 'e's in there again!"

"Tiff's gone visiting!"

"Yer dog's at his girl friend's!"

At four o'clock, all the builders would pack up and depart, closing the gate and silence would descend. Because it was midsummer, I managed never to turn on a light, for I had no wish to attract unwanted attention, but one night, that attention came to us.

Fern had already been out for the final time, when she asked to go out again. She became more and more insistent, and I had the back door only half open when she pushed through, and raced into the darkest part of the garden, behind the garage and out of my sight!

What on earth was she up to? Then I heard a sound that made my blood run cold, a sound to generate pure terror: the long, drawn out snarl of a threatening dog. And it was Fern! Beyond the fence, there was an answering dull crash, followed by brief scraping, then silence. Now Fern began to bark and bark with passion. The sounds fought to escape from her throat before exploding with vicious ferocity into the night.

Vague recollections of bloody newspaper and television stories rushed to mind. I realised I was hanging on to the cold metal of the door handle as if gripping on to life itself. I could hear my own breathing, swift and shallow. I would never, ever have believed Fern capable of such violent threats. In the distance, a car passed along Lincoln road. One started up close by and drove away quickly.

Suddenly, it was over. Fern came trotting back into view, hackles and tail erect, neck arched. She paused and glanced back over her shoulder, hackles now subsiding, before returning past me, and on into the lounge. She radiated a smug air of supreme satisfaction. It must have been a cat I decided, unconvincingly.

Returning from our walk the following afternoon, I happened to meet

Richard who told me someone had tried to steal the JCB during the night. He had found unidentified footprints around the digger, marks beside its door lock, and large tyre tracks beyond the gate. The digger had been parked behind our garage, alongside the garden fence.

All the complications of moving home had interrupted our agility training, and a further hiccup came in the formidable shape of the dog walk.

"I've heard it called the cat walk," said Sandy as she heaved the up plank into position. Whatever it was called, it was big! The cross beam was level with my shoulder, and although the regulation width of six inches, it seemed extremely narrow. At the bottom, both steep side planks had a short area leading on to the ground painted a contrasting colour. This was the contact area, which the dog must touch with its paws. It was a thoroughly intimidating piece of apparatus.

"We'll be one each side of her, and we mustn't rush her. She goes forward only when she feels she's able," said Sandy. "You urge her forward. I'll make sure her back legs don't come off."

I urged Fern forward. She wanted to go. She knew she should go, but she was very apprehensive. Two "marvellous feet" had gone readily enough on to the plank, but it took ages before the back two followed. Very tentatively, she started to climb, one step at a time, but she never seemed to have control of all four feet together! If her front feet were on the apparatus, then her back feet came off. When she had control of her back feet, then the front were all over the place! We supported her with our shoulders, all the time laughing and encouraging her. Her back feet came off so many times that I began to be afraid she might injure herself. I wanted to give up. Why should I put my dog through all this? Yet Fern wanted to do it! Her tail wagged, she looked upward, and she made no attempt to scramble off the side. Finally, we reached the top and the beginning of the long cross beam.

"We'll rest," said Sandy. "Let her look around, get used to being up there."

Fern did look round, and seemed mightily pleased with herself, elevated to a position above the "official" pack leaders!

It took almost as long to get her across the top! Because she was above us, it was very difficult to make certain all her feet stayed safely on board. She rarely seemed to have any idea at all where her back feet were! The down plank was somewhat easier, possibly because Fern could see that it was all almost over.

"Get her right down on the ground before you praise her, or you'll encourage her to get off early and miss the down contact in competition."

Competition?

"When all four feet are grounded, go mad praising her, go absolutely mad."

I'd hardly any breath left when Fern finally made terra firma, and certainly none left to ask Sandy what she had meant by competition.

Fern pranced about with delight. Or was it relief? Perhaps it was the praise and attention? But there was no rest.

"Back again!" Sandy called, laughing. "Lots of encouragement! Light and happy voice!" Where had I heard that before?

We set off again. It took Fern just as long, was just as scary and I was just as thankful when it was all over. I wondered if we had reached our limit. I decided not to ask Sandy about her reference to competition at all.

What I saw as a problem had now taken the edge off Agility for me, but not for Fern. I'm sure she knew it was Tuesday the instant she awoke! In the next lesson, Sandy took us through a line of five jumps from both directions, then added the tunnel before returning to the hut for the dog walk. Fern and Daisy were allowed off lead for a little respite, but Fern chose to follow Sandy to the hut, dancing around outside in gleeful anticipation. Sandy shook her head in amusement.

"That dog is absolutely desperate to learn!"

But again we faced a literal uphill struggle; across one way, praise, back again, more praise; break for tea, then try once more. We both agreed Fern's feet were more under her control now, because some of her weight had left our shoulders and we weren't taking quite such an age to cross. I felt a little better as the lesson finished with the line of jumps, and curved tunnel. Very soon now, the lead would be taken off I thought. Fern, as usual, showed only disappointment when the "big toys" were packed away.

The next time Fern and I arrived at the field, Sandy had already erected a small course and was jumping Daisy.

"Follow on!" she called as they were finishing, but Fern had other ideas. She was dragging me to the dog walk! At least she wasn't afraid of it I thought as I began to pull her away.

"No! No, take her on!" yelled Sandy, "use it, use it! Let her on!"

She flung Daisy's lead over a jump wing and walked towards us as Fern mounted the plank and slowly began the upward climb. I was terrified. Why didn't Sandy run? I didn't know whether to watch Fern's front feet or back feet! Sandy reached us and took up her usual position on the opposite side and together we made it to the top. It was then I realised, that neither of us had actually supported Fern's weight! Very slowly, her concentration obvious, she began to walk along the cross beam. Reaching the end, tip of her tail now wagging gently, she immediately began the descent.

"Make sure she goes right to the bottom with all four feet," Sandy whispered, "then you know what to do."

Did I know what to do? I needed no encouragement this time! I was so relieved! The three of us leapt around like lunatics! Daisy barked, wondering what on earth was happening.

"She's cracked it," Sandy shrieked in excitement, "she knows she can do it!" "Fantastic!"

"Brilliant!"

It was as if Fern had been practising in secret!

"Take her again. Don't try to be any quicker. Keep to her pace."

We repeated the exercise, so slowly, so steadily. Again, Fern did it entirely on her own, the lead remaining completely slack throughout. But this time, the moment her feet had all touched the ground, she didn't wait for her praise, but whipped round and started the ascent again.

"After her!"

We set off in pursuit, and we both had to walk just a little more quickly to keep up! We reached the end safely, all three again thoroughly delighted.

"After her!"

Fern had evaded our congratulatory hands and was back on the dog walk. Tail held out, head high, she broke into a near-normal, loose, swinging gait on the cross beam, her confidence growing with every step.

"Try to stop her coming back on, but don't say no. Try to distract her."

But Fern was having none of it! She was back on the dog walk again, and this time, we had to break into a little trot to keep up with her!

She again evaded us once more to return to her new conquest. She even had the time and confidence to look round at us from the start of the cross beam and I'll swear forever that she was laughing!

"Praise her and get between her and the plank! You mustn't forbid her, whatever you do!" Sandy's speech was an excited gabble. "I'll run to the jumps and call her over! Get the lead off if you can."

We reached the ground and Sandy raced off. Fern hesitated. She was torn between her disappearing friend and her newly found skill. The dog walk won!

Fern crossed and re-crossed that apparatus seven times before we managed to get her off: and that was only after we started counting!

The dog walk was the only problem in her training. The following months saw the opening of the Talbot Centre and the arrival of many new pupils. The long jump, tyre, weaving poles, flat tunnel, see-saw and awesome A-frame, were all carefully and successfully added to make Fern's Agility repertoire complete.

CHAPTER SIXTEEN

Phillip Court began to fill. First to join us were the Thomases. I hit it off straight away with mother Glen, a slim, attractive lady, and a great consumer of black mascara. Husband Martin, six feet four broad as well as tall, and known to everyone as Big Mart, was a generous, amiable giant, but one with whom it would not have been wise to pick an argument! He had a high powered job in gas turbines and spent a great deal of time abroad in exotic places, returning home for periods of extended leave of anything up to four or five weeks at a time. He could also be sent thousands of miles at a moment's notice!

Mark, seven, slim and studious, was their eldest son. Scott, two years younger, was Little Mart with Attitude. They were super kids, but both were terrified of dogs! Whenever they saw Fern, Mark would silently melt away, but Scott would scream blue murder, wave his arms about like a runaway windmill and charge frantically in all directions, until by chance, he happened upon a gate or door which would open to offer him sanctuary. Fern thought this was entertainment especially choreographed for her amusement and seemed to wind them up deliberately! Glen had no idea why her boys were like this and she was far too sensible even to have unwittingly taught them to be afraid. So whenever Mark or Scott came across to visit, Fern would stay in another room or be banished into the garden.

One afternoon, Scott took revenge on Fern for being a dog, by poking his cap pistol through the bars of my gate and firing directly into her face. Fern looked mildly surprised, turned, then walked away. Glen went ballistic and Scott went to bed. His protests, long and loud, fell on deaf ears.

Things came to a head shortly after. The boys were playing in the road and I couldn't have fastened my gate securely, because, suddenly, Fern galloped out to join them. Panic! Chaos! Mark shot back into his garden. Screaming like a banshee, Scott hurtled first in one direction, then

153

another, pursued by a delighted Fern who thought this a marvellous game. Whatever would the neighbours think of this dreadful racket? I was glad Big Mart wasn't around to see and hear his boys being "savaged", for there had been only limited opportunity for him to get to know Fern.

I hurried into the road just as Scott chanced upon the way into his garden, and ran, screaming, up the passageway between bungalow and garage. The problem was the Thomases didn't have a gate! Fern simply followed.

As I rushed into the passageway, to my horror, Big Mart himself appeared, carrying a large can of oil and heading for the garage. I hadn't even known he was at home! How on earth would he react?

"Fern sorting those two out?"

He squeezed past, showing not the slightest surprise at meeting a neighbour running into his garden.

"S'more than I can do."

He disappeared into the garage.

Fern had the boys at bay. Mark, with his back to her and his head as far into the corner as he could manage, was moaning softly and appeared to be marking rapid time. Scott, alongside, had his hands up to his face, but had stopped screaming now and was watching Fern through stubby fingers. Perhaps he was surprised he had not yet been eaten! Fern's tail was a wagging blur and she bounced up and down on her forelegs as she tried to restart the game.

"I'd leave her to it," Big Mart observed as he returned to the bungalow minus the oilcan, "seems like she's got 'em where she wants 'em."

He vanished indoors, totally unconcerned.

So I did just that, and stood out of sight in the passageway. Not one sound came from the little group in the corner. I continued to wait, hoping perhaps that Mart would be right and that left to themselves a kind of truce would evolve. Eventually, I was joined by Fern, who apparently found little reason to stay with two still and silent, small human beings.

In the days that followed, both boys touched Fern for the first time, then they walked alongside us, up and down Phillip Court. Next, they held her lead as we walked and I taught them how to tell her to sit.

That was as far as Mark went. He would never actually like dogs, but he would tolerate them and be terrified no longer.

Scott was different. Fern became, "My beautiful Fern", and was always referred to as such. I had to watch them closely, because Scott wanted to share all his sweets and crisps with her! On his birthday, I gave him a photograph of Fern in a small, brass frame. Glen told me that every night, he would turn the picture towards his bed, so that "My beautiful Fern can look after me while I'm asleep." When morning came, he turned the photo around because, "My beautiful Fern wants to see through the window." The photograph accompanied him during a short stay in hospital, where several nurses complimented Glen on their beautiful dog that Scott was always talking about. He has decided he will have two dogs when he grows up: one just like Fern and a bulldog! I suppose a psychologist might say that what happened in the garden that afternoon, was saturation aversion therapy!

I'd already skinned my knuckles and now I banged my left knee! Standing there, half-doubled up, uttering a series of heart-felt oooohs while waiting for the pain to subside, I realised there just wasn't room to unfold the folding bed unless I stacked the dining chairs first and that made the room look like a very small warehouse! The second bedroom, which I used as a dining room (guests only!) simply wasn't big enough and Margaret was coming to stay. She had been quite unwell recently. The hospital investigations seemed to be getting nowhere and I'd finally persuaded her that a few days of being cosseted would do her the world of good. I decided to use the folding bed for myself, putting it up in the lounge every night and Margaret would have my bedroom. I felt very pleased with myself to have found several vegetarian recipes with which to surprise her and it was in high spirits that I took Fern to collect her one afternoon. Nothing could have prepared me for the dreadful shock to come.

The first day of her holiday dawned fine and sunny. I made an early morning cuppa, then prepared breakfast while Margaret got up. And it was warm enough to eat on the patio! How good that felt as we sat there together! The garden might be very new, with bare gaps waiting to be filled in by the growing plants, but the geraniums brought vivid splashes of colour and the large circular pond, dug and built by David, already promised riches to come.

The gentlest of breezes stirred the leaves of the old willow which overhung the fence from the garden beyond. Margaret suddenly giggled as she buttered her toast.

"This feels really posh!"

It did, too, and it felt good! I had my own tiny family and the kindest, most understanding of friends. I was so lucky and at peace with the world.

"Are you coming with us?" I asked as I prepared to walk Fern, "or are you going to stay here in the sun? There's loads of books and some magazines."

Margaret chose to stay, but added,

"I've something to tell you when you get back."

Could I wait? I insisted she told me at once.

I was unnerved by the way she took my wrist and led the way back inside and into the lounge. Cool and dim compared to outside, its stillness did not generate any feeling of friendly peace, but instead, one of foreboding. We sat side by side on the sofa.

"You know all the trouble I've been having? Well, they've found out what it is."

I looked at her uneasily. Seated very upright, hands resting in her lap, her brown eyes were quite calm and clear, her voice measured and controlled. It couldn't be very bad I thought. But in that same moment, in that stillness, I realised there was too much control, too much calm, and I knew. I knew with certainty what she would say. Margaret continued to look at me, then spoke quietly, almost apologetically.

"I've got cancer."

How does one reply to such a statement? With sadness and commiseration, and risk depressing the sufferer even more? Or with cheerfulness and optimism, perhaps to be thought unsympathetic or stupid or both? And how selfish is it to think of oneself in such circumstances! My heart began to pound and my stomach sank with a once dreadful familiarity. Shocked into silence, I said nothing. It seemed ages before I could speak. I tried to be matter-of -fact.

"I am so sorry. How are they going to get rid of it?"

Margaret didn't reply at once.

"I can have some radiology. They say that should help."

Visions of my gentle friend being bullied by the purveyors of a system, which, out of necessity, rationed treatment, made me indignant. I completely missed the implication of her words and plunged on.

"What about chemotherapy? Or surgery? There's lots can be done!"

She dropped her gaze for the first time.

"It wouldn't help."

Suddenly, her tears came. From within her sobs, I heard only one word: "terminal."

Struck dumb, I could only stare at my dearest friend, separated from her by my own selfish world of sudden misery. The tables were turned.

She needed me desperately, and I did nothing.

"I'm going to die."

Her hand crept from her lap, seeking mine.

"I don't want to."

It was the pathetic cry of a child who does not understand why something enthralling but dangerous has to be taken away. Finally, we clung together and cried. I don't know how long we stayed like that, as if we might make time stand still and the ghastly thing Margaret had revealed would never become any worse. Then I repeated all the banal platitudes that well-meaning people trot out.

"We're all going to die. It's just that now you know when it might be."

"Someone's working on a cure this very minute."

I even said, "The doctors may be wrong."

I listened to my own voice, flinching as the words spilled out, so trite and so utterly pointless. Had circumstances been reversed, Margaret would have known exactly what to say or not to say. She knew when to speak, and when to be silent. She knew how to hold and comfort.

Margaret enjoyed her little holiday. She relished the early morning cups of tea in bed, the luxury of not having to plan and prepare meals. The vegetarian dishes surprised and delighted her. She came on some of Fern's walks, exploring the early autumn delights of Hartsholme Park and the South Common. At Fen Lane she slid many times down the children's big slide and didn't care who saw her. She met Glen, Mark and the impish Scott and we stole a beautiful day on the beach at Skegness.

I cried after she returned home. Mostly, I cried with shame, for I knew my tears were angry and selfish. Against all the odds, I had Fern, but now I was to lose Margaret. Why couldn't I have both? Why couldn't I keep the two most important beings in the whole world? When other people had such big families, it didn't seem too much to ask, just for two. Only two.

I tried hard to concentrate on other things.

New clients were appearing every lesson at the Talbot Dog Training Centre, and I tried to bury myself in all of this. What a variety there was too, both canine and human! From people with aspirations of competitive glory, often with little idea of the commitment involved, to those who wanted "Something for the dog to do"! From German Shepherds, through many varieties of spaniel, and crossbreed, to Westies and Jack Russells, but mostly, not surprisingly, the new pupils were Border Collies. Fern remained the sole Flatcoated Retriever.

Sandy was establishing a tradition whereby people were expected to bring chocolate biscuits in their birthday week and I adapted this! When Fern's birthday came around, I baked a chocolate cake and took it, so that everyone might taste a little of the pride and joy I felt in my dog's achievements, even though there was only Sandy and George who had any idea at all of Fern's unique background.

During actual training, the atmosphere was one of concentration, but there was still plenty of time for socialising. At tea break, George encouraged everyone to allow their dogs off lead, because they, more than anyone, needed to relax. We humans would sit at the picnic tables, drinking tea (some used to say we attended the Tea Drinking Training Centre!) and exchange stories about our beloved canines. We could also ask for any specific help, and listen to advice on all aspects of the Doggy Life from George and Sandy. These ad hoc and leisurely sessions were of immense value and, as a bonus, we were sometimes treated to hilarious stories of bygone Agility or Obedience from their endless repertoires.

The first fully fledged agility competitor to appear was Stella Baker. She had come to George for icing on her cake, to gain a finishing gloss to her years of competing with the object of progressing from also-ran, with the occasional clear round or place, to a win and its automatic reward of moving up from Starters classes into Intermediate. Solely for Stella, George had built a full competition course, the first any of us had seen at close quarters, so we all expected something special. Of course, we weren't allowed to use it (none of us could, anyway) but he took us "walking the course", a competition must, to explain its intricacies. What a fearsome eye-opener! Some of the handlers began to look forward to the day when they would be skilled enough to confront such a monster, but not me! I was definitely one of the "something for my dog to do" brigade. Whilst no individual piece of apparatus would be a problem, putting it all together would! I thought I would never remember any route with so many twists and turns!

Stella had no such qualms. She walked the course on her own, bending, waving, pointing and clapping the way to an imaginary dog, while the real one lay, impressively untethered, in front of the hut. Returning to the start, she called Tess, who ran immediately to sit on the line. A brindled Border Collie, Tess was calm and good-natured, with eyes only for her owner/handler.

George gave a nod. We held a collective breath.

"In your own time."

Slightly overweight she may have been, but Stella could certainly move!

"Over!" "This way!" "Down! Down, down!"

The commands came thick and fast.

"Come!" "Right over!" "Tyre!"

Her shouts became almost demented as Tess flew round.

"This way! Come, come!"

We were so impressed. Everything was dramatic, spectacular, like lightning! Could we ever be like this? Halfway round, it all came unstuck. Stella turned right to the A-frame. Tess shot straight on, over another jump, mindless of her handler's screams of desperation. Stella stopped at the foot of the A-frame.

"Come! Tess, come! Come!" Her arms flailed the air. "Come back here!"

Tess had stopped immediately after the wrong jump, and now looked first one way, then the other in confusion. Stella glanced round at an impassive George, grinned, shrugged and then took a few steps towards her dog.

"Tess, come!"

Tess suddenly made up her mind, came back over the same jump, and followed on towards the A-frame. Things went pear-shaped again in the weaving poles, where Tess dived in between poles two and three, instead of one and two. Stella got her back more quickly this time and finished at speed, out of breath, but smiling.

Standing there, in silent awe, we all thought it wonderful! I was particularly envious of Stella's confidence, of her shouts and massive gestures. She turned to George, who began to nod very slowly. Her smile grew wider.

"Ye-es, good, quite good, wi' a dog who's hard o' hearin'"

It was rare to hear praise of any kind from George. Stella's smile broadened even more, then she began to laugh.

"Tess's not deaf!"

"Wisp!"

In reply, George called one of his own dogs, and moved across to the starting line.

We exchanged glances. Were we about to see George himself do a round? If Stella had been watched with bated breath, then now the world stood still. At last we would see how well he put all his own advice into operation! George had a bit of a belly, and he must be around sixty. He couldn't possibly be as fast.

Wrong! We seemed to have time barely to draw breath before George had completed the course perfectly and near soundlessly. There was a stunned silence, then the man with the G.S.D. swore softly to himself.

George sent Wisp away, then called Tess.

"What's her command for the tyre?"

Stella's satisfied smile had vanished.

"Tyre."

George set off with Tess. In spite of going the wrong way before, she turned perfectly for the A-frame. The weaving poles were executed without a hitch. He made a great fuss of her, before returning to Stella's side.

"So why were you shouting at your dog?" he bellowed, as if their conversation had never been interrupted.

Stella's round was no longer impressive. We had seen The Master at work. George lowered his voice a little.

"What does "Right over" mean? Doesna "over" means jump, so what does right mean? Why ye got two commands for the same thing? "Down down"; is that the same as down? Why tell the dog twice? The dog's no deaf! So is it stupid? "This way." This way? This way? Ye're making a speech out there!"

I began to feel sorry for Stella. Often I had born the brunt of George's displeasure, but this was far worse. He was taking apart all her previous training, all her years of experience, and in front of other people. But he had not finished.

"I've no time for all that blather! No breath either, and you wouldn't have if you were going as fast as your dog could! And what was all this?" He whirled his arms like a windmill. "Your poor dog doesna know what to do to please ye'!"

Stella had been utterly humiliated. Just as I thought he had gone too far, George suddenly laughed, and slapped her on the back

"Cheer up, Pet! S'no all bad! The dog's good."

We all laughed, and the spell was broken.

"We can put the other stuff right if you'll work."

Then he turned his eagle attention to us.

Stella did work. She became a regular, even though I think she found it very hard at first, because she not only had to learn as we did, she had to undo much of her past learning as well! However, she saw the wisdom of

George's teaching, refined her act, and raked in more competition places, although I don't think she ever got out of Starters.

The man with the G.S.D. referred to George as Maestro ever afterwards.

Winter was fast approaching, and some clients now attended only spasmodically, but Fern enjoyed her agility so much that we never stayed away! She learned to work in frost, rain and wind. Only the wind disturbed her. Sandy said it was because she received so much scent information she could not concentrate. Saturday afternoon training was sometimes curtailed because it grew so dark and with the dark nights, another Christmas drew nearer.

"Oho! But you're only a very small ghost. I shall sniff and sniff and blow you away, said the big, black dog who was also very beautiful."

I sniffed. Mark sniffed. Scott sniffed louder.

"And the big, black dog who was also very beautiful, frightened the ghost away!" Mark permitted himself a delighted grin. Scott cheered and clapped. The boys were spending the evening with me whilst Glenn wrapped and hid their presents. The magic of Christmas filled my lounge in the glow of the fire and the twinkling lights of the Christmas tree, as I dreamed up an impromptu story to entertain two very excited little boys. By the time the big black dog who was also very beautiful had barked to frighten away the biggest ghost in the world and escorted the children safely to Father Christmas, Glenn had crept into the room, and nodded that all wrapping and hiding had been accomplished.

Thereafter, we indulged in the highly dubious, but gloriously messy attempt to toast mince pies by the fire for supper and we discovered Fern loved mincemeat!

On Christmas morning, the boys rushed across with a present for her; a football! She'd had it all of fifteen seconds before there was a pop, followed by a long hiss. But it was a good present nevertheless. The pieces kept her amused for weeks!

Both Glenn and Gordon had invited me to Christmas dinner. It was so kind of them, but I would have felt awkward; I would be an outsider, and I think I convinced them both that I would be quite happy with just Fern for company. Besides, Gordon's invitation had been to his mother's and I didn't think it right that he should issue invitations first, and then tell her afterwards! I recreated the tinsel-bedecked walk in Hartsholme followed by our own dinner and once again, it was wonderful! The magic lasted throughout the whole season.

161

With the New Year more people and their dogs arrived at the T.D.T.C. One pair became very special.

Owner Colin was of the something-for-the-dog-to-do brigade, whilst his young dog, Louis, was one of the do something, anything, anywhere, anytime but preferably right now kind. An all-black Labrador/Border Collie cross, he was friendly and brimming with energy, the kind of dog anyone would be justifiably proud to own and Colin was certainly that.

Tall and good looking, thick, wavy hair turning a distinguished shade of grey, Colin had led a colourful life, much of it in India. Whenever Louis' extrovert antics reduced the class to helpless laughter and Colin to distraction, he would let rip with a stream of what he claimed to be Hindustani. Louis would gaze up at him, amber eyes shining, ears pricked, head to one side, listening intently and completely unmoved!

The physical side of agility was no problem to this already super-fit dog, whose idea of fun was to run into a disused quarry and then to scale its sides while his bemused owner waited for him on the rim! Concentration was another matter entirely!

I seem to remember that it took only minutes for Louis to discover his perfect partner in crime. Perhaps it could be called love at first sight, because from the moment those tigerish eyes alighted on Fern, the die was cast! She felt exactly the same way about him, too. Both believed life should be lived to the full and both had a streak of disarming wilfulness that added to their charms.

We learned very quickly to keep them apart during training, but at break, they instantly made straight for each other and would play together non-stop. Each took turn to be victor or vanquished, but while Fern assumed her roles silently, Louis barked, whined, yelped, and growled incessantly. He was surely the most vociferous dog in creation! Their antics, together with Louis' vocal accompaniments, often terrified newcomers to the T.D.T.C., who thought they were witnessing the beginning of the fight of the century.

How wrong they were! Louis would have died for Fern. Her relationship with him rapidly became a canine anachronism. There may be the "one man woman" or even the "one woman man", but has there ever been a one dog bitch? Fern allowed Louis almost limitless liberties, but woe betide any other dog who tried it on! Her biggest scalps, a Dobermann and a Bull terrier, were allowed only a perfunctory sniff around her rear before she whipped round, teeth bared, growling menacingly. But while Louis could make eyes at any other bitch, he would become exceedingly belligerent should he catch any male doing the same to Fern! She, of course, was typical friendly Flatcoat, and, if I'm honest, a bit of a flirt as well, providing they didn't venture with intent towards her rear that is! It eventually became so much of a problem, that Louis received the ultimate coup-de-grace and was neutered. It certainly lessened his machismo, but not his devotion.

One day, the pair of them vanished during training.

How long they had been gone before anyone noticed their absence is hard to say. Agility was abandoned as many anxious eyes scanned the surrounding fields. A busy road ran alongside, its perfect straightness and speed de-restriction encouraging drivers, released from city confines, to put their foot down. Three fields further on, the road turned sharply through 90 degrees, then back on itself to cross the Witham. Fern adored water. The hedgerows provided cover for many rabbits. Chasing rabbits was a Louis speciality.

As time wore on, we all grew more and more worried. Almost sick with apprehension, I couldn't help but shiver as every car, every lorry, motorcycle, or van raced by. Why was the traffic going faster than ever this morning? What would happen if Fern was gone long enough to miss a feed? What if someone found her and fed her human food? Or dry dog food, which releases vast amounts of gas? Or gave her a normal amount? Had we come this far together to become a statistic in the Lost column of the local paper? Or worse?

People spread out through adjoining fields, calling their names, but the two dogs could be far away and anything could have happened to either or both of them! My only comfort was that they were together. But if anything had happened to Fern, would Louis allow anyone to approach her?

"Over there!"

The long grass of an adjacent field had begun to wave. The waving was definite and direct. It came nearer and nearer, until we could make out a single, dark figure.

"It's Louis!"

He came at a canter. As he grew closer, everyone could see he was liberally spattered with mud; his legs coated and his belly wet. He also had what could only be described as a silly grin across his face! He made directly for the water bowl, drank thirstily, then flopped on his side, taking care not to catch the eye of a mightily relieved and mightily cross Hindustani-spouting Colin.

But where was Fern? I knew Louis would never abandon her, and he certainly didn't seem agitated.

"Look!"

The man with the Boxer pointed across the field.

The grass had begun to wave once more. Fern? This was a brown dog! Yet it was her! Unlike Louis, she seemed oblivious to the upset she had caused and repeatedly sidetracked to investigate interesting dog phenomena. As she came nearer, we could see she was absolutely coated in mud. Even the aristocratic crown of her head was anointed! Innocently, she met everyone's gaze with a happy wag of her matted tail and the same satisfied, silly grin as Louis. She acknowledged my presence with a brief deviation on her way to the drinking bowl, took her fill, then turned to Louis. A brief mutual face-licking followed, then both dogs keeled over onto their sides, thoroughly exhausted and blissfully fulfilled. Neither did any more agility that day!

Then came another new arrival at the T.D.T.C: Gordon! He had called at Phillip Court one Saturday morning just as we were leaving for training, so I invited him along much to Fern's delight.

Thereafter, weekends began to change. Gordon would drive us to the Centre every Saturday. Even though he didn't bring a dog, George made him very welcome and included him in everything, just like any other paid-up member in fact. In return, Gordon made himself useful employing his strength in shifting the heaviest equipment and his carpentry skills in maintaining the same.

After Agility, he would stay for lunch, and in the evening, go home to change and then return to take me out to dinner. Back at Phillip Court, we invariably talked and talked until the small hours.

"Nothing going on?" repeated Margaret, a huge and knowing smile spreading across her face. "Nothing going on and you spend all day together, then still find something to talk about half the night?"

It was obvious too, that Fern shared Margaret's opinion, especially in the light of a strange little incident one Saturday during a break from training. Seven or eight of us, including Gordon, were clustered around George as he held forth on something. Several dogs were milling around, including Fern. As George finished, Fern walked across the circle and began to make a great fuss of him; not surprising, because Fern always considered herself closer to George than any of the other trainees. Her deliberate action drew everyone's attention. George responded in his usual extravagant way, and then for the very first time, Fern herself broke off the encounter. She re-crossed the circle to take up position in a classic sit beside Gordon's left leg and facing George. There was a brief moment of silence, then George laughed.

"Oho, now! What was all that for, ma girl? What're telling me, eh? You're telling me y've got a new Dad are you?"

He gazed around the ring in mock distress.

"Off wi' the old and on wi' the new! And here am I, thinking all dogs are loyal!"

Could Fern really have been telling George that things were changing?

CHAPTER SEVENTEEN

For several months, Sandy had been hinting that it was high time the more experienced T.D.T.C. students took the plunge and entered the world of Open Agility competition. Her hints grew ever stronger. Then she began to turn up with various schedules and to talk about the different venues. Finally, when the Cardinal's Hill club mounted one of their twice yearly shows, her suggestions burgeoned into threats! She caught us one day with our guards down and mouths full of Fern's chocolate third birthday cake. Now there really was no excuse; no pre-dawn departure, no marathon drive, just an early jaunt along the by-pass!

Dr. Hall's words sprang into mind: "You've come this far." Should we go further? I reasoned that one or two rounds of Agility spread over a day were far less physically demanding than any training session. Should we perhaps?

Sally, with the little spring-heeled Molly, gave in first. How I envied her happy-go-lucky attitude! Then Anne decided to have a go with Bearded Collie, Sophie, a rival to Fern in the happiness stakes. Sophie loved her agility and would bark non-stop with enthusiasm throughout her round!

"I will, if you will," the speaker was Janet, well experienced in Obedience. Elderly Border Collie, Jess, had taken so well to Agility, that her owner was convinced it had given her a whole new lease of life! Now everyone who was capable, at least on paper, had decided to go for it, did I have much option? I thought I might make a total idiot of myself, but that would be preferable to being the only one who didn't have the guts to try.

That same senseless, heart-racing fear I had felt first at the exemption show and then at the breed shows, kicked in about two weeks before the Great Day. Janet was no help. She seemed to latch on to me, perhaps instinctively recognising a fellow no-hoper.

"Are you nervous? " "Do you think we'll make a mess of it?" "Do you think you'll remember the course?" She even included me in her philosophy. "We'll never get round."

But I was no use to her, either. We simply talked each other down. If we didn't expect anything, then we wouldn't be disappointed, and everything would be all right.

What a stupid, pointless, thoroughly shameful attitude! Why couldn't I see the other side of the coin? I had a superbly athletic and confident dog who knew her job thoroughly; we had been trained by the very best, so why, oh why, did I assume we were destined for failure? Where on earth did that come from?

With hindsight perhaps, it was from my childhood. Try as I might, I could not live up to my father's expectations of sporting prowess. Even in his sixties, he would leave me standing in a sprint! Neither could I equal him in swimming. I floundered around in the shallows, while he scythed up and down from end to end.

It wasn't only in sport that I seemed the proverbial duffer either! At infant school, I still remember the hurt when not allowed to join a music class. I was so sure I would be good, yet I wasn't even allowed to try. And how I longed for a real part in those tiny, gorgeous extravaganzas staged for proud parents. But, no, I was automatic chorus material, destined forever to be a human backdrop.

At secondary school I also failed to make any mark. The compulsory entry for three events on Sports Day was a nightmare. Then there had been the school play. I'd always wanted to act, but absence made me miss the auditions, so I tried repeatedly to get the teacher to hear me read before the cast was announced. She was always too busy. Eventually, I stopped turning up every dinnertime only to be sent away in growing disappointment. There was always next year, I told myself. I attended that audition with high hopes. Even today, I remember every single word my character had to say in the statutory two pages of script each aspirant was allotted. They were near the bottom of a right hand page:

"Eighteen years and six months."

From my seat at the front of the classroom, I remember watching the grey-haired Miss Mattocks hold her pen over my name for a long, long time before crossing me out. I must have said eighteen years and six months quite well. But not well enough.

So when I took my place on the start line with Fern, I think I was already programmed for failure.

"In your own time."

167

Illusion

With stopwatch in hand, the timekeeper gave us clearance.

I remember little of the course, save that the first five or six obstacles were in a dead straight line, before a simple 90degree right hand turn, and that right at the finish, four jumps were arranged in something like a cross.

We flew that first line! I remember being surprised, but why should I have been? As Fern mounted the A-frame, the fourth apparatus in that line, my incredulity grew. She was doing everything right! My head was in a whirl. We're here! We've made it! We're in an Agility competition! Us! Fern got her both her contacts with absolutely no help from me.

Are you here, Man from Fen Lane? Can you see us? Can you?

But we shouldn't be here! Fern should be dead!

Dead! I formed that dreadful thought for the very first time then, racing alongside my living, breathing black beauty. But we'd done it! This was it! This was the reality! Such total lack of concentration could only ever bring one result. As we turned the corner, I lost my way. Desperately, I cast about searching for the next number in sequence. Dancing around on the spot, Fern grew anxious and decided for herself which way to go. It wasn't the judge's way. I set off after her, we negotiated some obstacles, then somehow found ourselves at the end of the course. Our first competition was over.

Elimination. But that was what I'd expected, wasn't it? Plus the cold, hollow fear and hot, back-prickling embarrassment that were my constant companions in such circumstances. Everything had gone to plan. Janet too, was eliminated, Sally had fifteen faults, but happy, barking Sophie earned the T.D.T.C.'s first Open Competition clear round.

Now that the plunge had been plunged, we were expected to continue. Sandy always had a fistful of schedules for us to examine at break. How many Starters' classes were there? How far was it? What were the roads like?

The next foray was over the Pennines to the suburbs of Manchester, Janet sharing Sandy's car and Colin with Louis, coming along with us for their debut. We had planned our respective routes carefully, Sandy deciding to by-pass Sheffield, whilst I would go directly through, because I knew the city didn't I? But how long had it been since I left? Even when we met road works preparing the way for Super Tram, I wasn't daunted! But coming up to where I expected a large roundabout however, we found ourselves face to face with what must be the tallest, thickest concrete wall ever built!

Colin spent much of the next quarter of an hour or so roaring with laughter as we weaved our way through unfamiliar landmarks, but somehow, I got us through and we escaped along the Penistone road towards our goal. We arrived some time after Sandy!

The weather had been poor for several days and now it deteriorated steadily. Each of the four rings began as grass with some mud, rapidly becoming mud with some grass as the rain became heavier. But this weather was a great leveller. Many dogs and handlers disliked working in the cold, wet conditions. Neither bothered Fern in the slightest, so I didn't feel quite as bad as I had done at Lincoln, poised on the start line. Would-be spectators had taken shelter in the organising club's hut and competitors in the queue were preoccupied avoiding the worst of the rain, so I pretended it was simply a training session, made easier by the absence of the eagle-eyed George.

"In your own time."

I kept to the course! Ten faults! I made a hash of our entry into the weaving poles, but had no idea of where the other five came from. I was delighted! Sandy put it in perspective.

"Your mind was on the next jump. You hadn't finished one before you were at the next. It worried Fern. She didn't know if she was doing right."

Concentration again!

Colin made an awesome start to his round, walking well out on to the course before turning and calling Louis to follow him over the jumps. There were very few handlers who could do this with such aplomb.

"I have to," Colin would explain whenever he was congratulated on this tour-de-force, "or I get so out of breath, I can't keep up with the b-----!"

After his brilliant start, it all fell apart and they ended up with something like a cricket score! Then Janet got lost again.

The Newton Heath club lived up to Sandy's complimentary description, for there were not only hot drinks but hot food as well available at lunchtime. However, I ate a cold and solitary packed lunch in the car, rain pattering on the roof, for I never dared leave Fern alone for long. The threat of possible torsion, which was always with us, increased at shows. Her strict feeding schedule could not be adhered to, and like any dog, she would pant with excitement, thereby taking in more air.

"Air has free entry into her gut." I must never forget those words.

Sandy was marvellous at these early shows, a mother hen looking after

169

her errant chicks. She explained how the rules we had learned worked, what the formalities were, the unwritten codes of acceptable behaviour and made sure that each of us was in the right place at the right time.

We had all entered the Starters' Jumping class in the afternoon: no contacts, thank heaven, so it should have been easier. Clear and almost home, Louis stopped for a sniff, cocked his leg and was eliminated. Janet found her way round successfully, but accumulated a multitude of time faults. Fern went faultlessly until very close to the finish, when she shot into the weaves behind pole two instead of in front and I totally lost it trying to get her back in correctly; another elimination!

We wondered who would tell George.

Middlesborough saw the next T.D.T.C. attempt at glory, but I decided that it was too far and the day would be too taxing for Fern. Neither Colin or Janet went for various reasons, but Sophie brought home another clear round and the man who referred to George as the Maestro, had two very promising five fault rounds.

Then, it was the big one! Several clubs in Norfolk combined to present a "Starters Festival" which lasted a whole weekend and included team events and many variations on a theme: exotic things called Take Your Own Line and Gamblers.

Sandy, Janet, Colin and myself would be there the entire weekend, while other T.D.T.C. members would drive down to compete on one day. H.Q. was to be Sandy's enormous tent which boasted three separate bedrooms! But Sandy would not allow dogs to sleep in her tent. That posed a problem for me, because I dare not leave Fern to sleep on her own in a car as the others did. Once again, my saviour came to the rescue. Gordon lent me his small dome tent, purple veteran of many steam and vintage rallies! Fern and I would sleep in there.

On a rather cool afternoon we were first to arrive, staking our claim near a sheltering hedge and, as instructed by Sandy, not near the porta-loos! I walked Fern across the Sports ground and into the field next door, already designated "Exercise Area", and where wads of small plastic bags hung from umpteen metal poles hammered into the ground.

This was so exciting, I thought to myself as we wandered round. Under canvas for the first time in my life, entering another sporting event! Whoever would have thought I'd be starting out in such things?

Returning to our claim, I watched more competitors arriving and slightly bemused, saw a colourful shantytown begin to grow. From cars and vans, but especially from battered Transits, there spilled people of all shapes, dogs of all breeds and tents of all colours and sizes. I passed the time predicting what might emerge from which and found a striking correlation between the Transits and Border Collies, and degree of vehicle battering with number of dogs emerging!

Sometimes, a caravan would pitch up and on rare occasions, it was towed by a 4by4!

Fern was beside herself with delight when Sandy appeared. As we erected the big tent, Colin and Louis arrived, followed by Janet and Jess. People were still rolling up as darkness fell, manoeuvring cars, vans and tents in the beams of headlights, or waving torches. The smell of frying sausages, the barks of excited dogs and the laughter of many voices filled the air. This really was some show!

Fern climbed into her bed readily enough, but in the eternal dim light of the countryside, I could see her ears constantly twitching as another intriguing sound erupted from nearby. I was too excited and too apprehensive to sleep much. Every time I awoke, Fern seemed to be awake, too.

Saturday morning dawned sunny but with a cool wind. Sandy emphasised how important it was for us to pay attention to the loudspeaker announcements, and should we find that any of our entries looked as if they were going to clash, then we must inform the steward in one of the rings that we were going to be late.

Colin had been brave enough to enter a Gamblers' class, but it didn't pay off, and neither did anyone else's efforts! In an agility class, I couldn't turn Fern and she shot away into the distance, then returned over the same jumps! We went on to finish, amazingly, well within time, but of course were eliminated. This time, Sandy didn't blame me and thought that Fern was "sky-high" with excitement. Louis, too, did his own thing, but Janet made it all the way round only to finish with time faults once again.

Our afternoon fared no better. I began to despair of ever receiving one of those wonderful, brilliant, shiny rosettes. If only I could win just one, only one, I would be satisfied; not even a place, just one clear round, one magical, marvellous Clear!

As each of us completed our programme for the day, we collapsed on varying sorts of seating in front of Sandy's tent, tired dogs tethered nearby. It had been an exhausting day for everyone.

"Erm…I think you have a problem with two of your dogs, the black retrievers."

The speaker was an earnest, middle-aged lady who had hurried from behind the tent. Sandy understood at once.

"The dog's humping the bitch," she stated, without moving.

Our informant looked uncomfortable.

"Well…um, yes, actually."

"That's all right, thanks. They're always at it."

Sandy stuck her legs out, folded her arms and lapsed back into silence. The woman looked non-plussed. Janet and I hurried to explain.

"It really is all right."

"They're just friends."

"They've both had the snip."

"They really are good friends."

The poor woman left in a hurry. Sandy put her head down onto her chest and sniggered into her jumper.

Hunger eventually galvanised us into movement, but the planned evening meal was chaos. No one wanted to sit at the table Janet and I tried in vain to prepare. We had volunteered to organise all the food, but Sandy and Colin especially refused to be organised! Residents and assorted gatecrashers preferred to rummage in any cool box, picnic box or packing case to find whatever took their fancy. Oddly, many of the gatecrashers brought food! We later discovered several items neither of us had bought on our supermarket sortie! The carefully planned weekend menus lay in tatters. Ignoring hoots of derisive laughter, Janet and I sat down to eat, using cutlery instead of bread doorsteps. Maintaining what we saw as a necessary decorum, we munched away, stuck to our planned menu as much as possible and did so for the entire weekend!

Sunday competitors began arriving before we'd finished breakfast. Today, there were several elementary classes, which meant that the jumps were at twenty-four instead of the standard thirty inches, and while height had never been a problem for Fern, the courses tended to be simpler and more straightforward than in Starters, which would benefit me!

Colin seemed to have entered everything again. Janet was in Starters' Agility and in the lowest of the low, Elementary jumping, with me.

I never dared enter Fern for more than one class in any session. Always with a watchful eye on her, I didn't have the chance to study any of my fellow competitors as George had said we must do, but waiting in the queue for our turn, I could hardly miss the fact that one dog demolished half the course, another decided to abandon the round halfway through to high tail it from the ring, whilst a third was eliminated because his handler hadn't removed his collar! At least, I thought, as we stood on the start line, we couldn't be as bad as any of that, not even if we tried!

"In your own time."

We were about to begin when I had to choke back the command, because Fern had suddenly started to scratch behind her left ear! The energy she put into it was embarrassing! Assuming a nonchalance I did not feel (Sandy later described it as looking like pure terror) I gazed around the course. It was simple; nothing like the horrors so often dreamed up by George. Nothing could possibly go wrong. Could it?

We raced through the finish. We'd not knocked anything down. We'd done the weaves cleanly. Were we inside the time?

There were so many entrants that score sheet after score sheet had been filled and posted while the class was still running! Eventually, the sheet which would show our score went up. I ignored the eliminations and the highest fault columns, searching the ten fault column first. We weren't there. Then I studied the five fault list. We weren't there either. Could we have time faults? No. So finally, I dared turn my attention to the zero column. I'd scanned up and down several times before I saw it. Fourth from the bottom, in blue biro, was two hundred and eighty seven: two, eight, seven. I stared at it: two, eight, seven. Two hundred and eighty seven. It didn't change. I hadn't misread it. It was there for everyone to see. Fern's number! Our number! We had our clear round! It didn't matter that tens and tens of other people had clear rounds. It didn't matter that this was the simplest course of the entire Festival. We had our clear round, and we would have our rosette; a rosette for genuine, top-class, Kennel Club Open Agility!

Then Janet got hers! Sandy put her arms around us and we all three jumped up and down like Olympic medal winners! I forgot about Colin. I forgot about the rest of our group, as Janet and I made our gleeful way to the presentation. Was I being selfish when, at that moment, I couldn't give a damn about anyone else?

Memories of that presentation remain as fresh as the soft breeze which sighed across the field. They remain as warm as the sun's rays which beamed on our tiny triumph. I suppose it was bound to be emotional. I sat on the grass with my arm around the muscular shoulders of my determined partner who had fought her way back into Life against all the odds and who still fought this dreadful disease which was a part of her, and I knew that there was no one else at that presentation who had more right to be proud of their dog.

Judge Queenie Teather made it special for everyone. This lovely lady knew that for many of her rosette winners, it would be the first time, indeed, for some perhaps the only time. So she made everyone sit on the grass, and gave a little speech about beginnings and pride and enjoyment. Then she not only presented all the place rosettes, but every single one of the clears, too. She must have smiled, said something encouraging and shook hands with getting on for a hundred people!

"Two eight seven, Brenda Tilsley with Fossdyke Illusion!"

It was the fourth time I had heard that announcement and it was the best time.

This rosette had two layers. Its outer frill was brilliant blue, the inner, pristine white. The ribbons trailed a long way down my notice board, as it shone from pride of place at the very top. "Norfolk Starters Agility Festival", it proclaimed in silver letters with those magical words, "Clear Round" circled beneath.

But now my appetite had been whetted! Was this clear round merely a "flash-in-the-pan"? Sandy knew of two dogs who had actually won out of Starters, one without ever having gained a place before and one who had never even been clear! In Intermediate, of course, they were totally out-classed and their handlers had a thoroughly miserable time. Was our clear one such fluke? Now I wanted a second rosette at least as much as I had wanted the first. I wanted proof that we could deliver!

The season was well over halfway through and Cardinal's Hill had their final show of the year. As soon as we arrived, to my delight, I spotted two Flatcoats! Fern, naturally, did the same! John, from somewhere rural in Suffolk, told me he'd always had Flatcoats in Agility.

"Never won, but we enjoy it!"

In the morning's Starters Jumping, we were almost home and still clear, when Fern suddenly veered off track, nose glued to the ground. She returned immediately on command, but precious seconds had been lost. We were clear, but not fast enough for a place and Cardinal's Hill did not give clear round rosettes.

The afternoon's Starters Agility was the final class, and we were drawn last to run. Practically everyone had already left for home when the final ten were called. Only handlers who believed they might have secured a place in the afternoon classes were left. As the queue shortened, I got into conversation with the bubbly, dark haired, girl immediately in front. She was on the end of a lead holding a Giant Schnauzer, a breed I had never before seen at Agility. Sharon, from the well-respected Scunthorpe club, was between Border Collies, and keeping her hand in with her brother's pet.

"She's useless!" she said, grinning from ear to ear, "but she enjoys it and its good fun. Gives her something to do. Stops her taking lumps out of things."

The queue grew shorter, my nerves more keen.

"I'm just hoping we go clear."

Sharon laughed again.

"You'll do a lot better than me! We've no chance! Greta'll wreck it!"

That unimaginably awful prospect didn't seem to bother her one little bit and how I envied that attitude!

With much cajoling and by sheer muscle, Sharon settled her charge on the start line, then called to the judge.

"Would you mind if I smack her on the nose if I have to?"

Competitors who deliberately touch their dog are eliminated. The judge hadn't missed the preparation and with a wry smile, shook his head.

"Sorry about this!" and she was off.

Greta downed pole after pole! Finally enticed up the A-frame with a mix of threats and encouragements, she then refused to come down! In spite of Greta's antics, it was nevertheless impressive handling. Sharon never lost her cool. She kept her eyes and mind fixed resolutely on her dog. Once down from the A-frame, Greta headed for the ring entrance. Sharon grabbed her from behind, delivered the promised smack on the nose, then turned for the see-saw. At the end of a very long day, the poor judge didn't know whether to laugh or cry! He was tired, he wanted to go home and with only one dog left to run, his course was being demolished, piece by piece! Greta negotiated the see-saw correctly and Sharon permitted herself a whoop of delight. Another pole then hit the ground, but the weaves began smoothly, if very slowly, until Greta became bored near the end and wandered off. Sharon took hold of her scruff and led her through the rest. Three more jumps; one cleared (another whoop) one barged flat, a final pole sent flying, and they were home. It is still, by far, the finest course demolition job I have ever seen!

I was so sorry I didn't get the chance to speak to Sharon afterwards. I would love to have asked her advice on how to develop such confidence to quell my rampant nerves.

We waited ages for the course to be re-built. It wasn't just a case of replacing top poles; whole wings had to be realigned and re-paced to their correct positions. I grew cold and massaged Fern's thighs to keep her muscles warm.

But as I waited, I realised Greta's demolition had generated something approaching confidence in me; added to which, there were only two or three people watching. Perhaps things would go all right.

"In your own time."

Fern immediately began to scratch! Then she settled, and we were off!

In that round, I was aware only of Fern and of our direction. I was so surprised at how quickly the finish came round, that I was convinced I must have missed some of the course. Otherwise, I thought we were clear.

"Pity you weren't next to last!" the judge remarked wryly as he passed on his way back to the hut while I was re-attaching Fern's lead.

Flatcoat John suddenly appeared at my shoulder.

"Brilliant! Brilliant! You'll get a place!"

A place? What? Me? What ridiculousness was this?

"We won't!"

"You will! Why not?"

"Well," I searched for an excuse for my conviction, "we wouldn't be fast enough."

"She's one of the fastest Flatties I've ever seen! Look, they're placing to twelve, and up to you, there'd only been eleven clears. You'll get a place."

I'll get a place? I began to make my way towards the hut. I'll get a place? Hope swelled into my lungs, forcing my breathing into deep, giant breaths. I felt light-headed. Please, please may it be true.

"Please, God, if I do get a place, don't let it be twelfth! Let it be eleventh, not twelfth. I don't want to be the one that just got in. But I will, if I have to."

Just? It had been a small class as Agility classes go, but I knew already that Fern must have beaten over ninety dogs.

"If you could make it single figures, God, if you could just make us ninth...." Tears stung my eyes at the very thought.

We reached the front of the hut. I wanted them to hurry. It was time to feed Fern.

I tried not to pray again. God had much more important things to deal with than the hopes of one woman for her dog, and hadn't He already answered my prayers?

The sun came out for the first time as it began to sink towards the horizon. Please let us be ninth. Everyone seemed to know someone else to talk to, but Fern and I stood quite alone. Flatcoat John must have gone. Please let us be ninth.

The dark haired woman came out of the hut with the judge and a list.

We weren't twelfth, nor were we eleventh. Ninth came and went and my hopes began to fade. Eighth, seventh: Flatcoat John must have it wrong. We must have been faulted.

"Fifth. Brenda Tilsley with Fossdyke Illusion."

Leaving Cardinal's Hill, I turned left, not for home, but for Margaret's. Fern could eat her tea there. As I drove, I couldn't stop smiling, yet what I really wanted to do, was to cry! I wanted to shed tears, to shout our triumph for everyone to hear! It was like that wonderful drive back from Whitegates after our visit to Christopher Day. My feisty, determined dog had taken on other dogs, who had nothing wrong with them, who'd never had anything wrong with them and had left all but four trailing in her wake! The stinging tears threatened to overwhelm and engulf me in a dangerous and delicious triumph.

Margaret understood. My joy was hers.

When we reached home later that evening, I rang Sandy, trying to keep my voice calm and level. Her reply was odd, almost as if she somehow knew.

"Can't talk now. I'm getting ready. I'm going out. I'll call round as I go. Half an hour."

I placed the rosette on the kitchen worktop, and covered it with an old sun hat I sometimes wore in the garden.

"I've something to show you," I said, when Sandy bounded through the kitchen door.

I led her to stand in front of the worktop and slowly lifted the hat. Two long, pale pink ribbons came into view.

"Ah...?"

The deep pink outer frill of the rosette emerged.

"Oh!"

I whipped off the hat, revealing the large, black number five. Sandy rushed to Fern.

"Oooh, you little beauty! You absolute smasher! You super dog! What an absolutely super dog!"

Then she turned to hug me, her face wreathed in smiles of pure delight.

"Brenda, I'm so pleased for you, so pleased. If anyone deserves it, you do."

I will always treasure that compliment, even though I don't agree with it, but all the fuss and hugs, cuddles and love from someone she respected and adored, were I'm sure, Fern's greatest reward of all!

CHAPTER EIGHTEEN

The phone rang unexpectedly just after midday when I'd returned from work.

"I'm sorry, but Gordon won't be coming round tonight."

I didn't recognise the woman's voice. She spoke in the carefully modulated tones of someone who thought the connection was bad.

"He's had an accident and he's in hospital."

My heart began to race.

"This is his mother, by the way. He fell off the steam engine at the museum last night and hit his head. The specialist's coming to see him this afternoon, so we'll know more then."

My stomach lurched. Specialist! A head injury! But the voice continued, seemingly unperturbed

"He thought I should let you know. We'll have to see what happens this afternoon. Bye-ee."

I was shattered! I hadn't liked to quiz her for fear of adding to her worry, yet she had seemed quite unmoved! Should I ring the hospital?

But I didn't even know which ward he was in, and they wouldn't tell "a friend" anything. The afternoon dragged. Should I ring his mother? There were too many Gibsons in the phone book. Would she ring me again?

"Specialist"; the title hammered round and round in my mind. At about half past three, the phone rang again.

"They've let me out. I'm sorry about tonight."

Gordon sounded so very weary.

"I'll come round tomorrow. I feel a bit rough now, but I'm all right. I've broken my collar bone."

My relief turned to indignation.

"They don't keep you in for a broken collar bone!"

"I banged my head as well. That's why they kept me in. Overnight,

178

with me living alone. I got concussion. It wasn't very nice," he added quietly.

How ashamed I felt that I'd spoken so roughly! I made him promise to go to bed early, and said that instead, I would call to see him tomorrow.

Watching T.V. that night, I found it difficult to concentrate. The thought of what life would be like without Gordon kept interrupting. Lying awake in bed, it was the same. I had grown used to him; to his voice, the boyish, slightly crooked grin, the dry humour and to the knowledge that he was, simply there.

I remembered Margaret's laughter, a month or two ago.

"Nothing going on?"

And now, suddenly, I knew she had been right to laugh.

It was nearing the end of the season, and our final sortie was to the East Of England Show. All the Agility rings attracted large numbers of spectators from members of the public, but we didn't earn any applause in the morning's competition.

The afternoon's jumping course had been set up before the lunch break, so there was over an hour in which to walk it; and I walked it! And walked and walked and walked! Since that glorious, to me at any rate, fifth in Lincoln, we had achieved nothing! I began to wonder if it really had been a flash-in-the-pan, a fluke. I imagined my T.D.T.C.fellows might even be thinking the same. I wanted another place desperately, not for myself, but for Fern. Her talent merited recognition and I usually let her down. So I kept walking that course. Often, I was the only one out there, taking my imaginary dog over the jumps while the real one watched from outside the ring. I paced between the obstacles, worked out which foot would be where, which direction my body would face, where my arms would be and crouched to get the dog's eye view. I knew that course inside out!

The beginning was pure George. Four jumps, each set well to the right of the previous one, with the fourth being the front side of a "square" of jumps, from which the dog was to exit over the jump on the left side. I thought this would pose huge problems for competitors and so it did. Waiting in the queue, I watched handler after handler get into a terrible muddle.

"Over! Heel!"

"Over! This way!" as each took a jump straight on, tried to turn their dog, square up to the next and waste seconds. Then came the attempts to prevent the dog going straight on through the square. If one could handle only with the dog on the left, then there were two options. With a very slow dog, handlers could run round the jump at the square's far side and towards the exit jump on the left, to encourage their dog, now inside the square, to turn and jump out over the correct number five. With dogs of more normal speed, the most favoured option was to enter the square with, or preferably marginally before the dog and try to block off the way directly ahead and somehow draw or send it out over the correct jump. This attempt to turn within the square often resulted in a collision between handler and dog or even with one of the sides of the square itself, the result of which was total confusion! On the rare occasions a dog was prevented from exiting over a wrong jump, it lost so much momentum, imprisoned within the square, that clearing any jump was virtually impossible.

Those who could handle their dog on the right, had still begun the round with their dog on the classic left. As the dog jumped number four onto the square, they crossed behind the airborne dog and in front of jump four. This had to be timed immaculately, or the result was that the dog slammed on the anchors and didn't jump number four into the square at all, but turned to follow the handler, jump number six and be eliminated. If the handler managed to prevent six being jumped out of sequence, the resultant confusion often still resulted in elimination, or so upset the dog that there was disaster immediately afterwards.

From my increasingly nerve-wracked place in the queue, I saw no one attempt what I had planned. I must be wrong. No one else saw the course as I did, not even those who, like me, could handle from either side.

"In your own time."

With the timekeeper's words, my lunch hour plans finally evaporated into the thin autumn air.

We faced the first jump. I was about to remove Fern's lead, when she began her scratching routine. This now seemed to be something she had to do before every competitive round. She never did it in training! But it did give me another moment to think. Why should I do what the others had done? I'd seen it didn't work. Why deliberately repeat mistakes? That's what would be stupid, I told myself, not that if I was unsuccessful in trying a different approach.

Fern finished her scratching. I screwed up my courage, turned round on the spot, walked several steps to my left and set her up again, but this time, she was on my right, and at an acute angle to the start line, well to the left of the first jump. What lay ahead of her now, was a straight row of jumps, "wider" but time saving, and I would already be on her left to draw her correctly out of the square. Pure, simple, George and it worked perfectly! Through the weaves, she was the fastest I had ever known her and I heard that appreciative, laughing murmur from spectators for the very first time. Two jumps, side by side; over one, turn immediately and back over the other in the exact opposite direction; no problem. Her paws thumped a furious drumbeat through the tunnel. The long jump was cleared with inches to spare. I managed to time changing sides behind her correctly, to negotiate the square from the opposite direction; a few more jumps, then we were finished and we were clear!

The icing on the cake came later:

"Ninth; Brenda Tilsley with Fossdyke Illusion."

I tried to work out which was best. Was it fifth from about one hundred and ten, or ninth from one hundred and ninety? Did it matter? That pale blue and white rosette proved our previous place had been no lucky fluke. It might be the plainest rosette I had, but it was my favourite. It has always remained so.

The season was over. How the year had flown! A crisp autumn arrived and dissolved through dull November into winter.

Now it was almost Christmas again: Fern's fourth! Of course there was no hesitation about fetching the decorations down from the loft, only expectation and happiness weaving their warm, secure spell!

One evening, whilst watching T.V., my attention was distracted by Fern, who had begun sniffing her way along the row of Christmas cards displayed in the bay window. Reaching one end, she turned and sniffed her way back again, then stopped at a card near the centre. Reaching out carefully, she turned her head to one side, picked it up, and brought it towards me. Tail wagging, she pushed it into my lap. Bemused, I opened the card. Inside it read, "Love from Sandy and K9's."

This year, there was so much more to do! More cards to send, more presents to buy, more celebrations to attend, with Fern of course, and, when I stopped to think about it, because of Fern! Gordon had been the proverbial tower of strength all year, readily offering the solution to any problem: what could I buy him to show my appreciation?

"Mum says would you like to come to Christmas dinner?"

This, surely, was serious stuff?

Apparently there was a gathering of the Gibson clan every year, but I would be the only non-family member there. I didn't think I would feel able to relax. I might feel as if I was on exhibition. I was an outsider after all. I also wondered if Gordon's mother had invited me out of imagined pity as much as kindness or interest, so with as much courtesy as I could muster, I declined the invitation. I invited Gordon to come for tea afterwards instead.

"Should we make it dinner then? I've never much appetite left for tea."

Another Gordon solution! But whatever would his family think?

On Christmas Day, I did all the things I had done last year, and the year before that. It was a beautiful morning in Hartsholme Park, but this time, there were three of us.

How I wish those pundits who would have us believe that dogs are little more than machines, driven inexorably by basic instinct, had witnessed an incident that Christmas afternoon! When we realised we hadn't seen Fern for some time, we called her. No response. We tried again: still nothing. We looked in the garden. The gate was fastened, she couldn't have got out. Back indoors, we looked in one room at a time. I found her in the lounge. She was sitting with her back to the door, hunched over an object on the floor.

"What you do?"

She didn't budge. I peered over her bent head. Right between her front paws, was a box, inadvertently left from the night before. Drool dripped steadily from her jowls, onto its lid as she stared fixedly at that most wonderful, most desirous of all things, chocolates! The box lid was soaked.

How long had she been there before we first missed her? How long had she fought this temptation? I picked up the soggy box, tossed it onto a cabinet, and then got down on my knees to hug her. Surely this was the triumph of intelligent learning over instinct?

Not long after Christmas, snow fell quite heavily during the night. It was Fern's first real sight of the cold, white stuff. She stared at it from the back step, glanced up at me, took a few steps to sniff it closely, then walked into it just as if nothing was any different. But it wasn't long before she discovered its true potential!

First, there was jumping around in it and scattering it all over, chasing the tiny bits which rolled along the top of undisturbed snow. Then there was racing through it, nose down, to create a growing bow wave. There was rolling in it or even trying to eat it, especially those large flakes as they wafted down deliciously from a leaden sky. Best of all was when Mum made it into snowballs, because they exploded when snatched from the air! Much as I loved to watch Fern's virtual aerobatics, this kind of play had to be limited because of the amount of air she couldn't help but ingest.

One afternoon, Glen, Mark, Scott and I tried to build what we intended to be the world's biggest snowman in the middle of Phillip Court. Fern had other ideas. She would watch, tip of her tail wagging slowly. As the snow mound grew, so did her tail wagging and when the mound reached an acceptable height, she would shoulder-charge it flat, so we'd have to start all over again!

Eventually, a three-foot high cretinous apparition rose on Glen's front lawn. It looked like a cross between a rabbit and a bear. We named it the rabear.

A giant snowball fared better, because it grew more quickly and was protected from Fern's demolition charges by the movements of its creators. But that didn't stop her trying! One gloriously hilarious moment saw her completely spread-eagled right across the top, all four feet well clear of the ground!

How she loved snow! Our long, silent walks by the river were excursions in a magical land. I felt sorry for those huddled indoors, who couldn't share these innocent joys of a true spirit. Fern found the deepest snow, and always forged her way through. She never retraced her steps, no matter how tough it became. But that was the Cupboard Top Kid!

Of course, the snow could not stay forever. As it melted, one small hollow near the hedge on the lower Fen Lane field, held on to its precious store for days, even when the rest of the field had turned green. The moment I released Fern's lead, she would gallop to that spot to bury her nose, roll and play.

One morning, it had gone. I caught up with her as she stood, staring into the hollow. Head down, tail still, she was the picture of dejection! She looked up. Her tail began to wag. Mum was here! She would make it right! Fern looked back to the hollow, then again at me. I saw the familiar frowning look she always gave when she wasn't getting her own way.

"Snow! Put it back! At once!"

And I wished so much that I could, but there was to be no more snow that year.

It had been a very long time since I had taken Fern into the Show ring, but as the snowdrops died and daffodils began to flower, I decided we should have another attempt. Perhaps she'd like it this time and I had thought out a strategy that might help calm my rampant nerves.

I was delighted to find the gun dogs outside, where they should be and the sun was surprisingly warm when we took our place in the ring. I tried to relax and let Fern sniff her surrounds as the other entrants came in. Yes, my strategy felt right. I would not care what the others might think. I would do only what was right by my dog, for I was George! My strategy was to think George!

Fern was full of herself as we waited for our examination. She gazed around, tail wagging in a blur of excitement. As the judge bent to examine her, I thought George as hard as I could. Gone were the Brenda thoughts:

"I hope she keeps still. I hope he likes her. I hope I don't do anything daft."

Instead, there were George thoughts:

"This is my dog. She's great, isn't she? You're lucky to have such quality in your class today. I know you'll appreciate it!"

Fern strode her triangle with power and aplomb and I felt pleased and proud as we resumed our place. But I'd found it very hard work pretending to be something I most definitely wasn't! I felt happy enough, but hot and exhausted!

As the judge continued along the line, I was able to relax, and crouched down to play with Fern. I was so relieved it was over, but Fern had actually seemed to enjoy herself today, perhaps because I'd handled her better. Maybe we should try again.

I was still dreaming and we were still playing when I became aware that all the other entrants had lined up, statue-like, for the judge's final inspection! Red-faced and with that familiar hot sensation of embarrassment prickling down my back, I struggled to my feet, stealing a glance at the judge. Yes, he had been waiting for me! The entire class had been waiting! Brenda came back with a vengeance! This was dreadful. And it had all been going so well! There and then I made up my mind never to enter the show ring again. I wasn't cut out for it. I was just too stupid. I looked back at the judge. He had not moved and when our eyes met, he raised his hand and pointed to the centre of the ring.

I looked. No one was there. I fiddled with the lead to give myself a moment to think. Applause had broken out and I heard brief cheers from two different voices on opposite sides of the ring. The judge's action seemed to meet with spectators' approval. But what did his action mean? I dared to look up again.

It was quite a plain rosette compared to the Agility ones. Only one layer of frills, but the gold lettering in the centre was splendid. Once outside the ring, I fastened it to Fern's collar. It looked so dramatic, but then, is there a more striking combination than black and scarlet?

I was so very proud! I couldn't wait to tell someone, anyone! Today, I knew that Margaret would be out, but Glen and Scot were thrilled to bits with Fern's success. Even Mark managed a wide smile and patted her elegant head. After feeding her, the first thing I did was to rearrange the notice board. The red rosette now occupied pride of place at the top, flanked by our two agility places. Beneath them, came the clear and the exemption rosettes. Not wanting to take my eyes away from feasting on the multi-coloured rewards of Fern's talents, I made the ubiquitous cup of tea, chose a chocolate biscuit and perched on the kitchen stool, continuing to gaze and gloat and marvel at the growing collection of rosettes on the cork notice board.

Of course, there was a down side to this triumph. It was months before I realised I had yet again made a colossal boob. We should never have been home that afternoon! All class winners go forward to compete for Best of Breed. Best of Breed goes forward for Best in Show. But there I was sitting at home, drinking tea. Just how much of a novice is it possible to be?

It was the following year before I dared show my face in the ring again! I was afraid someone might remember that I hadn't appeared for Best of Breed, even though logic told me that was ridiculous. And even if they had, so what? I took it all so seriously; I just couldn't see the funny side of my mistakes. It never even occurred to me either, that someone could have been very grateful indeed!

However, I scoured the schedules, chose the show and we set off once more!

This time, we were back inside, but something was different.

Watching the class immediately before ours, I became aware of the rumblings of discontent amongst the onlookers. The judge's decisions were not pleasing the crowd. This was the first time, as a competitor, that I had encountered the sporting phenomenon whereby the eyesight, ancestry, and/or financial arrangements of the judge are questioned. When it became our turn to offer ourselves to such unpopular scrutiny, I was wondering if I really did want to win!

I needn't have worried! Whilst we all stood, pretty much cramped and certainly immobile around the perimeter of the ring, the judge selected about half the entrants, approximately fifteen, and called us out to the centre. She then asked us to leave the ring and continued judging the remaining dogs.

"Thrown out with the rubbish!"

One man in particular was very angry. Most handlers accepted their fate as part of the ups and downs of Showing, but sometimes, a few voiced their feelings more strongly.

"The best dogs're out here!" a woman hissed in an indignant stage whisper, gold-rimmed spectacles bouncing on her nose, "never seen anything like it!"

There were murmurs of agreement.

"Look at the stop on that dog," another man in a thick sweater bristling with small metallic badges, gestured at the ring, "more like a b*** Pug!"

Mutterings of agreement again followed, which inspired Gold-rim to louder comment.

"Disgusting, that's what it is! Don't agree with mine, but that's just me. That bitch should never leave any ring without a place! Never! Not anywhere!"

"That bitch" was Fern.

Feeling somewhat embarrassed and certainly out of my depth, I melted into the background. As we picked our way through the crowd, I noticed the class had been judged. The winner was a black dog with slanting eyes.

"Eyes; not obliquely placed:" states the breed standard.

But Fern continued to love her Agility. In the following seasons, clear round and place rosettes began to creep their multi-coloured way down the board, and I enjoyed nothing more than having to re-arrange them to accommodate another!

Whenever work permitted, Gordon would be with us, but the very first time he came to a competition, we learned that he could not actually watch!

Fern had been going extremely well. Over three-quarters of the course had been completed, fast and faultless. Then the direction in which she must work turned directly away from where she had last seen Gordon. She stopped dead, looking round and scenting the air.

"Come! Fern, come!"

Her head twitched this way and that. She looked back at me, then out over the spectators. The clock ticked on. Realising what was happening, Gordon had dived for cover behind a marquee.

"Fern! Come!"

Nothing like this had ever happened before, not even in her early training. She took a step towards me, glanced over her shoulder, then took a few more tentative steps in my direction. Suddenly her mind was made up. She turned and raced from the ring.

I looked round at the judge to apologise. He looked surprised, even sympathetic! Strangely, I wasn't embarrassed. It was clearly not the undisciplined action of a dog entered into competition before being ready. It was obvious that she had been looking for someone; someone more important to her than a round of agility.

Moments later, she and Gordon were re-united as they reached the car simultaneously. Several spectators who witnessed the incident sympathised that their husband/brother/sister/ whatever, could never watch because their dog would always leave the ring to go to them. Henceforth, we had to leave Gordon in the car. He would then sneak off to watch us if there was a suitable vantage point and be back at the car before we returned.

George had now found a better location in which to run his school. The field was drier, completely flat, more accessible and with good parking. It was even within walking distance had we wanted to expend energy in that way! Many more dogs and their owners began to arrive, but Fern still remained the only Flatcoat.

I was not to know that as my birthday month of February came round (yet again!) my life would change once more. Oddly, Gordon had insisted that he would come round that Wednesday after work. Odd, because Wednesday evenings were sacrosanct and always spent in the company of Sylvie, Harriet, Maud and John. I had never known him to miss their company before. It was the French aristocrat, Sylvie, who had hurled him to the floor and put him in hospital! I had warned him not to trifle with her affections again, but here he was, ignoring the potential violence within her temperamental eight tons, in favour of me! I was surprised he could tear himself away from the museum and its steam engines! What was wrong with coming on Tuesday or Thursday? They weren't the fourteenth were they? They weren't Valentine's Day!

The evening began much as they always did: a welcoming cup of coffee and a "rough house" with an ecstatic Fern, then suddenly it was ten o'clock and I still hadn't found out why he had been so determined to come round. I had a lovely card, a heart-shaped balloon and we had made great inroads into the box of hand made chocolates he had brought. Perhaps it was just that.

Illusion

We were side by side on the sofa, when, with a finesse I had no idea he possessed, Gordon slid smoothly to the floor, went down on one knee, turned to face me and took one of my hands within the both of his.

"Will you marry me?"

I gasped. I was taken aback, astounded! Confirmed bachelor meets career woman! We'd both been on our own so long! I sat there, open-mouthed, while he returned my gaze calmly and with patience. My mouth became dry. I thought of Mum. I wondered what Margaret would say. Could Gordon and I both find the necessary give and take to make it work, I wondered? Was either or both of us too set in our ways? All kinds of logical reasons to maintain the status quo flooded into my mind. Why change what was working? Gordon interrupted my whirling thoughts

"You don't have to say, not now. If you want to think-"

I'd always thought that my head ruled my heart. It would be sensible to wait, wouldn't it? To be sure. Not this time!

"No. Yes!"

We hugged each other. A fine, black muzzle pushed and wriggled its way into the centre of the embrace. Gordon returned to the sofa.

"I suppose we ought to get a ring now," he said, with the enthusiasm of a man who thought rings were really something only to do with pistons!

CHAPTER NINETEEN

Within a few days, we had fixed the date: July 26th, five months away. Some may have thought we were rushing. Hadn't we already waited long enough for each other?

First we told Gordon's parents. They happily accepted the forthcoming marriage of their only son as if it were an everyday occurrence! From there, we drove straight to Margaret's. I had phoned first, just to make sure she was in. If she was surprised at our unexpected visit, she didn't show it. I thought her face a little more lined, her voice a little quieter, as though it were more effort to speak, as her awful disease took its relentless toll.

We exchanged the usual pleasantries.

"We've something to tell you."

She hugged and kissed us both, then bent down to a cupboard in her sideboard -and extracted a bottle of wine. Festooned from its neck were several long, narrow white ribbons and a white card.

"Congratulations on your engagement. With much love for your future happiness from Margaret and David."

As Gordon drove home, I kept my face averted so he did not see the tears filling my eyes. Why did Margaret have to suffer so much? Why had she only more pain to look forward to? Why did she stand near the End, whilst I stood at a Beginning?

There was someone else I ought to tell, too. At sometime I had already mentioned the "man in my life," but I went there in person to tell Mary about the coming wedding. Fern of course, remained outside in the car.

This time, Mary approved whole-heartedly of my plans and I was instructed to bring Gordon to meet her as soon as possible. She was full of enthusiastic suggestions for our wedding; more like the Mary I knew. In fact, I was wary of this, for it would have been so easy to allow her to take over completely! She would have master-minded a marvellous occasion with consummate ease, but it wouldn't necessarily have been what I wanted, so I beat a hasty retreat to the car. Mary came with me. She said that I must not leave Fern outside next time.

Three weeks passed, before Gordon and I stood on her doorstep. I was promptly sent back for Fern, who amazingly, was allowed free run of the entire bungalow and garden! As we talked, Fern explored, unhindered. Eventually, she returned to the lounge and lay across the doorway into the garden, one forepaw curled beneath in her usual manner, the other stretched elegantly across in front of her chest. The sun streamed onto her shining coat and her fine head was profiled against the bright lawn. Used to Fern's beauty, even I permitted myself an inward smile of pleasure that day. But Mary had seen the same.

"You know, I used to think that Chico was the most beautiful...but really....." her voice trailed away. Suddenly, she was on her knees beside Fern.

"Oh, Fern, I was so horrible to you, so horrible and you've brought your mistress so much happiness. Can you ever forgive me?"

Gordon and I gazed open mouthed at each other in total astonishment.

Although always friendly towards Mary at their subsequent meetings, Fern would never greet her with the unbridled enthusiasm with which she greeted everyone else and which is so typical of the Flatcoat.

An amethyst birthstone, surrounded by diamonds! The ring had been a surprise and was entirely Gordon's choice, but we had both been disappointed when it needed to be sent away to be made smaller. Now it was back and where it should be!

I wore it at a Tuesday morning agility session. Sandy was first to notice and let out a wild shriek.

"You're not! You are!"

The others had been pleased to see Gordon on his day off and must have thought the bottle of wine something to do with Fern's fifth birthday. But this was a double celebration!

They were all so pleased, even thrilled! I told of the classical romantic proposal. We promised wedding invitations for everyone. They asked things like where were we going to live and were we going to stay in Lincoln and Colin agreed to be our video-photographer.

The sun shone, we ate the traditional chocolate cake and drank wine. It was a lovely morning, sitting there, discussing future plans with the wonderful people who had first become my friends and were now friends to us both. I thought I must be the luckiest person in the whole wide world.

Perhaps it had been with the intention of keeping my feet on the ground that I entered another Breed Show. Maybe I courted some disappointment at that time just because I was so happy. To be so happy felt unreal, almost wrong. I hadn't done anything to deserve all the wonderful things that were happening. Surely something would come along to spoil such riches? But if I entered in Breed then it would be like taking out insurance to safeguard all the rest of the delights that were raining down on me. If I made this my disappointment, then everything else might remain safe.

Perhaps it was this strange attitude that allowed me to be a little more relaxed in the ring. I wore my engagement ring of course. I wondered how noticeable it was, for it looked very new, and very, very sparkly! Each time I moved my hand, it twinkled that I was loved and special to someone and that was a wonderful feeling. With such a feminine phenomenon constantly reminding me that I was lucky to be me, it was virtually impossible to "think George" again, however hard I tried!

So there were three people on the other end of Fern's lead that day; the nervous me, the loved me and the pretend George! A combination for total confusion!

Yet we won! Again! And this time, I did know to remain in order to go forward to Best of Breed.

Of course we had to wait for all Flatcoat classes to finish. There was also a lunch break and by the time B.O.B. was announced, we had been hanging around for almost five hours. Fern's "emergency rations," which I always kept in the car, had been used and she was bored stiff. I'd taken her for a walk around the entire perimeter of the showground to occupy her, but in that wide-open grassland she had been on lead and that, in her eyes, had been unforgivable!

Standing in the class winners' line-up, there was only one dog whose tail did not wag. Only one whose head was not up and alert. I tried to gee her up, but Fern remained resolutely detached. She did perk up however, when the judge came across.

"Oh, I'm so glad you've cheered up," he said.

We weren't Best of Breed. Neither were we Reserve Best, but the judge invited us to follow those two dogs on their lap of honour, explaining that the decision had been very close and that I really must try to "Get more life into my bitch," who was "very lethargic in the ring."

If only he knew the half of it!

As soon as there was a decent spell of weather, Gordon introduced us to his caravan. Fern took to the life as a duck to water! But the holiday was the proverbial steep learning curve for him, for he found out how well Fern knew her own mind and just how determined she could be!

A fine but cool afternoon found us strolling beside the Carsington reservoir. Yachts with jewel-like sails billowing in the breeze passed in the distance, whilst a couple of rowing dinghies creaked their more leisurely way nearby. Of course, Fern raced at once into the water. In a small bay, she wacked first one marvellous foot, then another onto the water in a rhythm of delight, making as much splash and noise as she could. She swam beneath the overhanging trees and through the reeds, but her favourite game was trying to catch the droplets from the handfuls of water scooped up and thrown at her by Gordon. She wanted more and more, but this game had to finish, for, as ever, we needed to be wary of how much air would be entering her gut.

We continued our walk, with Fern now on the lead to ensure a quiet time. But she was not happy, and when we chanced upon another sheltered inlet, her demands to be allowed back in the water grew more insistent.

"No."

Gordon pulled her back and we tried to continue.

"No!"

He shortened her lead, gave a firm tug and tried to move on.

But Fern was having none of it! With a sound halfway between a bark and howl, she threw herself onto her back and raged, punching the air with all four legs! We stared at her in disbelief; this twisting, twirling demented creature venting her frustration. She was throwing a tantrum, a full-blown, histrionic tantrum! Somehow, we got her up and turned inland. Her indignation started to subside at once, to be replaced by the frown, but by the time we reached the caravan, her sunny nature had re-emerged. What an awesome display of Cupboard Top Syndrome! Yet I admired her for it and loved her all the more!

Plans for our wedding now began to take over.

Mum-in-law-to-be, Audrey, would make the cake. Gordon and I visited a wedding emporium, where he instantly selected the invitations. Rather elegant and unusual too: maroon lettering on a cream ground. But I did wonder if his choice could have been influenced by the fact that they were in the first book he took and that it fell open at that page! How much more simple are these things for a man! I realised also, that men can get away with "the suit" (weddings, funerals, assorted formalities) but I would need something very special. I wanted to look like the bride, not the bride's mother, but I didn't want to look like mutton dressed as lamb either! I needed time to think. So we just ordered the invitations and left with a book on etiquette.

Gordon took over the formalities for the Register Office, while I scoured venues for the reception and found that of all places, the pavilion at Fen Lane was available for hire! The main hall was just the right size, there were plenty of small tables and lots of chairs, a big kitchen with every facility and we would be allowed to hang decorations and to have it all day. Perfect! Then I had to find a caterer. A local firm was the most impressive and we decided to carry Gordon's maroon and cream theme through to the hall and table decorations and even to the icing on the cake!

We enjoyed our second holiday in the caravan, a long weekend that also included an Agility show and one I won't forget in a hurry, because I was on the receiving end of a strong dose of the renowned Flatcoat humour!

It must have been at Elementary level, for the rigid tunnel was fully stretched. We approached straight on, at speed.

"Throoough"

But Fern ignored the gaping entrance right in front of her and swerved to gallop down the left side. Absolutely dumbfounded, I stopped. At the far end of the tunnel, she slammed on the anchors, turned to look back at me, and then dived into its exit, emerging from the entrance to race up to me, pink tongue hanging out. I will swear forever that she was laughing!

I remembered a car sticker I'd once seen: "You wouldn't understand. It's a Flatcoat thing."

Preparations for The Day continued. The cake was cooked and maturing in Audrey's capacious larder and I began to attend fittings for my outfit. Long accustomed to letting down hems or sleeves and taking in waists when buying off the peg, I decided to push the boat out and to have it made! Armed with my own sketches, I plucked up the courage to enter a very swank shop at the top of the high street.

My design of a starkly plain, sleeveless, knee-length dress in cream, topped by a maroon short-sleeved lace jacket with a curved hem, met with the approval of the proprietress; apart from the fact that she couldn't find any suitable weight maroon lace anywhere! Suppliers had cream lace, blue lace, black or scarlet lace, even gold or silver lace and each with its own name! There was a second gold lace too, a filigree of fern fronds, unsurprisingly called "Fern", but I was disappointed to find the old gold dingy and unattractive. It would have been so appropriate! I settled on the scarlet. She would make the dress first, and warned me neither to lose nor gain weight!

After three weeks, and three fittings, the dress was ready. Beautifully made, it simply flowed into place, fitting perfectly. Just to make sure the chosen lace was the right one, all the alternatives were again brought out, to be draped, in turn, from my shoulder. I hadn't wanted to bother, especially when the dull, old gold lace made its reappearance. But this time, what a transformation! Against the cream of my dress, it looked superb; the two complemented each other perfectly. My jacket would, after all, and so appropriately, be "Fern."

I wanted to find something to make the day extra special for Mark and Scott, but pageboys were, I thought, a bit over the top for a Register Office, so what on earth could I find for two small boys in so short a ceremony? Ring Bearers! Scott could carry the rings secured to a fancy cushion (in maroon and cream) and Mark could take them from the cushion and pass them to the registrar! Both boys would feel they had equal responsibility. We practised hard.

"This is as good as it gets," I whispered irreverently to Gordon as I took my place beside him on an overcast and humid Friday. But those weren't the first words spoken at our wedding: those had been Gordon's when he'd hissed at our photographer;

"You've got your lens cap on, Colin!"

Colin's reply was not in Hindustani, nor was it a whisper and I suddenly felt an overwhelming desire to giggle as I walked in, Margaret at my side. All my meticulous planning appeared to be going up in smoke but I didn't care at all!

Everything had gone swimmingly that morning. The minute by minute timetable pinned up in the kitchen had gone without a hitch. Walk Fern at Fen Lane. Meet Gordon's family at the pavilion on the way back to check on the readiness of the hall. Ring caterers to make doubly certain they were coming and with the right stuff. Go to hairdresser. Return and prepare sandwiches for lunch. Feed Fern. Meet Martin, the husband of Gordon's youngest sister and be taken to town for make-up. Afterwards, Mary would be waiting outside the salon in her car to bring me home. The flower be-decked car was to be driven by her right-hand man, Fred and they would already have picked up Margaret. Give them all lunch. Say goodbye to Mary before she was picked up by mum and dad-in-law-to-be and taken to the Register Office. Leave Fern's next feed ready, give the door key to Margaret, then we'd both leave for the ceremony in Mary's car. Margaret would later give the key to Sandy, who, after the ceremony, would feed, then bring Fern to the Reception: after adding the special white rose to her collar!

Apart from the lens cap, apart from Fred most uncharacteristically scraping the front bumper of Mary's beautiful car and apart from two long

194

pauses caused by having to force rings onto swollen, sweating fingers, it all went like a dream!

The two boys stole the show! Scott carried the two rings on a tasselled satin cushion with the greatest solemnity, while Mark untied the ribbons and passed the rings to the registrar with enviable, unhurried confidence. Everyone assumed we were leaving on honeymoon that same day, but we managed to evade practical jokers by driving off with empty cases in the back and taking a circuitous route back home, where we skulked about until darkness began to fall. Even the Thomases opposite were unaware of our presence until we emerged in jeans and t-shirts, to fetch a fish and chip supper! We washed it down with champagne!

Immediately after our return from honeymoon, we began house hunting. Much as we both loved the bungalow and location of Phillip Court, we agreed it would be better to find "our " house and to make a fresh start. We also needed more space!

But now, we encountered a problem. Whilst Fern had always wanted to be with Gordon, we soon realised that she believed he had joined the Pack as its lowest ranked member! This was plainly evident by the manner in which she ignored his commands when they didn't happen to suit and her imperious demands that he must play, stroke, or cuddle her at every whim. Sandy had the answer.

"Sit in her bed."

Sit in her bed? Apparently, pack leaders, then the highest ranked pack members have first choice of sleeping quarters. We were incredulous, but we trusted Sandy and so, one lunchtime, Fern came trotting down the hall towards the kitchen to find Gordon sitting cross-legged in her bed, reading a newspaper. She was thunderstruck! Stopping dead in her tracks, she stared at him in total dismay. Then she backed away up the hall, took another long, hard look and returned to the lounge. Thankfully, Gordon uncoiled himself.

It was a good five minutes before Fern reappeared. She stood at the kitchen door, watching Gordon intently, the slowly wagging tip of her lowered tail betraying her anxiety. After a moment, he called her over for a cuddle. That was all that was needed. The new order had been established.

Unforeseen and sad circumstances now forced Fern into making another adjustment. It happened at her annual check-up. (Annual! How I loved that!) The waiting room was packed but unusually, there was only one vet on duty: sadly, it was Nigel.

Illusion

Following an incoming phone call and a brief consultation with the nurses, Nigel transferred to the smaller of the two surgeries, continuing to see patients there. It seemed an odd thing to do.

Suddenly, a middle-aged couple with their G.S.D. hurried in and were immediately ushered into the big surgery he had vacated. Within the minute, he joined them. Something was obviously very wrong. Every owner in the waiting room knew. It had been apparent in Nigel's preparation, and in the pale, distraught expressions of both the man and the woman. Everyone there felt the tension. No one spoke, but every single person in that room gathered their pet closer and seemed to be very busy stroking, cuddling or simply holding.

It became unnaturally quiet. Little sound came from the surgery, save the intermittent murmuring of Nigel's voice.

Suddenly, the door opened and the woman, tears streaming down her face, fled through the waiting room, to escape outside. Her husband followed, to stand distractedly in the middle of the floor, one hand in a pocket, looking around for someone, anyone, to help him in his bewilderment and misery. A nurse led him gently after his wife. Grim-faced, Nigel returned to finish his surgery from the small room.

We all knew what had happened behind that closed door. Fern knew what had happened, too, and she could see no reason for it at all. Nigel was never to be forgiven.

At subsequent meetings, she no longer greeted him with joy, but acknowledged him with great deference, even fear. She would not meet his eyes, her head and tail remained down and she was only happy when leaving the man whose skills and dedication had saved her life.

At training, we now became aware of worrying rumours that the T.D.T.C. was, unbelievably, going to close! George himself said nothing and so I dismissed the idea as preposterous.

Janet told us all about a big exemption show to be held at a country fair in the seaside town of Mablethorpe. She had already entered Jess in two Obedience classes, and many of us decided to make this a Talbot Day Out!

We were surprised at the size of the show, on the local secondary school's playing fields, but it was summer with the population swelled by an enormous number of holidaymakers. Stalls, demonstrations and all kinds of entertainments, as well as the Dog Show, kept everyone busy!

Jess won both her Obedience classes. Fern came third in hers, at a more basic level! In the so-called Fun Agility, our first place earned us money; a £5 voucher to be spent at B&Q! In fact, all the Talbot dogs came in the top ten. But poor Colin still did not have a single rosette to his name and was becoming a little dispirited.

A plan was hatched. When Louis was in the fun class for "Waggiest Tail", I would lurk, with Fern, behind the spectators then, at the appropriate moment, we would appear! All I had to do, was to make sure that Louis saw Fern, his tail would become an aerodynamic blur and the winner's rosette would be his!

But before that, was the class for Best Condition. Everyone from T.D.T.C. had entered their dog, and so it seemed, had everyone else on the field! There must have been approaching forty dogs in that ring, but the judge was undeterred. She divided us into two groups and each had to circle the ring while the others stood by. From this, she selected dogs to go forward to a second round. I noticed Colin and Louis from the other group were through.

Each dog now underwent an individual physical examination, and it was as thorough as at any breed show! Then followed another circuit of the ring, with this keen judge scrutinising every step.

To my surprise and delight, she held out her hand to us. We had won! I couldn't help but sneak a little grin to myself, wondering what the outcome might have been had the judge known that her choice suffered a chronic, life-threatening illness!

But the best was to come! Louis was placed second! At the presentation, the judge said she found the two dogs to have "outstanding musculature" but that she had given first place to the bitch because of her "superb coat".

Colin was well pleased.

"They've both got muscles because they both do agility," he explained, "and actually, you've chosen boy friend and girl friend!" he added with a grin.

The judge laughed. Perhaps Louis and Fern were not convinced the judge had really understood, so there, in front of everyone, they began a demonstration!

The duck was broken. Louis then came second in Waggiest Tail: and without Fern's help!

At the end of the day, we all headed for the beach, everyone happy with their haul of rosettes. Jess won unofficial Talbot "Scruffiest Dog" because of her habit of getting slightly damp, then rolling in dry sand, which stuck like glue. Fern of course, was Talbot "Wettest Dog"!

CHAPTER TWENTY

We found our new home! A small estate was being built on the outskirts of town and we located another bungalow at the end of another cul-de-sac! We also persuaded the builders to build the inside back to front, so that our lounge and kitchen would overlook fields instead of the road!

But at the same time, came devastating news: the T.D.T.C. really was to close. Sandy told us on one of those wonderful Tuesday mornings where training took equal place with the feelings of warm comradeship as we sat at the picnic table, sipping tea, whilst our dogs played happily together. After the initial total disbelief, I felt bereft! Not simply because there was now nowhere for us to train, but because I would lose so many good friends. No more Sandy, no more Colin or Janet or Louis and that was just the tip of the iceberg! Of course, George didn't owe us any explanation for ending it all so suddenly, but it would have been more kind and certainly more thoughtful if we'd received some warning of such a sudden and drastic step.

Sandy immediately tried to find somewhere for us all to train. There was a dog club only nine miles away at Branham, and one sunny morning, Sandy and I, with Daisy and Fern, arrived at the training ground to try out their agility section.

There were about twelve people already there, and two elderly men had a full course almost built. This looked promising! We were immediately welcomed and made to feel at ease. Sandy and I exchanged delighted glances.

Strangely, no one appeared to be in overall charge. Occasionally, the more experienced handlers might offer advice, but otherwise, people simply took turns to pilot their dogs over the whole course. After a couple of weeks, I realised with dismay, that this was all that ever happened! No set pieces, no contact practice, no exercises: this agility club seemed more like a social club!

Sandy could, of course, have begun a real training programme, but she is not the sort of person to put herself forward unless asked. And no one asked, even though they saw her expertise with Daisy and Fern. Everyone there was quite happy with the status quo, which of course, was fair enough. Sadly, it wasn't the club for us.

But I did want to stay a while to grab the rare and exotic carrot dangling before my eyes! The club gave dog-handling demonstrations, and I had been promised that Fern could be trained to take part in their Grande Finale where she would leap through blazing hoops! First, Fern and I would work with the strange looking, and evil smelling jump itself, then, once she was happy with that, the hoop would be added, and then the smell of fresh paraffin. Next, the horizontal bar would be set on fire, then it would be the turn of the hoop, and finally, both bar and hoop would be set ablaze!

Gordon and I went with them to a demo at a country fair in Derbyshire because Fern had a place in the agility team. The demo was well presented and with an excellent commentator, but the Grande Finale fell apart. Gordon had joined us to watch the promised spectacular ending, but only the second of four dogs completed the fiery run. One refused to start at all, another ran out after two jumps and the fourth, having jumped two, refused to go on! The end of the show was a disaster, and that would be what spectators remembered.

"And now, for the first time in public, Brenda and Fern will attempt the Burning Hoops! Now, you've all seen this lovely little Flatcoat in the agility, and didn't you just want to take her home with you?"
I felt my jaw drop.

"Now, if she doesn't do it, just remember that it's her very first time in public with anyone watching…."

I was totally dumbfounded. I lost what else he said. What on earth was he playing at? How could he do this, do this to Fern and me? But he continued.

"So come on then, everyone, a big round of applause for Brenda and Fern."

Spectators began to clap. We were expected in that ring.

What if Fern refused? Such an experience could totally frighten her off agility itself! Should I risk it? How dare he put me in this position! But there was a row of four agility jumps still lined up at one side of the ring. If Fern did refuse, then I could take her over those so she would be able to finish on a positive and happy note. Perhaps I should try? But what if Fern left the ring to be with Gordon? We would be jumping towards him.

I would never have attempted it had those agility jumps not been there. We walked forward. I took a route alongside the burning hoops. Fern glanced at them, mildly curious and sniffed the air. We turned to face them and I settled her just as if it were an agility competition.

"Over!"

Fern slammed on the brakes so close to the first jump I was afraid she would burn herself. The crowd aah'd their disappointment. One more try I thought, then its over the agility jumps. Laughing and tickling her ears as we went back, I turned immediately for the jumps.

"Over!"

Sandy's meticulous early training now reaped its reward. Fern jumped through all four blazing hoops. The crowd loved it and I was so proud of my bold and brave partner.

Over the tannoy, the commentator congratulated us extravagantly. It was only a long time afterwards I realised no one else from the team had said a thing!

Gordon managed to video our moment of glory. Whist I thought Fern had jumped normally, the video showed differently. Before each jump, she had put in an extra, small stride.

Tuesday mornings were kept alive at the old Whisby gravel pits. Everyone who could met there at ten o'clock with their dogs. Fern would immediately rush off on her own to the "beach" on the opposite side of a large lake, only to race back to us, minutes later, soaking wet, bark at us to hurry up, then disappear once more. She usually managed the round trip three times before we finally caught up with her! Invariably, she would be standing out in the clear water, tongue lolling from open mouth in sheer happiness whilst her wagging tail made gentle swishing sounds across the surface of the lake.

Poor Louis! His Labrador traits did not include a fondness for the wet stuff. He would fuss and fret at the water's edge whilst his girl friend swam or simply frolicked in the water making as much splash as she could.

Fern was always excellent at retrieving from or across water and never had to be taught or even encouraged. In fact, this inbred ability, allied to her individual determination could be a frightening combination. Gordon and I once watched in growing alarm from the beach at Robin Hood's Bay, as Fern surface dived repeatedly to try to retrieve a pebble thrown by a well-meaning passer-by!

But Louis could never come to terms with Fern's watery antics. Standing in the shallows, water lapping just over his feet, he would whinge and whine ad infinitum!

The search for suitable training went on. Next we tried Gainsborough, where a husband and wife duo, both experienced competition handlers, ran the Agility. This looked like being our answer, but almost as soon as we arrived, they moved house and the agility section lost its raison d'etre.

It seemed Fern's competition days were over. To my surprise, I was deeply disappointed! I'd only come into this sport as "something for the dog to do", and here I was, thoroughly upset that it appeared to be all over! I still suffered the most dreadful nerves, which began days before a show, so why on earth should I want to perpetuate the terror? One can become addicted to adrenalin; perhaps it was that. Or perhaps I wanted Gordon to see how good Fern could be. But I believe the prime reason was that I knew I had a dog of immense talent, both physical and mental, and I knew that I let her down time after time, so perhaps one day, if I kept trying, I just might not. So I'd kept trying, but now, any opportunity to redress the balance was fast disappearing. I decided we'd finish at the end of the year.

Another Wednesday was now about to become a red-letter day but in a strange and frightening manner. It was evening and Gordon was out ministering to the needs of Sylvie and co. Fern was stretched in front of the radiator, occupying as much floor space as caninely possible, and I was sitting in front of the T.V. I phrase it that way deliberately because it was one of those occasions on which we kid ourselves that we are actually doing two jobs at once! I was darning the thick, dog-walking socks that Gordon wore to make his feet fit his wellies, and also educating myself, courtesy of "Panorama."

One single phrase suddenly leapt out from the screen:

"-Chronic disorders of the digestive system."

The programme was exploring the controversy surrounding the human M.M.R. vaccine. I already knew that some scientific thought blamed the combined vaccine for the onset of autism, but I had never before been aware of any possible link with digestive disorders. I listened, incredulity growing, as more detail unfolded.

The programme suggested the presence of an inherited genetic tendency to viral damage in early life, and that children with this genetic make-up were vulnerable to permanent damage if the number of viruses thcy cncountered was extremely high. These children, vaccinated with the combined M.M.R. during this "window", developed autism, and or, digestive disorders.

Christopher Day's words returned to haunt me.

I saw him shake his head again. I saw the sad resignation of his expression as he looked at Fern and now I looked at her with the same feelings. The socks slid to the floor. My blood ran cold and my eyes filled with tears. For the multi disease M.M.R. vaccine for children, substitute the multi disease Primary vaccine for puppies! Had I done this to her?

It fitted perfectly as any jigsaw puzzle. The canine Primary Vaccination contains not three, but five viruses. It is injected into a tiny being less than one tenth the size of a child. The more I thought, the more sense it made! And I couldn't wait to have Fern vaccinated! Did she have the genetic tendency and had I not only chosen the very moment when her window was open, but open at its widest?

"Inherited genetic tendency:" Fern and Magic! Had Jill happened on a similar window for her? Magic was bigger than Fern. It was logical to assume she had been a bigger pup and therefore more able to withstand the massive onslaught of microorganisms. Even though digestive disorder had finally killed Magic, her problem had not seemed as severe as Fern's; perhaps her window had not been open quite as wide as her daughter's.

My thoughts were in a maelstrom! I wished Gordon were home. I was afraid my imagination would run away, allowing me to distort possibility into fact.

But his reaction was similar to mine. Everything seemed to add together. But we mustn't be carried away. We took turns to play Devil's Advocate.

Skipper was vaccinated at eleven weeks, and unaffected. But perhaps he didn't inherit the gene combination. The rest of Magic's litter was unaffected. It was also possible that none of them had the deadly inheritance and also that they were vaccinated at the more usual time of twelve weeks and one week is a long time in the life of a tiny puppy. Two of the pups had died in tragic accidents under the age of three months and their reaction to vaccination remains unknown.

Dr. Hall had spoken of damage to Fern's digestive nerves. Those nerves had once functioned perfectly! Then their function diminished steadily. Was this as the vaccine took effect? But if vaccination could have such a devastating effect on dogs, even though, as in children, only a tiny minority is affected, then why were we unaware of rumblings in the dog world? The answer, as we know now, is that there are questions being asked, and those questions grow more insistent.

I ask any vet I happen to meet for an opinion. None of them blame vaccination for Fern's condition, and quite rightly so. There is no actual proof. But neither has any one of them ever said vaccination could not have been to blame.

None of this whirlwind of ifs and buts affect what had already happened. I have a dog with a potentially catastrophic disease. Nothing will ever change that.

After a few days, we both felt a little better for knowing what might have caused Fern's condition.

Some months later, I would learn that the measles virus can often lie dormant in the human gut. Both Nigel and Dr. Hall had found the areas known as Peyer's Patches in Fern's gut to be mysteriously inflamed. Inflammation is a symptom of disease.

Finish agility? This was the year I began to tackle it as I always should have done! And all because I watched an Agility class for the very first time! Having to watch Fern instead, I had never studied any competition handling, only being aware of very few from my nerve-wracked place in the queue to start. Observing others, and learning from good and bad handling was something I had never been able to do, but now whenever Gordon came with us, I could rely on him to keep Fern safe and happy. He was content to remain in the car, devouring motor magazines, until I returned!

So, after three years of competition, I really watched a class for the first time. It was at the Rutland Agricultural Show. Although ABC Open Agility had been going for some time, it was a totally new concept to me. The letters mean Any Breed but Collies and that also included Collie crosses. Open meant that all dogs, from Starters to Seniors were eligible. Fern and I were drawn 52, so with her safe in Gordon's care, I had time to make my way to the ring for what George had always said was of paramount importance.

A familiar face passed by with an unfamiliar dog. Sharon had her Border Collie pup!

"Just socialising him, getting him used to the atmosphere!"

She was here simply for a day out, supporting her fellow club members and was most surprised to hear of the closure of George's school, for she well knew his outstanding expertise and he had sometimes competed for the Scunthorpe club.

I continued on my way to the ring.

This ABC course was highly controversial! Apparently, no one had yet gone clear, and neither had anyone, regardless of faults, completed it within the time! Club officials had even asked the judge to lower her time of 48 seconds, but she had refused.

As I watched, ideas began to form. Fern could do that better, I thought. I'd have made that clearer. Fern's quicker than that. I wouldn't have done it that way.

When we took our place on the start line, still no one had gone clear! But this time, something was very different. I was different. The recurrent theme running through what I'd seen had brought about an enormous change in my attitude. I could barely believe it myself! I no longer hoped we'd go clear. I knew we would! There was nothing to worry us on this course! Neither did I hope for a place. I knew we'd get one! As we stood there, unbelievably, outrageously, my only hope was for an outright win! The timekeeper had become bored by constant failure. His tone was patronising.

"Now let's see what a Flatcoat can do. In your own time."

Fern immediately began her scratching ritual.

One or two in the queue oohd and aahd, then someone giggled. I didn't care. I knew what was to come.

"Just watch," I thought, "just watch and eat your heart out!"

Fern stopped scratching and sat up, looking straight ahead; one jump, then the weaves. Almost a third of the dogs I had seen, had faulted here. From the dog's eye view at the start, the weaving poles were the first obstacle; the jump before was well above their eye line, but at the T.D.T.C. we were used to such ploys and how to deal with them. All I had to do was to emphasize that first "Over" and to give the command before I moved a muscle. I was so buoyed with confidence, I even decided to play up to the erroneous "Scatty Flattie" image.

"There's a jump before the weaves, kid. Don't forget to do that first," I said clearly.

Then it was down to business.

"Over!"

She flew! One jump, then through the weaves, head down, body flexing like a snake. Round in a tight circle to the A-frame, both contacts well struck. More jumps, dog walk, again with both contacts well and truly landed; flat tunnel, change sides to pick her up on my right and off down a row of jumps. Then suddenly, a complete break, where she must leave that enticing row, turn back on herself, and run alongside the jumps she'd just completed, to enter the rigid tunnel. I'd opted to allow Fern to get ahead of me (not difficult!) then to call her back. There was enough room to position myself well away from those jumps so that when Fern turned, she would see a clear line straight back to me. It might have appeared to be a gamble to some, but I knew Fern invariably returned instantly on command when in a strange place and I'd seen many handlers get into terrible trouble as they attempted to prevent their dogs continuing the line of jumps. True to form, she whipped through almost 180 degrees and raced towards me. Rigid tunnel, jump, jump, seesaw, again with clean contacts, jump, 90-degree turn, jump, another turn, jump and we were home! Would we be first to go clear?

As I picked up her lead from where it had been tossed from the start, to my delight, I heard clapping. I knew we'd been faultless in the ring, so were we within that notorious time? Were we clear?

I glanced over my shoulder. The judge was looking in our direction and smiling! Then she did something I will never forget; something, which to me remains unforgettable! She raised both arms above her head to clap. We were clear! We had not only proved that the time could be beaten, we had blown it away! How I longed to go back to that patronising timekeeper! I almost did. But there was no need. He'd seen what a Flatcoat could do!

I spent the rest of that morning yo-yoing backwards and forwards between the car and the ring. Could anyone beat our 42.98 seconds? "We're still winning!"

I watched one handler try my method of drawing his dog out of the line of jumps and returning to him. But he stood too near the line and his dog returned by re-jumping the same hurdles into elimination.

"We're still in the lead!"

I kept Gordon informed.

"Still there!"

The tannoy sent out the Final call. I ran back to the ring. When the course had proved so difficult, how many dogs from a final ten could possibly beat us?

Numbers in the queue dwindled. I was on frightening, glorious, tenterhooks! But what a wonderful, marvellous, unbelievable position to be in!

Five from the end, a greyhound from Intermediate beat our time. Next to last, another Intermediate, a large cross-breed, raced into second place. We were third.

Illusion

An unusually large number of people were at the Presentation and I found myself beside Sharon. As usual, she bubbled with enthusiasm and was delighted with our third place.

"You'll be in the final, then!"

I didn't understand.

"The ABC Final! This's a heat! There's ten, or twelve, I think, all over the country! The first three go through to the Final!"

I felt my mouth drop open. Sharon laughed and pumped my arm up and down.

"It's next year, July I think. You'll get all the bumph. They'll tell you."

I had no need to reply, for the presentation began. To cheers and shouts, Dweezle Music Maker received his winner's rosette and with it, a large envelope. More cheers and whistles for the second placed pair. Now I felt very alone. There would be no one to cheer or shout for Fern and me, no supporters from our non-existent club. I had reckoned without Sharon.

"Third, Brenda Gibson with Fossdyke Illusion."

Cheers and shouts! Whistles and clapping! Sharon had primed her fellow members to adopt us!

The judge shook my hand and presented our rosette. Someone gave me an envelope and wished us luck in the Final. I walked back on air to a widely grinning Gordon.

The afternoon saw us in Starters' Jumping. I remember nothing of the course, save that we were drawn almost at the end and I had hung around so that, as at Cardinal's Hill, we could run last. The results were already being collated as we made our way back past the ring. I overheard one official.

"The little Flatcoat that's just gone must be well up."

We collected a rosette for fourth place.

Gordon drove all the way home. Fern snoozed in the back. Two rosettes glowed above the dashboard. Two runs, two places; what a super day!

Now it must be "official," my indomitable Fern was surely amongst the best non-Collie Agility dogs in the whole, entire country!

And we had nowhere to train.

The "bumph" duly arrived: The final was sponsored by Pedigree and would be organised by the Newton Heath club at Tatton Park, Manchester, on June 13th, next year. Fifty dogs from heats held throughout the country would battle it out under judge, Brenda Tenten. I had once spoken to her at a show when I happened to pull up alongside in the car park. She had called Fern, "Absolutely beautiful" and I remembered that "absolutely" with pleasure! She had a formidable reputation as a course builder with the emphasis on handling ability! A win under her was a victory to savour!

The competition would take place around the middle of the day, and all other activity would be suspended. And there was another prize too, a once-in-a-lifetime prize of glittering seduction. From the dogs who went clear, one representative of each breed would be invited to compete in the "All Stars Grand Final" at the end of the year Christmas show at London's Olympia.

Fern at Olympia? The idea stole my breath away! Fern running, jumping, turning, twisting beneath the arc lights of that famous arena? Fern on national television? Fern, who never knew when she was beaten, at that marvellous Christmas show? I had to take a firm grip on myself. There was the final first! There might be another Flatcoat there, even more than one. We may not go clear. But in those following months, thoughts of Olympia were never far from my mind. They glowed from the future, enticing, beckoning, a dream beyond belief! But with that dazzling thought, there always followed one other: we had nowhere to train.

I investigated the Scunthorpe club. They would welcome us! The facts that we were trained by George and in a national final opened the door to their top classes. But normal training routines were being temporarily disrupted by circumstances dictated at their Council controlled training ground, and the only suitable class would not recommence until just before the final. Also, that class would be held in the evenings, the very time when Fern was always at her "fattest". I couldn't risk it.

The next nearest club was in Norfolk: a round trip of almost two hundred miles for an hour's work: obviously not an option. What on earth were we to do? Thoughts of scratching from the final occurred to me. It was logical, but when had Fern ever done the logical? When had she ever given up? I dismissed the idea. At least long walks and plenty of play kept her fit.

"I'm in hospital. I didn't want you going to the house for nothing." It was Margaret's voice. She said she had been admitted for "a rest." I felt a chill of real fear.

Visiting the next day, I found her alone in a narrow room off the

207

corridor leading to the main ward. She lay, thin and fragile, fully dressed on her bed. A small cabinet and one of those hospital chairs with the high seats were the only other things in the room. I wondered where the rest of her clothes were. I wondered if she was eating. Our conversation was boringly, achingly normal.

"A rest'll do you good."

"Nice not to have to cook and clean."

"Not to have to go shopping."

"Yes. Let someone else do it."

"Or to have to think about what to get for meals."

"It's a lovely day."

Margaret smiled with pleasure and nodded towards the row of tiny windows. They were so high, all she could see was the sky, a cloudless, brilliant blue sky.

"Everyone's so good. They're always looking in. I tell them I don't mind being on my own, but they're always looking in. I had three cups of tea in the night!"

She must have lain awake for a long, long time. The thought made me so sad.

"Jammy bod! How d'you manage that?"

We talked of anything and everything. I tried to convince myself that this was indeed "a rest", and that Margaret just needed temporary respite to recharge her batteries, to continue her fight, but in my heart, I knew this wasn't so. Margaret was not here for temporary rest. I did not believe she would ever return to her cosy little home and the garden she loved so much. Margaret had come here to die, and she was going to die in a room that looked as if it had been fashioned from a cupboard. It broke my heart.

Standing at the sink two days later, I stared through the kitchen window at one of those ghastly November days when the sky is uniform leaden grey and you can't tell where that ends and the distant ground begins. I hadn't intended to visit Margaret that day, but then I thought of what she must be seeing through those tiny windows, and abandoned my housework.

A keen wind had sprung up since I'd walked Fern earlier and the cold drizzle now angled sharply against the windscreen as I drove. Fern sat in her "Barbour" jacket in the boot, head resting on the back of the rear seat as usual.

Margaret was tucked beneath the sheets and she was racked with guilt.

"I just fancied it. Right out of the blue. I don't know why. I only said it as a joke and they made me one! Straight away! I don't know how! But it was nice," she smiled at the memory, "it was so nice. I really enjoyed it."

"It" was a small chicken sandwich. I tried to salve her vegetarian conscience to little avail.

"Whatever will David think of me?"

Margaret was so bothered by this lapse from her principles, as we discussed it from every possible angle, that she almost forgot to tell me her news. Moments before I arrived, she had been told that a bed had been found for her at St. Barnabas, the very hospice where she had worked as a volunteer for many years.

I was delighted she would be going to such a wonderful, happy, and caring place, where staff already knew and loved her, but with that knowledge, came the realisation that any glimmer of hope to which I'd clung was now gone.

A bespectacled, round-faced man suddenly stuck his head in the doorway.

"Mrs. Walker?"

He came in, shirt-sleeved and cheerful.

"I'm your driver! There's a nurse coming to get you ready. I'm your posh chauffeur!"

Not one, but three nurses came. Several more dropped in to say goodbye. Every one hugged Margaret. I saw the tears in one nurse's eyes as she hurried out. She knew. Only Margaret, gentle, calm, smiling, seemed unaware.

"I'll give you a day to settle in. Then I'll come and see you."

From habit, I allowed Fern out of the car to relieve herself. I turned my back to the strengthening wind, and waited.

Fern wandered along the grass verge, raindrops forming a cap of diamonds on her gleaming head. Suddenly I knew that Margaret must see her! I locked the car and we hurried across to the corner of the main drive. Every vehicle had to pass there.

Several delivery vans and a couple of private cars splashed by. Some drivers stared. It was not the kind of day to be hanging about anywhere, but we stayed, getting colder and wetter.

Illusion

The car came slowly, weaving round puddles. I waved an arm above my head, then pointed down at Fern. I think that by some miracle of canine sixth sense, I'd expected Fern to know that she was saying goodbye to the friend who loved her so much and who still called her Ferny-pup. But there was no poetic, spiritual finale. Fern was intent only on investigating the grass, oblivious of Margaret's gaze. She turned in her seat as she passed, pale face pressed against the window and I could see she was talking to the driver, no doubt explaining the strange pair who hovered on the drive in the wind and the rain.

I watched long after the car turned from my sight, as if, by remaining there, I could stop time and keep Margaret forever. But the drive was empty. I listened to the raindrops on the grey, pitted concrete and the sighs of the wind as it cut across the stark brick corners. I watched it sculpt strange shapes on the surface of the puddles.

Suddenly, without warning, Margaret's words from years ago came rushing back up that windswept drive.

"She will do something for you. Something special. Something only she can do."

It was then I knew the truth of her words. I went home to weep in the comforting arms of the husband I had taken so long to meet.

Flowers adorned every surface. The curtains and bed linen were patterned with roses. Soft lace curtains, festooned away from the window, revealed the beauty of a garden beyond. Birds darted to and fro between the feeders hanging from the gentle arms of a silver birch and a small fountain twinkled in the pale sunlight. Inside the room, a dressing table of palest wood held a huge basket of flowers that beamed their fragrance to the bed opposite. It was a lovely room; calm, and peaceful.

Margaret had not left her bed since her arrival. I sat very close because she wanted to hold my hand. She was so serene and, dare I think, even happy? Her vicar had visited both yesterday and this morning and she had enjoyed their talks together. Her beloved David would be coming this evening, and tomorrow, he had a whole day off work. Yes, she was happy. I promised to return the day after.

She squeezed my hand, and spoke softly but clearly.

"It won't matter if you don't see me. I'll be all right."

On the way home, those words echoed round and round in my mind: "Don't see me." 'Don't.' It seemed odd. "Can't" would surely have fitted better.

210

The next morning dawned like a new world! After Gordon had left for work, I stood washing breakfast pots by the kitchen window and watched as the brilliant orb of the winter sun rose over the distant hill. Shafts of golden sunlight pierced into a cloudless sky. Dawn was like Spring that November morning.

The sun was shining from a brilliant blue sky when David rang.

CHAPTER TWENTY-ONE

Certain music has always reminded me of particular people. My father is "Rhapsody in Blue", Mum is the "Minute Waltz", whilst a favourite aunt is "Softly Awakes My Heart". We left the church at Margaret's funeral to the sound of Wet Wet Wet's "Love is All Around". That will be forever Margaret's signature.

I missed her so much. Her understanding and compassion, tempered by a gentle humour and an almost child-like enthusiasm are qualities rarely encountered and I cherish her memory dearly. We had been friends for barely seven short years. At her funeral, the church overflowed. Many other people loved Margaret, too. David had devised a unique and beautiful service for his mother and was totally overcome when reading a poem for her. I longed to jump up and to read it for him.

The sadness and darkness of the lengthening nights were eventually lifted by preparations for Christmas. Illuminations went up in the city, the local roads were closed off for the annual Christmas Market and the ritual preparations began. But the roller coaster of stressful events continued.

I rang Jill with season's greetings and learned two things, both of which I would have preferred not to know. Firstly, she had recently lost Skipper, to that scourge of our breed, cancer. I had always planned to take Gordon along to meet Illustrious, but now he would never know Fern's "twin" and I so regretted my human frailty of never having got round to it. Fern heartily disproved such procrastination! But Jill had even more to say.

"She's the last."

At first, I didn't understand. Jill interpreted the silence correctly and explained.

"As far as I know, she's probably the last of Magic's litter." *

Amazement, disbelief and finally pride, surged through me! So much pride that my eyes filled with tears. Might Fern really be the longest lived

* I now believe Fern to have been outlived by Fossdyke Impressario.

of all twelve puppies? It was beyond belief! What volumes it spoke of her courage, her indomitable spirit! But for the first time, it made me aware of her mortality. I even thought of how our life together might end. That it would be both unexpected and dramatic I had no doubt. Fern was not one to fade gently. She had faced every adversity and won every battle, but even she could not do that forever.

Christmas Dinner, as usual, was at Audrey's with the closest family.

The Gibson tradition of waiting to open presents until after dinner continued to drive me mad! How could anyone possibly wait so long?

After the present opening, came the Games. Father-in-law, Harold, a most laid back and charming man, kept "Give Us A Clue" alive the entire holiday, suddenly and earnestly springing into action at the oddest moments, calling out "I've got another!" Myself, sister-in-law Anita and husband, Martin, thought this hilarious, but neither Audrey nor Gordon is endowed with Harold's enthusiasm and patience, which to us, perversely, made it even funnier! Sister-in-law Sue would escape outside for a cigarette while Uncle John would smile benignly and return to whatever he happened to be doing which was usually sleeping!

Fern thought it all wonderful. Apart from Sandy and George, the people she loved most were together under one roof; true Flatcoat philosophy! But it was Anita who came in for the most attention. A little wary of dogs, she did not relish being licked. Fern picked up on this and never gave up trying to reassure Anita of her good intentions in the only way a dog can: by licking! The more Anita shrieked and wriggled, the more enthusiastically Fern would lick! These sessions became known as "being mugged".

On Boxing Day, everyone came to us. I had little time to remember the "old" tradition.

Later, when the decorations had been returned to their cotton wool beds, D-I-Y began in earnest. Having moved into a brand new property, one might have expected there was little to do: wrong! Plants in temporary pots, which we had brought from Phillip Court, needed protection, so my multi-talented husband built a greenhouse. Then he laid a patio, to try to prevent some of the dirt and grit being trailed into the house by four feet and four paws from reaching our new carpets! On both these projects, I was labourer, and tea-masher. Fern was Quality Control, thoroughly examining each component and conducting minute inspection of the finished product.

Although the two-of-everything syndrome had been largely defeated,

213

we still had two lots of books and magazines, two collections of tapes, videos, vinyl and CDs. So Gordon built shelves all along the window wall of the smallest bedroom and we grandly renamed it the study.

As winter began to lose its grip, I sat in there and started the ritual of sending away for Agility schedules, for this was the Year of the Final. We planned three early shows, then, aware of Fern's fragile boredom threshold, we would leave May and the first part of June free. She would be fresh for the ABC Final. But there was still the problem of her training. Having tried to locate a suitable club and failed, I did what I thought I would never do, and returned with her to Cardinal's Hill. There was no other way.

Agility training had apparently ground to a halt not long after our fifth place, neither had there been any shows there, but word was out that things were to be re-born, so I investigated. Yes! Training was to recommence almost immediately and scheduled after the usual Sunday obedience (and pet!) classes. The dark haired lady whom I had spoken to when inquiring about the pet class, Sybil Wheeler, was in charge. I signed up and paid up. A new beginning for us and perhaps for the club? After all, a local dog, already with Open Show places to her credit and qualified for a National Final, was bound to be an asset to a club about to re-establish its agility credentials, I thought.

There were about eight of us the first Sunday. Five jumps, a short run of six widely spaced weaving poles and a seesaw were the only equipment drawn from the huge stock in the hut. It appeared that all the other dogs were either beginners or very inexperienced, because they used jumps at the elementary height of two feet and with a second pole below to prevent any running underneath. When it came to Fern's turn, I had to hurry round, changing the jumps to those in competition by raising the top pole to its full height and removing all lower poles right from the course. This, in effect, more than halved Fern's actual training time, mainly because I was stupid enough to feel I was depriving others of their time and that it might look as if I was showing off. I wasn't very happy as we returned home. Here we were, preparing for a national event, preparing to face Intermediate and Senior dogs, by working in an elementary class! Things must change.

The dog walk made its appearance the following week, with most of the time being spent watching the beginners coaxed along its formidable length, even though no dog was ever allowed as long as Sandy had allowed Fern in her early attempts.

Hoping to demonstrate my commitment to the club, I attended their Annual General Meeting. It seemed that finances had taken a dive, and it was due to the lack of revenue previously generated by the Agility Shows. Members wanted the shows to restart yet no one seemed willing to help Sybil with their organisation! I thought it might seem presumptuous had I volunteered to do so after my two weeks' membership, although had anyone suggested so, I would have agreed at once.

In the following Sundays, nothing even approaching a full course was ever put out, but then there was only Fern capable of tackling one.

Putting out equipment wasn't the only problem; putting it away was just as fraught! Some members always found reason to hurry away before the end of the session, leaving the few who were keener or just plain daft enough to put up with this, to return it all to the hut. I wondered why the club did not make it clear on their application form, like Scunthorpe, that in joining, members accepted their responsibility not only to put out, but to return everything they had used. Whilst George always preferred to have things ready when people arrived, early departures were extremely rare. I think everyone felt they learned so much and their dogs had enjoyed so much fun, that no one was in any hurry to leave! At least George would say things like thank you, or, see you next week, or slip a treat to a shy dog, so that we all felt we were an integral and valued part of the T.D.T.C. Sybil never volunteered a thank you or even a good bye. Training became a grim chore.

April found us going round in circles, literally! En route to our first show of the season in Manchester, we couldn't find our M66 exit from the M62. This was because the authorities had renumbered it M60, but left no indication of the change until four miles along the M66, or 60! When we finally arrived, late, we discovered we weren't the only ones! But the efficient Newton Heath club rose to the occasion, and allowed those who had been caught up in the traffic chaos to run later.

Still upset up over the delay, I slipped on soggy ground in ABC Agility, flinging out an arm to regain my balance. Sadly, but understandably, this was interpreted by Fern as "Go that way!" which she did and into elimination. In the afternoon's Starters Agility, we finished 9th, from 168 entrants; another top ten place, but only just!

Back at Cardinal's Hill, numbers began to dwindle. Occasionally, a handler with dogs in Senior Agility from the earlier obedience classes would appear briefly to take her dogs round once or twice. Apparently Sam had plans to set up her own school, and she liked Fern's boldness and good humour. I liked Sam and sought her advice whenever possible. It was she who suggested I invest in some studded shoes to prevent slipping in wet weather, and within days, I was the proud owner of a pair of black football trainers, which sported lurid green "Go faster" stripes down their sides! I wished I could have worked with Sam, but she rarely came and she wasn't in charge.

"Can we have the A-frame out?"

"Are you going to lift it on your own?"

We were getting nowhere. Far from being seen as a dog to renew interest in the club's Agility, Fern was being ignored. If she ever was considered at all, then because of her very different needs, it was as a nuisance.

Gordon began to come, simply to lift more equipment in and out of the hut, willingly standing around for the hour or so in between. But our hope of more appropriate training for Fern was short-lived. He made the error of "taking" Fern on the seesaw, and was told that, as a non-member, the club's insurance did not cover him and he was not to do so again. We accepted this, but it raised the question of how he had been able to "use" that same equipment by lifting it in and out of the hut. He stopped coming.

Numbers continued to drop.

One Sunday, I arrived to find the hut being locked by someone from the earlier Obedience classes.

"Agility? Oh, I don't know anything about that. I don't suppose there is any."

I swallowed my surprise and anger at this treatment which, at best was discourteous and at worst, breath-takingly arrogant. I felt embarrassed and awkward, as if I was at fault in repeatedly wanting something to which I was not entitled. It never occurred to me to ask, no, demand the key. Why ever not, for I was a member, wasn't I? I simply took to ringing the club every Sunday to make sure the scheduled class would actually run. Often, two or three calls were needed to locate Sybil and to secure an answer: sometimes yes, sometimes no.

Not surprisingly, numbers decreased still further until there was just three of us left; a lad with his Border Collie, interested only in Obedience, but who wanted a really fit dog and an elderly man who hoped agility might give his painfully shy Sheltie some confidence.

Why, oh why, did I accept all this without demur? The club had accepted my joining fee to do agility with my fully trained and experienced dog readily enough. All we were getting was the occasional beginners' class! I felt utterly frustrated. Fern had come all this way, and now it was all falling apart. How can any athlete, human or canine, enter any level of competition without preparation?

Sandy listened gravely as I raged impotently. She showed not the slightest surprise.

"Do you want to try in my garden? I've got some old equipment. It's sound. There's enough room to do set pieces."

The wheel had turned full circle.

Fern always knew where we were going. I varied the route. I approached from three totally different directions just to see if I could fool her. I never did.

Sandy's garden was laid to grass, very long, but narrow. She had four complete jumps, a full set of individual weaving poles, a seesaw and a battered dog-walk. But what was lacking in facilities, Sandy made up with her ingenuity in building "set pieces", the more fiendish, the better, and she even taught Fern to, "weave on the right", although she might dispute that!

Dogs must always enter weaves between the first and second poles, passing the first pole with their left shoulder. Entry anywhere else is penalised. Depending on the difficulty of the course, the line of poles may be approached from any angle, which is determined by the position of the obstacle immediately before. Should that obstacle be to the left of the start of the poles, then there is temptation for the dog to enter incorrectly. Most handlers have to "run round", so that they and their dog are both on the correct entry side, but this can waste precious tenths of seconds, or even whole seconds, so Sandy decided we must learn correct weaving from every conceivable angle, so that no matter where I was on the course, I would be able to send Fern ahead correctly.

The obstacle on the approach would be gradually moved round, positioned further and further to the left, and brought nearer and nearer to the poles in tiny stages; the idea being that the dog remains unaware of those gradual changes and simply continues to weave correctly. That was the theory.

But when had Fern ever done what was expected of her? She began to enter the weaves anywhere, and to our dismay, leave them anywhere, something she had never, ever done! We were three weeks from the Final, and all we had succeeded in doing was apparently to destroy her previous excellent weaving!

Illusion

For the first time ever, Sandy was cross with her. I was surprised at her comment.

"The little cow's doing it on purpose! She's taking the mickey!"

It rather reminded me of some of George's comments. Her remedy was drastic. There was to be no more weaving at all, until immediately before the final, in the hope that Fern might forget it all and revert to normal.

I accepted this. By now, I'd have accepted anything from anyone. Thoughts of a Final place were in tatters. Olympia no longer dominated the future. My hopes, my dreams were all but in ruins. I'd tried hard, really hard. My attitude had improved enormously, but now things seemed to be running away from me, and I felt powerless to do anything about it.

"They're on the wrong side!"

"That's because you're weaving on the right."

I had expected to weave in the usual manner.

"Just tell her and get on with it. She'll do it."

I didn't care any more, so I did just that. I told her. And she did. Without any hesitation, Fern ran right round the poles to enter correctly. She did so again when we changed the course, and yet again.

Sandy made no fuss of her protégée beyond a "Good girl" and a swift pat.

"That's the way to teach this dog," she said to me quietly, "sail in with what you want, make it clear and she'll do it. I knew she was taking the mickey."

Yes! I remembered George had once described Fern as having two fingers and what she did with them!

We walked in Tatton Park the evening before the final. Through trees, by a lake, past a herd of grazing deer, we were inevitably drawn to the show ground. The middle of five empty rings was sited directly in front of a large marquee. Across the marquee entrance, a huge yellow and red banner proclaimed "Pedigree Chum ABC National Final." I saw it and quaked. I wondered if Fern was the only Starter in the line up. She was likely to be the oldest finalist, for she was officially a veteran now. We would certainly be the only ones who hadn't prepared within the auspices of a club. It was unthinkable that any other dog there had not trained properly for over a year and done all her preparation in a suburban back garden! What possible chance could we have?

About three weeks previously, I'd realised all the old negative attitudes

218

were staging a comeback, so I'd tried to combat this by sitting down and writing a list of pros and cons. I thought of that list now. The cons had been a long list, full of sense and logic. The pro side had only two entries: "Very Best start" and then just one word; "Fern." Logic said she had no chance, but when did Fern ever do the logical thing? She had always done it her way.

But as I tried to sleep in the caravan that night, my thoughts were not of what would go right, but of what could go wrong. Once again, I had become afraid of failure.

Saturday dawned grey and showery and to my dismay, windy as well. The final was scheduled for lunchtime when all morning classes had been completed and there would be no other activity.

I was used to gauging when we might run and adjusting Fern's feeds, but this time, the problem seemed more complicated than ever. I found out the number of entrants for all the morning classes, then chose the largest Agility entry, which always takes longer than Jumping, and learned the course time. Now, all I had to do was multiply that time by the number of entrants and I would have an idea of the times to feed Fern. But that took no heed of faster or slower individual times: would they balance each other? There was no allowance either for the intervals between contestants, scratched entries, or of any necessary course rebuilding, or judges' and stewards' break times. Today, everything seemed such a hassle, so complicated, when today was the day I just had to get it right.

One good thing; Fern was the only Flatcoat in the final! All we had to do was to be clear in a decent time and we would be in the All Stars at Olympia. Olympia! The kind of dream which comes true only in books, yet it was a dream within our grasp! Fern certainly had the skills. All I had to do was nothing silly and we would be there. I tried to focus on this.

Gordon and I tried to keep things low-key. We shortened Fern's morning walk, but of course, she knew it was short and it met with her frowning disproval.

We were sitting in the 'van, sipping coffee and trying to talk about anything other than dogs, agility, weather, time or food, yet always with one eye on the clock, when a dusty red car drew up alongside. Sandy! She had driven all the way across the Pennines that morning!

"Wouldn't have if I didn't think it would be worth it, would I?"

She had meant to bolster my confidence, but her appearance only added to the pressure. I already feared letting her down, but how much worse would it be if I let her down when she was watching and after

219

she had come all that way? She had done so much for us, trying to find adequate training, then working in her garden when all else failed.

She came with me when it was time to walk the course. No wondering and waiting here; the tannoy announced a full half hour, but continued that "Trainers and supporters" were not allowed in the ring with the handler. Sandy circumnavigated the outside.

"There's only one problem for you here," she announced. "Get her past that gap and you're home and dry!"

About a quarter of the way round, the end of the dog walk poked enticingly close between two jumps which were part of a sequence of jumps running at ninety degrees to its tip. Fern was always keen to get on the dog walk.

"She'll want to veer left onto the dog walk."

Whenever I allowed any doubt to creep in about where we should go next, Fern invariably chose to go left.

"Don't let her. There's nothing else here to bother you."

Yes there was! There was no opportunity to shave seconds by weaving on the right!

I left Sandy at the ringside and went back to walk the course again; and again! She had disappeared when I left the ring. I would not see her until afterwards.

Now I stood alone. It was here. Within the hour, it would all be over. It had ruled my life for a year, now it was here. It: another It. I had known many Its before with Fern. The two ghastly occasions when she barely escaped full torsion; then waiting for Dr. Hall to tell me what was wrong with her; the time It had seemed to be all over and we were to "Enjoy the weekend together." The It in Christopher Day's surgery as I waited, heart in mouth, to find out if It really was the end. Yes, I was used to Its. If anyone should know how to handle an It, then it should be me. I went to fetch Fern.

Judge Brenda Tenten was elegantly dressed and wore a large spray of flowers in her lapel. As the final began, I took Fern to the exercise area to relieve herself. The sky was gloomier now and a few drops of rain began to fall. The wind blew cool. I shivered, but not because of the wind. I remember walking slowly back towards the ring and watching the luridly striped "Go-faster" shoes squeeze water and mud from beneath the grass. I pressed my weight one way then the other and played pointless games guessing where the water would squirt next. There wasn't enough time to return to the caravan, and too much time to stand about.

"How'd you get in, then?"

The question was posed by a small, wiry man with a brown cross-breed, but I didn't want to talk. I watched a dog turn directly onto the dog walk from the line of jumps: elimination.

"Empingham, third."

He laughed.

"You took my place! Came fourth! Had to try again at-"

I never heard where. Another dog lost a great deal of time confused between the dog walk and jumps. Then one raced onto the dog walk in the correct sequence, but so fast that it overbalanced and came off over the side! A turn at the top of the course was also causing problems. But it all seemed unreal, as if it had nothing to do with us. Were we really here? Was my dog, who should be only a puppy memory, really waiting in her veteran years, to compete against the best ABCs in the country? Was the novice who had wanted "Something for the dog to do," really waiting for her turn to compete in a national event?

"Brenda Gibson with Fossdyke Illusion. They qualified-"

The spectators turned their eyes and expectation on us. It was time! "It" had come. The tannoy boomed on, but I could no longer decipher the words. Where was Sandy? Was Gordon watching? It didn't matter now. There was only us: one ordinary woman with her extraordinary dog.

"In your own time."

One jump into the course and I knew Fern was not at her best. She was moving swiftly enough, but that deceptive, long-striding speed of hers just wasn't there. Suddenly, I realised she had not gone through her scratching ritual on the start line! With dismay, I realised she must have picked up my nervousness and it must have unsettled her! As we turned into the weaves, I tried hard to focus. Concentrate! I was in a National Final and all I could think about was that my dog hadn't scratched! Turn the corner. Change sides. Get between Fern and the dog walk. We had passed Sandy's "only problem"! Relief almost brought a smile! It cannot have been coincidence now that Fern found her speed! Turn left,180 degrees; turn right, 90. I raced alongside the dog walk. But where was Fern? Then I heard her paws scrabbling for a hold and my heart sank. I shot a glance behind, knowing with fear that I'd never before looked at her from this angle. She had the up contact, but I realised I'd allowed her on at such an acute angle, that her momentum threatened to carry her over and off the side. Of course! I'd seen several dogs fault in this way, yet still hadn't had the presence to slow her down! I'd been too high on having passed our "only problem!" Concentration! Inwardly, I cursed myself. But Fern knew the rules. She knew her job; she knew she must stay on. Somehow, those marvellous feet kept her on the dog walk, helped regain her balance, and she picked up her stride, and raced past me. She struck the down contact cleanly and was over the next jump.

I became aware of the judge close by. Her arms were still. She hadn't signalled any faults! Jump, turn, jump, turn: now we faced three jumps, positioned side by side. Over the middle, turn sharp left and back over the farthest, turn left again, pass the face of the middle jump, turn left and over the near one. Twice, Fern turned beautifully, virtually on the spot. Now she was going like the proverbial wind, and then we'd only have the A-frame and two jumps to go! The A-frame had never been a problem, and Fern had only ever downed two poles in competition, and we'd be clear and we'd be going to Olympia and I'd already committed the cardinal sin. My concentration gone, my focus elsewhere, I allowed her to clear the middle jump again.

I didn't try to stop her. Hitting both A-frame contacts, clearing both jumps, she completed the course in great style to sympathetic applause and understanding murmurs.

We would not be going to Olympia.

My beautiful, talented partner had been denied her deserved glory. I hugged her, and re-attached the lead. Automatically, I headed for the caravan.

It was all I could do to stop myself crying and stamping like a frustrated child. Gordon sat silently on one bunk, Sandy opposite him on the other. With my back to them, I began to prepare lunch. I washed lettuce with ridiculous care, studying the stream of water running over each leaf. Couldn't it be the go-faster shoes squeezing out water from the grass? Then I'd have my time over again. Then I'd know what to do. I wouldn't make any mistakes.

I wondered if I might forfeit my grown-up self-control, and rage like a child to invite their solaces, but perhaps they had none to give. Poor Sandy had given so much of her time and energy to prepare us and I had let her down. She described it as "One of those things", but she must have been bitterly disappointed.

Chopping cucumber was difficult. My fingers wanted to get in the way.

Gordon had said nothing. I know how dearly he would have loved to see the dog, who so keenly sought his company and changed his life forever, do well or even win the greatest sporting accolade open to her. We ate in silence. The lettuce leaves still had grit on them.

In bed that night, neither of us spoke of the Final. We held each other briefly, then turned away to our separate disappointment and misery. All the hopes and dreams which had lighted my life for more than a year were gone and it was I who had extinguished them. I could not believe it was all over, finished. Perhaps this was the dream. Perhaps I'd wake up to find I still had the chance to let Fern reap the reward she so deserved.

I thought dawn had broken many times before its grey light finally trickled around the curtains. I forced myself to think ahead and tried to take stock. The future no longer held any inviting promises. There were no dreams, no great goals to aim for. So what mattered now? It must be Now! But hadn't Fern always taught me that? Surfing a joyous wave of infectious enthusiasm, she awakened each morning, fully expecting that, although yesterday had been wonderful, today would be even better. She had held true to that belief throughout her life and this morning would be no different. It mattered not to Fern that I had ruined her chance of a transitory fame; she had enjoyed it out there. She had exulted in her gifts of intelligence and athleticism and would continue to do so, no matter what I, or anyone else did. She would be herself. I think that is why I loved her so much. Without upsetting anyone, without causing hurt, she was always herself, determined and proud. Yes, I loved her and I envied that sweet, unshakable self-belief.

We had a class of Agility later that day. We came tenth from over two hundred entrants.

CHAPTER TWENTY TWO

Gordon built a summer- house later that year, with a brick barbeque close by. His uncle and aunt came over from Australia and we held a big party for all the family, making full use of the new facilities. Even the weather behaved itself! Fern was in her element: so many people, such excitement; and so much food! Australian Andy fell utterly in love with her. I overheard him once when he was sitting on a couch with Fern between his knees and looking up at him.

"Geez, but you're beautiful!" he had said, thinking only she could hear.

We decided to holiday in Scotland just before the schools broke up for summer, and in view of the difficulties of travelling with Fern, we had to take the journey in easy steps. A weekend Agility show was scheduled at Barnard Castle, about 123 miles north, so it was decided to make that our stopover. Although Fern hadn't trained at all since the ABC final, only a few weeks had elapsed and she remained very fit.

The ubiquitous Bacon Butty van was already frying when we arrived on Friday afternoon. Much to Fern's disappointment we didn't pitch alongside, but left the farm yard and crossed the field to set up beside a hawthorn hedge. Four rings were already marked out in the next field, with stacks of multi-coloured agility equipment ready in the centre of each. An adjacent field was the exercise area. Thick woodland ran the length of its far side; and that was where Fern headed immediately! She loved trees. Reminiscent of her first walks with Gordon in Stapleford Woods, for Fern, trees were synonymous with great happiness.

The usual agility mobiles began to arrive. We watched one woman "level" her caravan by walking round it and seeing how far the floor reached up her leg! Then a middle-aged couple with four collies, tails wagging so hard they threatened to become airborne, drew up in their camper van next to us as Gordon manipulated the gas bottles.

"Don't worry!" called the driver, "we're quiet."

"We're not!" was Gordon's tongue-in-cheek reply. When he straightened, to his horror, the camper van and whirling dogs had vanished!

I chose an Agility class for Saturday and a jumping class for Sunday. I can't remember how we came to be eliminated on Saturday, except that we were part of an extremely large and rather miffed club, but Sunday is the competition that will live forever in my memory!

There was a special, hollow-stomached excitement from the very time I opened my eyes that morning. Maybe it was the irrational hope that there would be some kind of magical poetic justice, for we were drawn third from the end and surely I could fiddle the queue so we were the last to run? Remembering those two previous occasions on which we had gone last, this could only work to our advantage and my attitude had improved by miles since then! Or perhaps it was because we were entered in only one class where there were no contacts to worry about, or the fact it was scheduled for the afternoon, and I expected to have an entire lunch hour to walk the course and to be able to do so alone without having to manoeuvre around other handlers. But whatever had sparked that feeling, I had now fully accepted what George and Sandy had always told me. I had a superb dog and at long last, reaching the end of her career, she finally had a handler who was showing some signs of living up to her.

I planned the day carefully. In spite of her entreaties all that morning, Fern had only two short walks, and both with me. She did not go to play with "Dad" in those woods nearby as she so much wanted! Her frowning disgust was obvious, but I was determined all her energy would be channelled into her jumping, and that when the time came, she would be ready to work her socks off!

When lunch hour came and I did have an hour to walk the course, I could not believe what I found! It was huge, dramatic and it could have been built for Fern! The jumps were their maximum distance apart, with two great, long straight runs, one the full diagonal of the course. Here, she could really open up! These two runs made the turns acutely sharp. Whereas frequent bends and wide turns simply slowed Fern, sharp turns were a speciality. I could barely wait for the afternoon to pass! I counted the minutes to competing! A rare and wonderful feeling!

"Final call for Starters' Jumping. The class will close in five minutes. This is the final call for Starters' Jumping."

I re-laced the go-faster shoes even tighter, and pinned on my number, took down Fern's agility lead and slipped it over her head. When I opened the door, Fern rushed through and almost yanked me off my feet! Gordon would eventually follow to lurk at some suitable vantage point as usual. I checked in with the steward, but did not immediately take my place in the queue. We sauntered back and forth, but no one else arrived and so we took our place on the start last of all. There were three jumps to the weaves. I reckoned that if I reached the weaves along with Fern, and got her in with her head down and concentrating, then it was all over. This was her course. This would be our best-ever result; of that I was certain.

"In your own time."

Fern went through her scratching ritual.

"Over!"

I was at the weaves! A split second's delight, but now I was at a standstill and Fern still wasn't with me! Looking back, I saw her sailing over the third jump, head in the air, gazing sideways at the spectators. It reminded me of an old photo I have of her in the beginners' attitude of "sitting" over a jump. Her whole demeanour was wrong!

"Boring!" it proclaimed, "don't want to do this! Boring!"

She landed safely, but instead of racing into the weaves, she slowed to a trot! As she progressed through the poles, the trot became a walk, the walk a lackadaisical stroll. I was horrified! I couldn't believe what was happening! Previously I would have thought she must feel unwell, that she had some discomfort or even pain in her gut, but today, I knew absolutely this was not the case. Her feeds had been on time, she had been given plenty of rest and she had virtually leapt from the caravan, brimming with pent-up energy. I urged her on, but she took no notice, eventually ambling out of the weaves into a complete standstill! She stared round at me, over her right shoulder, her expression one of pure belligerence! I was thunder struck! There we were, not one-third into the round, standing still with the clock remorselessly ticking away! A course built for Fern, a big, flowing course where her long-striding and powerful hurdling would surely reap their just reward, yet here we were, stock-still, staring at each other!

Utter disbelief, then I yelled at her! It was only the second time I had ever done such a thing. I forgot my training. I forgot my commands. I yelled at her as a frustrated mother might yell at a disobedient child.

"Why are you doing this to me?"

She stared back defiantly. I became aware of the spectators. Many of them would be handlers who had achieved a good time and come back to see if they'd gained a place. I remembered the phrase "Scatty Flattie" and the patronising timekeeper at Empingham. I remembered throwing away the ABC Final and I became even angrier. These spectators would never know how good she was. They'd think she really was scatty; beautiful, but dim and it enraged me!

"Everyone'll think you're a pillock!" I bellowed irrationally.

Could she possibly have known what I meant? It must have been my tone, my body language, a frustration and anger she had never known before, but whatever it was, she erupted into action. She turned to hurl herself over the next jump. I set off after her, but she drew further and further ahead. Any chance of winning had long gone, but at least, I thought, the spectators would see what she could really do. At the first turn, I was far enough behind to cut across and pick her up on my right as she came back towards me. With barely any change to her stride over the jumps, she caught, and passed me. Now I forgot my anger. I forgot the spectators. This wasn't a dog with a handler. We were as one, one whole being, perfectly in tune! This was total exhilaration! The second turn loomed. Much more acute than 90degrees, it was in a corner of the ring.

"Back!"

I had to shout the command, she was so far in front. I saw her head come round, then her body began to follow as she began the turn whilst still over the jump! Her forelegs hit the ground and, as her momentum tried to carry her on, she somehow forced her back legs round to drive herself further into the turn. Pushing off with her back feet, she sent two great divots of soil and grass hurtling towards the spectators! Afterwards, I would remember a fleeting glimpse of people ducking for cover.

Eyes fixed on Fern I turned to the diagonal line, to keep her on my right. She caught and passed me once more, seemingly without effort. This was Fern at her best! She had never been better! I urged her on. Now I had to turn her to the right this time, and although the distance between us was increasing with every stride, I knew with absolute certainty that not only could I turn her, but could do so at precisely the right moment.

I began to cut right, through the diagonal line she was completing, so far ahead of me.

"Heel!"

She turned right instantly.

"Over!"

I raced across and right through the row she had just entered and in doing so I was able to see her hurdling towards me. Never will I forget that sight or that feeling! A beautiful, living metronome: take-off, land, stride, take-off, land, stride! We were one! We were invincible! Three jumps from the finish, we were alongside each other for the first time.

"Over!" This command was a mere whisper.

"Over!"

"Back!"

"Over!"

We were through the final turn.

Now I could feel the sweat between my shoulder blades and I realised I was trembling. My breath coming in deep, thirsty gulps, I bent to pick up her lead. Suddenly back to earth, that glorious feeling I experienced out there on the course replaced by burning cheeks and spectacles sliding uncomfortably down my nose, I wondered how far outside the running time we must be. Perhaps we'd been eliminated after the weaves. We shouldn't have been, for Fern had neither disobeyed a command or strayed away from the course, but judges can make strange decisions and what had happened out there was very strange indeed. It was like having two totally different dogs! But I would always cherish memories of the second! I had forgotten everyone and everything. The whole world had been Fern and me. No one and nothing else had existed!

It was as I slipped the lead over her head, I remembered something I must have read, or perhaps heard in an interview, and I realised the truth of that glorious feeling out there. It had been that rare time of perfection of which all athletes dream: "The Zone." Its spiritual and physical exhilaration are beyond mere words for those who have never been there, but now its fleeting wonder had been revealed to me. Fern had taken me into the Zone. I will have that memory and be grateful forever.

"What happened there?"

The judge had come across and was gazing at us, totally perplexed.

I shook my head.

"Don't know," I managed, between gasps.

He, too, indulged in a bewildered shaking of the head, before moving away.

I saw Gordon coming towards us. What on earth would he make of this performance? Fern had seen him, so I dropped her lead and she raced off. He caught the lead, then inclined his head towards the woods. I waved agreement. There was no reason to save Fern's energies now. She may as well go and enjoy herself.

I set off towards the caravan, grappling with the strange contradictions of what had just happened. Disappointment, pride, disbelief, frustration and gratitude surged through me. I had tried, really tried! I had been in

228

exactly the right frame of mind. The course, the weather had both been perfect. Fern had never been better prepared. I had truly expected this to be Our Time, but it had been Fern herself who quite deliberately threw it all away.

I glanced over my shoulder to look at this strange dog as she and Gordon neared the wood. In spite of myself, I smiled as I saw her purposeful, rolling gait. Even from here, anyone could see how happy she was.

And in a flash, the answer came! I knew "what happened there." Of course Fern had rushed from the caravan to go out! She had wanted to go out with the person she loved most and to play beneath the trees! Learned obedience and a prize in competition were not for her, but a spontaneous celebration of life and of love! The pup from the cupboard top had not wanted to do agility and had once again made her wishes crystal clear. I had every right to be cross with her for such defiance, and yet, how dare anyone say she was wrong? Were the values she judged to be greater really inferior to mine? I stood and watched them vanish into the trees.

We went to the presentation for I was curious to learn our time if we hadn't been eliminated. When we arrived, it had already started. Placing to twenty, and with few clears, it shouldn't take long before I was able to examine the score sheets. I waited at the edge of the crowd as the rosettes were awarded.

"Twelfth. Brenda Gibson with Fossdyke Illusion."

Twelfth? Twelfth? I couldn't believe my ears! Twelfth, and we'd walked almost a third of the course? Then we'd stood about, motionless, and we were twelfth?

As we walked forward, I refused to allow myself to think along the lines of what might, or should have been, but I did allow myself the indulgence of one perverse satisfaction. I knew Fern had finally wreaked her revenge for all the hapless handling she had previously suffered at my hands: the most awful, Ultimate Revenge!

It was weeks before I revealed the details behind the elegant navy and white rosette to Sandy. She listened in silence, but her expression of incredulity grew.

"....So, well, I think we might have… got a better place….maybe our best," I finished lamely. There was a brief silence. Then Sandy's feelings exploded.

"Place? Place?" she repeated the word as if she had never heard it before. "Place?" Then she turned to Fern.

229

Illusion

"Oh, you cow! You little cow!"

She turned her frustration on me.

"Bre-enda," she made it sound like an insult, "come on! You walked half the course, then stood still and held a conversation with your dog! Come on! You know how much time there is between the top places!"

She ran both hands distractedly through her red hair.

"You won that! You won that and you won it handsomely!"

Turning back to Fern she added quietly but with fearsome intensity, "You absolute bitch."

We finished our agility career the following month. Neither Fern's enthusiasm or speed were showing any signs of diminishing, but we had nowhere to train, so our "Indian Summer" could not last forever. I decided to call it a day with Fern at her peak.

Our final competition was at Barnwell in Northamptonshire, and our career ended as it had begun. Fern was going superbly, fast and accurate. She had landed all her contacts and there was only the rigid tunnel and several jumps to go. Immediately after the dogwalk, I had sent her on over a jump, cut across and was already at the mouth of the next obstacle, the rigid tunnel. There should have been no possibility of error.

"Throoough!"

But I heard the patter of paws on wood. Fern had deliberately ignored me and swerved, returning to the piece of apparatus she had just completed and which had been our undoing on so many occasions; the dogwalk!

"Oh, no!"

That was from the judge!

Fern came to a halt on the cross-plank. She knew full well she had done wrong. Her tail wagged slowly, her eyes were on me. Once before she had deliberately played such a trick when she should have entered a tunnel. Once more the renowned Flatcoat humour had struck: another Flatcoat joke and I was again the butt!

We had, of course, been eliminated. I knew it had all come full circle. It was over. I reached up to tickle her ear and her tail began to wag furiously.

Yes, it had been a good joke. Mum thought so, too.

It had all been good. I remembered words from the past. "She's putting two fingers up at you, Brenda!" "She's taking the mickey Brenda!" I remembered the Olympian dream which remained a dream, the "win" that wasn't and I didn't care. I'd had an unforgettable time with a dog

230

of great character, boundless talent, wicked humour and an unshakable determination to be herself. How could anyone ask more?

We finished the course and crossed the line together.

Fern settled happily into her life as purely a pet. If she missed the excitement of Agility, she didn't show it. Gordon and I usually took turns to take her for walks and varied the routes as much as possible. I think she preferred the outings with him. She usually returned in some state of wetness that varied between damp and soaked! When her ears were really wet, the hair used to crinkle up into tiny Marcel waves that would gradually straighten as they dried.

"Old Crinkly lugs!" Gordon would say as he attempted to dry her, with the hit and miss technique perfected by men doing their best. She loved that too! Once, he returned with a real rarity: a green spotted Flatcoat! Fern was plastered with duckweed!

She enjoyed all the caravanning, but especially, I think, the times we spent at Scarborough. When the tide was out, she would swim in the pool formed where a stream from the Yorkshire moors empties into the sea. People would stop on the prom, or on the small footbridge across the pool to watch her joyful antics.

Her only concessions to advancing years were the appearance of a little silver hair beneath her chin and a tendency to put on weight. Much to her disgust there was only one way to bring the latter under control!

April 29th 2001. The date had come at last! More than eight years ago, standing on the top step at Whitegates, I had set the target of double figures. Now that target had been reached. Fern was ten! She was old in any doggy terms, but especially in Flatcoat terms, yet strangers would guess her age at anything from two to five for she was a typical Peter Pan. Defying all logic, Fern had lived, and how she had lived! Not a thin, weakly, cosseted existence, but a vibrant life, filled with fun, and laughter and achievement.

The chocolate cake no longer had its usual destination, but tradition had to be upheld and I knew someone who had one chocolate biscuit for elevenses, but who deserved more, much more!

"For us?"

The familiar brown eyes creased into their warm smile.

"Really for us?"

Cathy threatened to put on weight and Francis frowned with mock gravity.

"Mmm...but does he deserve cake?"

231

Illusion

Back home, my mind returned to the beginning. I hadn't chosen the puppy who would become Fern, she had been chosen for me. Why? I had often wondered. I reached for the phone to ask the one person who knew.

"Of course I know what date it is!"

Jill's manner was as direct as ever but I could hear the pride and pleasure in her voice.

"Give her a hug from me! A big one, bless her cotton socks!"

Then I asked the question which had always intrigued me. Why had she chosen the determined puppy with the marvellous feet to be Fern?

"Instinct," she replied in her brisk, no-nonsense manner, "always follow my instincts. You two just seemed to go together."

EPILOGUE

It began as a faint cough not long after that milestone birthday. Antibiotics made it vanish temporarily, but it soon re-asserted itself. Nigel's X-rays (taken without anaesthetic) then revealed the presence of a solid white mass just behind Fern's breastbone amidst the normal dark clarity of her chest.

He referred us to a specialist at a veterinary hospital in Derby, and there, after further x-rays, blood tests and scans with state-of-the-art equipment, we learned the truth. Fern had an aggressive and advanced lung cancer that had most likely already metastasised to other parts of her body. Her death was only months, more likely weeks away. There was a drastic operation, but the chances of it effecting a cure were remote. It might prolong Fern's life a few more weeks, even months if we were very lucky.

Gordon and I agonised for two days. Eventually, we concluded it would be wrong to put her through such tremendous trauma for the dim prospect of so little gain. We would care for her, spoil her, love her and the moment we saw the sparkle in her eyes begin to fade, we would know the time had come to say goodbye. We would fill Fern's final days with all the things she loved to do and take her to all the places she loved to go.

Nigel understood. Sarah Smith, Fern's specialist at Derby, understood. We hoped everyone else would. In my mind, I set a kind of target as I had done so often before: we would have Christmas together. But this target lacked the sharp determination of ten years ago and this time, I knew exactly what I had to lose.

A kind of peace followed our decision, but it was very short-lived. The following morning, I shook Gordon from his sleep.

"We've only looked at it from our point of view!"

He knew at once what I meant.

"We've never looked at it from Fern's! What would she do if we could explain it all to her, tell her there was this chance, that it's slim, very, very slim, but it's there…"

Three days later, we were back at Derby. However could we have thought the Cupboard Top Kid would be satisfied to give in, to simply wait to die?

"She'll fight. She'll help you every inch of the way."

Sarah smiled.

"I know she will. Your vet said so and we can always tell those who fight," she added as she began to lead Fern away. She paused, then turned to look straight back at us.

"So will I."

Five hours later, still begowned and with a mask hanging around her neck, Sarah almost ran into the waiting room, her face beaming with surprise and pleasure.

"I can't believe it! How well she's done! She never gave us one moment's worry under the anaesthetic! She's marvellous! She really is!"

I leapt to my feet. Of course she is! This is Fern!

"She's already chewed off her drip!"

I took a deep breath. Had my indomitable Fern beaten all the odds once more? Had she again grasped her chance from another sea of despair? She wouldn't give in now. It simply wasn't in her nature. We weren't out of the wood by a long way yet, but we were on our way!

Just over an hour later, we were allowed to see her.

We were led through an avenue of two tiers of cages. The nurse bent to open one at floor level, so I got down to my knees. As she opened the door, unbelievably, Fern pushed straight through, tail wagging furiously, to climb onto my lap. A huge, thick, bright blue bandage swathed her entire body between front and back legs. She seemed perfectly normal, happy and alert! It was so difficult trying to stroke and fondle her without touching that bandage, so difficult to see that bandage through the tears.

Then she caught sight of Gordon, behind me. Instantly, she was up and hurrying to him. The nurse too, was thrilled with Fern's recovery.

"Just think how we'd be after an operation like that!"

I wondered what lay beneath the blue cover. Did her ribs hurt? How far had they been forced apart? Was she terribly bruised? How much of her lustrous coat had gone? I didn't allow myself to think about the ugly thing that had been growing within her beauty.

"She'd better go back now."

Fern didn't want to go back. She wanted to stay with Gordon. I made myself speak firmly to her.

"No," I said clearly, placing the flat of my hand directly in front of her face. I stood and took a step backwards. As the nurse closed the cage door, Fern thrust one sad, protesting paw into the narrowing gap.

"A marvellous foot," I thought to myself, suddenly reminded of that first time I had seen her.

It was the last time I saw her. She died in the early hours of the following day.

The nurse had taken her to relieve herself. Everything had seemed fine. Putting her back into the cage, the nurse had talked happily to her as Fern calmly curled herself into the back corner, preparing for sleep.

At the next check, the nurse found her in exactly the same position, curled in sleep. But it was the sleep from which she would never awake.

We refused the autopsy a disbelieving and tearful Sarah offered. We will never know the catastrophe that struck so swiftly and silently, but a friend believed she knew. She said Fern would be aware her cancer had not gone, and that having seen us once more, had wished to spare us further heartache.

I can believe this bitter-sweet answer. But even if this is so, then I know with certainty that Fern would not have made her choice for that reason. Fern would have chosen that way for herself. She would never have given her vitality, her beauty and strength, little by little, to a vile and unseen enemy. With one final, defiant shout, Fern met Death on exactly the same terms she met Life: her own.

She was cremated and her casket buried in our garden on the third anniversary of Margaret's death. A standard white rose marks her grave. Her image stands proudly atop a weather vane, looking out over the fields, past the old Talbot Dog Training Centre, and towards the river.

I did not take her along the arduous road to seek the Championship she so richly deserved. Neither did I allow her to fulfil her capabilities in Agility. I will forever regret how much I failed her, even though I know she would forgive me.

"Never mind Mum, we had a great time! We had fun!"

Two shoe boxes filled with rosettes lie on the top shelf of my wardrobe. A larger box holds her toys, worn "Barbour" jacket, collar and two leads. The old horse brush lies there, too. None of these valueless, precious things will ever be used again.

As I look through the window to see which way the wind is blowing, another dog, bigger than Fern and with a deep auburn coat, strolls across the lawn. She is already nine, and the rescue dog I planned. She, too, is a

Flatcoat. Our names wait on two more rescue lists.

For Gordon and myself, Fern transformed our lives forever. He is my soul-mate, I am his, and we were brought this greatest of all gifts by Fern. Within myself, I have the confidence to be me, not what people think I should be. Less hampered by fear of failure, I am more likely to seize opportunities when they arise and to laugh at my own many short-comings. I can look at the stars, but am content to be me.

Fern's signature music eventually came; not the lovely classic I expected, music to evoke the beauty of her form and movement, it was a loud and raucous pop song, pounded out to the strong beat of insistent drums. But hadn't Fern always done the unexpected? Hadn't she always marched to the beat of her own drum? There are periods of quietness, but always the same relentless, unstoppable rhythm, drives its way inexorably forward. It seemed to personify my beloved Fern, forever determined to do it her way.

Not being any sort of pop fan, many days passed before I was able to identify it and when I did, it evoked such a strange feeling! The only way I can describe it, is to say that it brought peace and the satisfaction of knowing her story to be complete, and that sweet self-belief I so envied and admired, remains as strong in death as it was in life. Tina Turner's "The Best" is Fern's music.

"Take my heart and make it strong," says one line. Fern did exactly that.

No my dear Mr. Day, when you said I "Owe this dog nothing," you were wrong; very, very wrong.

With deepest gratitude to
Jill Saville,
whose knowledge, skill and love brought Illusion to reality.

Illusion

Illusion